THE SEX PROBLEM
IN
MODERN SOCIETY

THE
SEX PROBLEM
IN
MODERN
SOCIETY

An Anthology

EDITED BY

JOHN FRANCIS MCDERMOTT

THE

MODERN LIBRARY

NEW YORK

Random House IS THE PUBLISHER OF

THE MODERN LIBRARY

BENNETT A. CERF · DONALD S. KLOPFER · ROBERT K. HAAS

Manufactured in the United States of America

Printed by Parkway Printing Company   Bound by H. Wolff

ACKNOWLEDGMENTS

THE editor gratefully acknowledges his indebtedness to the following for the use of the material incorporated in this book:

American Mercury; Bookman; Dodd, Mead & Company; Doubleday, Doran and Company; Harcourt, Brace and Company; Harper & Brothers; Alfred A. Knopf, Inc.; Horace Liveright, Inc.; The Macaulay Company; *North American Review;* W. W. Norton & Company; *Outlook and Independent;* Greenberg: Publisher; Dr. Charles Francis Potter; Miss Grace Potter; Charles Scribner's Sons; Simon and Schuster, Inc.; The Viking Press.

J. F. McD.

FOREWORD

THE twentieth century has witnessed on the subject of sex a change in the attitude of thinking persons from that generally held in the nineteenth. People then professed to believe that the only excuse for the indulgence of the sexual function was in the propagation of children. Sex was not to be discussed, not to be thought about, not to be investigated. It was to be spoken about only in whispers. Its only motives were to be piety and patriotism. Today the subject is, on the whole, freely discussed, it is much thought about, and it is thoroughly inquired into.

Paradoxically, the change which has been brought about arose from the spirit of scientific investigation which characterized many people of the past century. They did not, it is true, show much inclination to make a study of sex, but the general breaking down of taboos, which began in that time, weakened remaining prohibitions, and the interest in and pursuit of scientific (especially biological) knowledge led to a consideration of the physical part of man. The study of his body has caused man to have a greater curiosity as to his bodily functions and made him aware that sex is one of the principal functions of the body.

The actual change in attitude, however, has been brought about chiefly by the work of sociologists such as Havelock Ellis, whose monumental *Sex and Society* is a frank acknowledgment of the importance of sex and of the necessity of understanding its relation to society; by the work of such a psychologist as Sigmund Freud who has practically founded a new philosophy in which the love function is the center of all human activity (in one sense it does not matter whether

Freud is right or wrong: he has stirred up a vital interest in sex and its problems; by the work of such a social philosopher as Bertrand Russell who has insisted on the humanity of sex and its relationship. As a result of the work of these men, of many others, and of their numerous followers, sex and its functioning are now looked upon as a basic study toward the understanding of human nature, which is, after all, our most immediate problem.

Yet, though in recent decades much has been accomplished towards the increase of man's knowledge of sex and though there has been some dissemination of this knowledge, the non-scientific man is still in need of a wider distribution of findings on the subject. The editor of the present book, therefore, has gathered together a number of papers on various aspects of sex and attitudes towards it. The volume which he has made is not intended to represent one rigid editorial point of view. The editor is not concerned to express his private views through his selections; it is his aim, rather, to present papers on several principal features of the sex question today. The essays, written by persons well qualified to speak on the subjects of which they write, are intelligently constructed and are genuinely enlightening in their respective fields. By offering points of view which are current at the present time, the essays will give the lay reader a definite idea, in a small compass, of what the leading thinkers today feel about sex.

The editor has, consequently, decided that articles on the sexual ethic, on the psychology of sex, on love, on marriage, on eugenics, on birth control, on the adolescent and sex, and on sex in literature may prove of interest and of value to the reader. In order, however, that no one idea of or attitude toward sex might solely be developed in the book, the editor has offered in each section at least three essays, presenting different points of view on or different approaches to the general subject of the section. For instance, in the section on the psychology of sex, the reader will find a re-

statement of the Freudian point of view, but he will also find
a chapter from Adler, who minimizes sex as a vital influence
and elevates over it the ego. In the section on marriage, the
reader will discover essays by such divergent personalities as
Robert Lowie, Will Durant, Ben Lindsey, and V. F. Calverton. In the section on birth control, he will see articles by
one of the chief advocates of it and by a writer who does not
at all believe in it, together with an article by a minister and
another which is concerned with birth control as a check on
population. The last section of all, on sex in literature, dis-
cusses both the widespread use of sex as a principal motif in
modern literature and the relation of sex censorship to literature. In this way the editor has compiled what he hopes
will be both an interesting and a useful volume for the lay
reader.

JOHN FRANCIS McDERMOTT.

CONTENTS

xi

I

THE SEXUAL ETHIC

WHY A SEXUAL ETHIC IS NECESSARY [1]

By Bertrand Russell

In characterizing a society, whether ancient or modern, there are two elements, rather closely interconnected, which are of prime importance: one is the economic system, the other the family system. There are at the present day two influential schools of thought, one of which derives everything from an economic source, while the other derives everything from a family or sexual source, the former school that of Marx, the latter that of Freud. I do not myself adhere to either school, since the interconnections of economics and sex do not appear to me to show any clear primacy of the one over the other from the point of view of casual efficacy. For example: no doubt the industrial revolution has had and will have a profound influence upon sexual morals, but conversely the sexual virtue of the Puritans was psychologically necessary as part cause of the industrial revolution. I am not prepared myself to assign primacy to either the economic or sexual factor, nor in fact can they be separated with any clearness. Economics is concerned essentially with obtaining food, but food is seldom wanted among human beings solely for the benefit of the individual who obtains it; it is wanted for the sake of the family, and as the family system changes, economic motives also change. It must be obvious that not only life insurance but most forms of private saving would nearly cease if children were taken away from their parents and brought up by the state as in Plato's *Republic;* that is to say, if the state were to adopt the rôle of the father, the state would, *ipso facto,* become

[1] From *Marriage and Morals.* New York: Horace Liveright, 1929.

3

the sole capitalist. Thoroughgoing Communists have often maintained the converse, that if the state is to be the sole capitalist, the family, as we have known it, cannot survive; and even if this is thought to go too far, it is impossible to deny an intimate connection between private property and the family, a connection which is reciprocal, so that we cannot say that one is cause and the other is effect.

The sexual morals of the community will be found to consist of several layers. There are first the positive institutions embodied in law; such, for example, as monogamy in some countries and polygamy in others. Next there is a layer where law does not intervene but public opinion is emphatic. And lastly there is a layer which is left to individual discretion, in practice if not in theory. There is no country in the world and there has been no age in the world's history where sexual ethics and sexual institutions have been determined by rational considerations, with the exception of Soviet Russia. I do not mean to imply that the institutions of Soviet Russia are in this respect perfect; I mean only that they are not the outcome of superstition and tradition, as are, at least in part, the institutions of all other countries in all ages. The problem of determining what sexual morality would be best from the point of view of general happiness and well-being is an extremely complicated one, and the answer will vary according to a number of circumstances. It will be different in an industrially advanced community from what it would be in a primitive agricultural régime. It will be different where medical science and hygiene are effective in producing a low death rate from what it would be where plagues and pestilences carry away a large proportion of the population before it becomes adult. Perhaps when we know more, we shall be able to say that the best sexual ethic will be different in one climate from what it would be in another, and different again with one kind of diet from what it would be with another.

The effects of a sexual ethic are of the most diverse kinds

—personal, conjugal, familial, national and international. It may well happen that the effects are good in some of these respects, where they are bad in others. All must be considered before we can decide what on the balance we are to think of a given system. To begin with the purely personal: these are the effects considered by psychoanalysis. We have here to take account not only of the adult behavior inculcated by a code, but also of the early education designed to produce obedience to the code, and in this region, as everyone now knows, the effects of early taboos may be very curious and indirect. In this department of the subject we are at the level of personal well-being. The next stage of our problem arises when we consider the relations of men and women. It is clear that some sex relations have more value than others. Most people would agree that a sex relation is better when it has a large psychical element than when it is purely physical. Indeed the view which has passed from the poets into the common consciousness of civilized men and women is that love increases in value in proportion as more of the personalities of the people concerned enters into the relation. The poets also have taught many people to value love in proportion to its intensity; this, however, is a more debatable matter. Most moderns would agree that love should be an equal relation, and that on this ground, if on no other, polygamy, for example, cannot be regarded as an ideal system. Throughout this department of the subject it is necessary to consider both marriage and extra-marital relations, since whatever system of marriage prevails, extra-marital relations will vary correspondingly.

We come next to the question of the family. There have existed in various times and places many different kinds of family groups, but the patriarchal family has a very large preponderance, and, moreover, the monogamic patriarchal family has prevailed more and more over the polygamic. The primary motive of sexual ethics as they have existed in Western civilization since pre-Christian times has been to secure that degree of female virtue without which the patriarchal family becomes impossible, since paternity is uncertain. What has been added to this in the way of insistence on male virtue by Christianity had its psychological source in asceticism, although in quite recent times this motive has been reënforced by female jealousy, which became influential with the emancipation of women. This latter motive seems, however, to be temporary, since, if we may judge by appearances, women will tend to prefer a system allowing freedom to both sexes rather than one imposing upon men the restrictions which hitherto have been suffered only by women.

Within the monogamic family there are, however, many varieties. Marriages may be decided by the parties themselves or by their parents. In some countries the bride is purchased; in others, e.g., France, the bridegroom. Then there may be all kinds of differences as regards divorce, from the Catholic extreme, which permits no divorce, to the law of old China, which permitted a man to divorce his wife for being a chatterbox. Constancy or quasi-constancy in sex relations arises among animals, as well as among human beings, where, for the preservation of the species, the participation of the male is necessary for the rearing of the young. Birds, for example, have to sit upon their eggs continuously to keep them warm, and also have to spend a good many hours of the day getting food. To do both is, among many species, impossible for one bird, and therefore male coöperation is essential. The consequence is that most birds are models of virtue. Among human beings the coöperation of the father is a great biological advantage to the offspring, especially in unsettled times and among turbulent populations; but with the growth of modern civilization the rôle of the father is being increasingly taken over by the state, and there is reason to think that a father may cease before long to be biologically advantageous, at any rate in the wage-earning class. If this should occur, we must expect a complete breakdown of traditional morality, since there will no longer be any reason why a mother should wish the paternity of her child to be indubitable. Plato would have us go a step further, and put the state not only in place of the father but in that of the mother also. I am not myself sufficiently an admirer of the state, or sufficiently impressed with the delights of orphan asylums, to be enthusiastic in favor of this scheme. At the same time it is not impossible that economic forces may cause it to be to some extent adopted.

The law is concerned with sex in two different ways, on the one hand to enforce whatever sexual ethic is adopted by the community in question, and on the other hand to protect the ordinary rights of individuals in the sphere of sex. The latter have two main departments: on the one hand the protection of females and non-adults from assault and from harmful exploitation, on the other hand the prevention of venereal disease. Neither of these is commonly treated purely on its merits, and for this reason neither is so effectively dealt with as it might be. In regard to the former, hysterical campaigns about the White Slave Traffic lead to the passage of laws easily evaded by professional malefactors, while affording opportunities of blackmail against harmless people. In regard to the latter, the view that venereal disease is a just punishment for sin prevents the adoption of the measures which would be the most effective on purely medical grounds, while the general attitude that venereal disease is shameful causes it to be concealed, and therefore not promptly or adequately treated.

We come finally to the question of population. This is in itself a vast problem which must be considered from many points of view. There is the question of the health of mothers, the question of the health of children, the question of the psychological effects of large and small families respectively upon the character of children. These are what may be called the hygienic aspects of the problem. Then there are the economic aspects, both personal and public: the question of the wealth per head of a family or a community in relation to the size of the family or the birth rate of the community. Closely connected with this is the bearing of the population question upon international politics and the possibility of world peace. And, finally, there is the eugenic question as to the improvement or deterioration of the stock through the different birth and death rates of the different sections of the community. No sexual ethic can be either justified or condemned on solid grounds until it has been examined from all the points of view above enumerated. Reformers and reactionaries alike are in the habit of considering one or at most two of the aspects of the problem. It is especially rare to find any combination of the private and the political points of view, and yet it is quite impossible to say that either of these is more important than the other, and we can have no assurance *a priori* that a system which is good from a private point of view would also be good from a political point of view, or vice versa. My own belief is that in most ages and in most places obscure psychological forces have led men to adopt systems involving quite unnecessary cruelty, and that this is still the case among the most civilized races at the present day. I believe also that the advances in medicine and hygiene have made changes in sexual ethics desirable both from a private and from a public point of view, while the increasing rôle of the state in education is gradually rendering the father less important than he has been throughout historical times. We have, therefore, a twofold task in criticizing the current ethics: on the one hand we have to eliminate the elements of superstition, which are often subconscious; on the other hand we have to take account of those entirely new factors which make the wisdom of past ages the folly instead of the wisdom of the present.

THE DISCIPLINE OF SEX [1]

By Edward Sapir

WE are in the habit of complimenting ourselves on the healthy attitude which is coming to prevail in America toward questions of sex. There is some justification for this, for it is obvious that an attitude that looks upon sex as intrinsically evil, and that seeks to rescue it from condemnation by confining it into conventionally fixed and approved channels, is a repressive and unhealthy one. But I am not willing to grant, for all that, that the present excited and puzzled attitude, shifting back and forth in a single individual's mind all the way from orthodox acceptance of the restraints of Puritanism to a reasoned religion of promiscuity, is a healthy attitude. The very notion of health implies the presence of a certain balance and of a fundamental surety of the significant outlines of behavior. The most that one can say for the sex mind of radical America is that it is in a state of transition and that a certain willingness to experiment dangerously is in the long run a safer thing than a premature striking of the balance. This may be a just interpretation of the few; of the many, who bless you for a formula for noble weakness, it is but psychology gulled.

A realistic view of actual sex opinion and sex behavior leads to the feeling that on every hand life is being measurably cheapened by an emotional uncertainty in matters of sex, matters that no healthy society can long brook uncertainty of. An individual can create true personal values only on the basis of those accepted by his society, but when nothing is accepted, he has no room for the growth of any values that are more than empty formulæ. The "enrichment of per-

[1] From the *American Mercury*, April, 1929.

sonality" by way of multiple "experiences" proves to be little more than a weary accumulation of poverties. These shibboleths are given the lie by the uneasy eyes of the bored adventurers who drawl them out. Human culture, it seems, is so constituted that the individual dare never face his own organismal responses skeptically. These fundamental responses must somehow be taken care of, by implication, in the patterns of social conduct, and the individual who is constantly being called upon to create such patterns anew never gets beyond the point of struggling with nature. His "freedom" is but the homelessness of the outlaw.

The present sex unrest has been nibbling at more or less reliable information reported by anthropologists from primitive communities. Any primitive community that indulges, or is said to indulge, in unrestricted sex behavior is considered an interesting community to hear from. Such a community is at once equated with "primitive man" in general and has the great merit of bringing us back to that primary and glorious man that wishful romanticists have always been dreaming about.

It does not seem to occur to the readers of excited books about pleasure-loving Samoans and Trobriand Islanders that perhaps these communities are not as primitive as they seem, that there are perhaps other primitive groups that have developed an ideology of sex that is not so very different from that of our happily extinct Victorian ancestors, and that in any event there may be social determinants in such societies that make the question of value in sex conduct of lesser urgency than among ourselves. It is true that many primitive societies allow of erotic and marital arrangements that shock the sensibilities of our conservatives. But what should be denied is that sex conduct is truly unregulated even in these societies. A closer examination shows that the community has certain very definite ideas as to what is allowable and what is not allowable.

As the conception of the permitted and the illicit, however, in such groups is rarely calculated to interest us unless we happen to be objective students of primitive culture, it is not so obvious why we should think of the license, or approximate license, that we read into their sex behavior, as of any special concern to us. If we cannot sympathetically understand their sex taboos, why do we pretend to understand their freedom from our sex taboos? Obviously they are in no better case than we ourselves. Historical factors have set certain specific bounds to the expression of the sex impulse in these societies, as they have set more or less specific bounds in our own, and a primitive reformer who attempted to break down every possible barrier to the free play of sex would receive small comfort from his fellow men.

But it is simply not true that sex freedom is the norm for primitive societies. It is, as a matter of fact, very much the exception, and the presence of sex taboos, of institutionalized deferments of sexual gratification, and of all manner of sex ideals, so far from justifying us in wringing our hands at the perversity of mankind, might more rationally be expected to lead to a psychological inquiry into the reason why human beings have so persistently gone out of their way to put obstacles in the way of the immediate satisfaction of the sex impulse. A certain type of historian is ready with his answer. He tells us that these restrictions have merely come in as a by-product of the conception that women are a form of property. This is one of those theories that are too plausible to be true. The institutionalizing of marriage in terms of property can be amply illustrated in both primitive and sophisticated societies—this no one doubts—but we are far from having the right to take it for granted that ideas of ownership are the root of all sex restrictions. We know too little as yet about the psychological causes of sexual modesty and secrecy, of the universal dread of sex squandering, of the irresistible drive to hedging sex about in one way or another, but we may be certain that these causes are not of a trivial nature and that they are not to be abrogated by a smart and trivial analysis of sex by intellectuals who have more curiosity than intuition.

For reasons which can only be dimly guessed at, man seems everywhere and always to have felt that sex was a quintessential gratification that it was not well to secure at too easy a price, that it held within it sources of power, of value, that could not be rudely snatched. In short, mankind has always known that sex needed to be conserved in large part and made over into more than sex. Freud's theory of sublimation has always been man's intuition, and sex has always restlessly striven to become love.

Nothing seems more difficult than to convince the all-wise modern that the emotion of love, quite aside from the momentary fulfillment of desire, is one of the oldest and most persistent of human feelings. It is far from being the secondary or adventitiously superimposed thing that it is so often said to be. On the contrary, much that is generally interpreted as primitive, because unromantic, may well be interpreted as a superstructure imposed upon the sex life by considerations of a relatively sophisticated nature—economic, social, religious, or political.

It may be well at this point to relate a brief story which I collected a number of years ago from the Sarcee Indians of Alberta, Canada. The story goes back to the early days, before the Indians were seriously bothered by the white man's morality or his license. It will seem all wrong to some, for it is nothing but an old-fashioned love story from anywhere and any time.

Here, once upon a time, they were camped in a circle. They were putting up the Sun Dance.[2] This one young man was making love to her; he and the girl had love for each other. Every time that she came in she would sit down close to where the people were singing and her young man would peep

2 The Sun Dance is the most important communal ceremonial of the tribes of the Plains, and the most sacred object in the ritual is the center pole of the Sun Dance lodge.

in between the lodge-poles which were leaning against each other. And so it was that his face paint would always be left on the poles.

After a while it was said that they were about to go on the warpath, so this young man went to his sweetheart and said to her, "Do not get lonesome for me. We shall see each other again." And then the girl gave him a little of her hair which she had cut off and she tied it up and they kissed each other and parted. Now they went off to war and the girl's heart dropped.[3]

When the Sun Dance was over, the people broke up camp; they were to come together again at this place at a stated time. They moved off in different directions. Now, as to these people who had gone off on the warpath, they were sighted by the enemy, who sat down in ambush for them. When they got in sight of the enemy, they were attacked and all of them were killed.

After a long time the people came together again at the place that had been mentioned, and when they were all assembled the news was brought that those who had gone off to war had all been killed—so it was said. This girl heard about it. And then she went to the Sun Dance lodge and came here to the place where her sweetheart had been in the habit of peeping in. She saw his face paint on the pole against which he used to lean. And then she returned to her people's lodge and, having arrived there, she took a rope. And then she went back to the Sun Dance lodge and climbed the pole which stood in the center of it. She tied the rope to the pole and looped the other end of it about her neck. And then she sang the song which her sweetheart had been in the habit of singing.

After a while a certain one discovered the girl and what she was doing, how she was singing while seated up there on the pole. He spoke of it. They rushed out to her, but before they could reach her she had jumped off and strangled herself with the rope. Though they cut the rope off at once, she was already dead. That is how the girl strangled herself.

[3] The native equivalent for "she was brokenhearted."

This story proves nothing, but it gives pause for thought. It contains all the elements of romantic love and it subjects that romantic love to the final test of all values, which is the test of tragedy. It is not an isolated instance, by any means, though I should not like to be misunderstood as claiming it to be an average or even a typical incident of primitive life or of any other form of life. It is one of those comparatively rare but basically typical examples of the form that a natural value will take in almost any culture if it is supported by an underlying passion which is pure and intense. To speak of frenzy or madness is beside the point, for frenzy is the climactic test of any value.

What is the meaning of this strange passion of love, which crops up at all times and in all places and which the modern rationalist finds it so difficult to allow except as a superficial amplification of the sex drive under the influence of certain conventional ideas and habits? It is as difficult to state clearly what the emotion consists of as it is easy, if one is willing to be but honest for a moment, to comprehend it. The sex nucleus is perfectly obvious and no love that is not built up around this nucleus has psychological reality. But what transforms sex into love is a strange and compulsive identification of the loved one with every kind of attachment that takes the ego out of itself. The intensity of sex becomes an unconscious symbol for every other kind of psychic intensity, and the intensity of love is measured by the intensities of all non-egoistic identifications that have been transferred to it. It is useless to argue that this is madness. In a sense it is, and we have yet to learn of a value or an ideal that is not potential madness.

Why is it, then, that a sentiment which is as much at home in our despised Victorian yesterday as in the obscure life of a remote Indian tribe needs to be discussed with so much apology today? There is a complex of factors which explains the present temper and we need only examine them to make us realize how transitory is likely to be that temper.

First of all, the old Puritan morality, which looked upon the sex act as inherently sinful, is still too painfully near to us, and the revolt which was bound to set in sooner or later has concentrated all of its energies on the annihilation of this notion of sin. Naturally enough, it has had little patience with the arduous task of retaining that in the inherited ideology of sex which was psychologically sound or, at any rate, capable of preservation as a value without violence to nature. What has happened is that the odious epithet of sin has been removed from sex, but sex itself has not been left a morally indifferent concept. The usual process of over-correction has invested sex with a factitious value as a romantic and glorious thing in itself. The virus of sin has passed into love, and the imaginative radiance of love, squeezed into the cramped quarters formerly occupied by sin, has trans-figured lust and made it into a new and phosphorescent holiness. Love, a complicated and inevitable sentiment, is for the moment sickening for lack of sustenance.

But the anti-Puritan revolt is much more than a revolt against sex repression alone. It is a generalized revolt against everything that is hard, narrow, and intolerant in the old American life, and which sees in sex repression its most potent symbol of attack. Many young men and women of today who declare themselves sexually free are really revolt-ing against quite other than sex restrictions. They glory in the reputed "sin" because they see it as a challenge to the very notion of repression.

The revolt complex is powerfully strengthened by an in-sidious influence exerted by modern science. It has been one of the cheerless, yet perfectly natural, consequences of the scientific view of life that nothing.in human conduct is sup-posed to have reality or meaning except in the ultimate physiological terms that alone describe life or are said to describe life to its scientific analyst. If life is nothing but physiology, how can love be other than sex, with such immaterial reinterpretations as no hard-headed modern need take seriously?

Even more important, at least in America, is the great psychological need of the modern woman to extend and make firm her symbols of economic independence. Every attitude and every act that challenges the old doctrine of psychic sex difference is welcomed, no matter where it leads. The most obvious differences of motivation between the sexes are passionately ignored and a whole new mythology has been evolved which deceives only the clever.

The virulence of this reinterpretation of the significance of sex differences is tending to die down, but we are still suffering from the psychological aftermath of the feminist revolt. Who has not met the essentially frigid woman who uses her sex freedom as a weapon with which to feed her ego? And this all too common sacrifice of love and the possibility of love on the altar of an ambition which is essentially insatiable, because it is so much of a compulsion, is met by the complementary need of "fair-minded" men to accept the free woman at her word. Hence the cult of pseudo-nobility, what Wyndham Lewis so aptly calls the new sex snobbery, which makes an intellectual fetish of freedom and abolishes jealousy by a fiat of the will.

The psychological falsity of these attitudes and liberations is manifest enough and leads to a new set of most insidious repressions which owe their origin to the subordination of the natural impulse to reason. It is questionable if these new and hardly recognized repressions, these elaborate maskings of the unconscious by the plausible terminologies of "freedom," of "cumulative richness of experience," of "self-realization," do not lead to an even more profound unhappiness than the more normal subordination of impulse to social convention that we hear so much about.

The truth of the matter is that in the life of the emotions one can make too few as well as too many demands, and the life of love is naturally no exception to the rule. Men and women who expect too little of each other, who are too nobly eager to grant each other privileges and self-existences that the unconscious does not really want, invite a whole crop of pathological developments. The chronic insistence on the notions of freedom and self-expression is itself contrary to the natural current of the sex life, which flows away from the ego and seeks a realization for the ego which is in a sense destructive of its own claims. Sex as self-realization unconsciously destroys its own object by making of it no more than a tool to a selfish end. There can be no doubt that much modern sex freedom is little more than narcissism, self-love. Applied narcissism, in our particular society, is necessarily promiscuity.

A further consequence of an uncritical doctrine of sex freedom is the lack of true psychological intimacy between lovers and between husband and wife. Abstract freedom is poor soil for the growth of love. It leads to an unacknowledged suspicion and watchfulness and a never-satisfied longing, which in the end kill off the finer and the more sublimated forms of passion. The modern man seeks to save the situation by analyzing sex attachment into the fulfillment of sex desire plus such intimacy as constant companionship can give.

This is, of course, totally false psychologically. It is merely a feeble synthesis of dissociated elements arrived at by an inadequate analysis. The easy physical accessibility of the sexes to each other at an early age, the growth of a spurious "pal" spirit between them, with sex itself thrown in as a bribe or as a reward—all this, so far from bringing the sexes together in a finer intimacy, has exactly the opposite effect —of leaving them essentially strangers to each other, for they early learn just enough to put a more intuitive seeking and longing stupidly to sleep. Is it a wonder that the sexes unconsciously hate each other today with an altogether new and baffling virulence?

In extreme cases—one dreads to acknowledge how frequent these extreme cases are becoming—the constantly dampened, because never really encouraged, passion between the sexes leads to compensation in the form of homosexuality, which, if we are reliably informed, is definitely on the increase in America. This surely is a strange point of arrival for a gospel of delivery from repression, but it is a perfectly explicable one. Love having been squeezed out of sex, it revenges itself by assuming unnatural forms. The cult of the "naturalness" of homosexuality fools no one but those who need a rationalization of their personal sex problems.

In estimating the significance of the social and psychological currents which are running in the sphere of sex today, it is important to do justice to both cultural and personal factors. It is dangerous to ignore either. Our culture of today is not the creation of the moment, but the necessary continuation of the culture of yesterday, with all its values. These values need revision, but they cannot be overthrown by any scientific formula. The intellectuals who declare them dead are very much more at their mercy than they care to know. It is not claimed that all individuals can or should make identical adjustments, but in an atmosphere in which no norms of conduct are recognized and no values are maintained, no man or woman can make a satisfactory individual adjustment.

It is peculiarly dangerous in dealing with the sex problem to let petty verbal analogies do the work of an honest analysis. The problem of jealousy is an excellent illustration of this. Owing to the highly individualistic and possessive philosophy of so much of our life, the image of possessiveness has been plausibly but insidiously transferred to the marital relation, finally to the relation of love itself. Sex jealousy is therefore said to imply possessiveness. As one emancipated young woman once expressed it to me, it would be an insult to her and her husband to expect fidelity of either of them. Yet what is more obvious than this—that jealousy can no more be weeded out of the human heart than the shadows cast by the objects of this world can be obliterated by a mechanism that gives them an eternal luminosity? Every joy has its sorrow, every value has its frustration, and the lover who is too noble to be jealous has always been justly suspected by mankind of being no lover at all. It is not the province of men and women to declare out of their intellectual pride what emotions they care to sanction as legitimate or admirable. They can only try to be true to their feelings and to accept the consequences of the fulfillment or denial of these feelings in the terms which nature sees fit to impose.

The supposed equivalence of sex jealousy to the emotion of resentment at the infringement of one's personal property rights is entirely false. Sex jealousy, in its purest form, is essentially a form of grief, while the combative feeling aroused by theft or other invasion of one's sovereignty is of course nothing but anger. Grief and anger may be intermingled, but only a shallow psychologist will identify them. Perhaps the linguistic evidence is worth something on this point. It is remarkable in how few languages the concept of sex jealousy is confused with the notion of envy. Our use of the English word *jealous* in two psychologically distinct senses has undoubtedly been responsible for a good deal of loose thinking and faulty analysis. It is an insult to the true lover to interpret his fidelity and expectation of fidelity as possessiveness and to translate the maddening grief of jealousy into the paltry terminology of resentment at the infringement of property rights. These crowning psychological absurdities were reserved for the enlightened mentality of today.

We are beginning to understand how much we are swayed in the unconscious by obscure but potent symbolisms. There is a certain logic or configurative necessity about these symbolisms which it is hard to put into words, but which the intuitively-minded feel keenly. Sex conduct offers singularly potent examples of the importance of such symbolisms and of their arrangement in a series of cumulative values. I refer to the general symbolism of human intimacy.

Every normal individual is unconsciously drawn toward or repelled by another individual, even if the overt contact is but brief and superficial. These feelings of intimacy and withdrawal have their symbolisms in gesture and expression, which differ from individual to individual but tend none the less to take typical forms under the influence of social forces. Of necessity, the most potent symbols of intimacy are those that lead to the touching and handling of bodies. To put the matter crudely, we are not in the habit of embracing people to whom we are indifferent and of standing frigidly aloof from those that we are psychologically intimate with, unless, of course, there is a conflict that paralyzes expression.

Now, of all known forms of intimacy among human beings the sex relation is naturally the most far-reaching. It necessarily takes its place in the unconscious series of symbolisms of intimacy as the most valued and the final symbol of all. I do not claim that all human beings are equally sensitive to symbolisms of this sort, but there is enough of a psychological common ground in most of us to make it impossible for the normal person to transgress the unformulated laws of symbolic expression beyond a certain point.

It is exceedingly likely, it seems to me, that the obscure, though of course unacknowledged, feeling of shame felt by prostitutes and by those who indulge in promiscuity is by no means entirely due to the fact that they transgress the social code, laying themselves open to a conventional censure. It is likely that this shame is also in large part the resultant of an elusive feeling that a natural scale of values is being transgressed because the expressions which are their symbols are, by implication, arranged in a psychologically impossible sequence. In a deeply symbolic sense, then, the prostitute is "illogical," and her only psychological escape is to refuse to identify herself with her body. And it is no mere accident that so many of the protagonists of sex freedom despise their own bodies.

In sober fact the erotic landscape in contemporary America

is by no means as depressing as these observations may lead one to believe. I have wanted to point out the psychological fallacies in the contemporary cult of sex freedom and the ultimate implications of those fallacies rather than to give an accurate description of contemporary sex life. Sex irregularities, while numerous, are not necessarily as indicative as they seem to be of the deeper-lying set of our erotic philosophy. Unless I sadly misread the *mores* of America, there are many reassuring signs that the reign of so-called Puritan morality is not likely to come to a sudden end even among the sophisticated and that, while the negative elements of that morality are sure to be cast aside by the intelligent and their rigor mitigated by all, its essential core will survive.

Europe may laugh and shrug its shoulders but America can be shockingly stubborn on what she feels to be the fundamentals of life. It would be nothing short of a cultural disaster if America as a whole surrendered to continental European feeling and practice. With religion in none too healthy a state and with the æsthetic life rudimentary and imitative, America needs an irrational faith in the value of love and of fidelity in love as perhaps no other part of the occidental world needs it today.

The moral atmosphere in America is only superficially similar to that of continental Europe. One of the surest signs of the essential difference in outlook is the rapidly increasing divorce rate. Bewailed by domestic moralists and deplored by our European visitors, the ease of obtaining divorce in America is actually an indication of our restless psychological health. Were the institution of marriage and the family actually divorced in sentiment from the sphere of sex indulgence, there would be no reason why a tolerance of marital infidelity should not come to be accepted in America as it has long been in France. But anyone who imagines that America can with a clear conscience settle down to the reasonable and gracious distribution of individual pleasures and familial ceremonies that seems to suit the French genius knows very little about the American temper.

The very youthful intellectuals who are clamorous in their determination to "go the limit" are unable in practice to "play the game," for they cannot learn the rules. Do what one will, sex relations in America have a way of calling up romantic images and implications of fidelity that make this country seem a mysterious, an incredible, realm to the emancipated foreigner. Incompatibility of husband and wife of necessity leads more speedily to divorce than in sophisticated Europe. I am leaving Russia out of the picture, for we know too little about the psychological realities of contemporary Russia to speak of it with profit.

Closely connected with this stubborn unwillingness of the typical American to save marriage and the integrity of the family at the cost of erotic honesty is his peculiar unwillingness or inability to make a fine art of sex indulgence. The "kick" of sex freedom in America lies precisely in its being "sin," not an honest way of life. Americans make poor Don Juans. Nor does the graceful and accomplished *hetæra* of French life seem to flourish on our stubborn soil. Many young women have tried the part but even the most successful of our amateurs in the erotic arts seem compelled by the very nature of the culture in which they have been reared to pay a heavy price. Our intellectual mistresses of sin play a sadly pedantic part, their ardors are in the head rather than in the heart zone.

To put it bluntly, the "free" woman of sophisticated America, whether poetess or saleslady, has a hard job escaping from the uncomfortable feeling that she is really a safe, and therefore a dishonest, prostitute. The charge seems unreasonable to the mind, but the spirit cannot wholly throw off the imputation. The battle shows in the hard, slightly unfocused, glitter of the eye and in the hollow laugh. And one can watch the gradual deterioration of personality that

seems to set in in many of our young women with the premature adoption of the new sophisticated sex standards.

Psychiatrists have often burned their fingers in this matter and perhaps there is nothing they need to keep more
steadily in mind than that in proffering advice in matters of
sex they are addressing themselves not merely to intelligence
and to desire but to certain obscure and unacknowledged
values that cannot be flouted with impunity. If they are of
foreign birth and culture, it would be well for them to take
a little more seriously some of the "resistances" they encounter and to ponder, on occasion, the possibility that in
exploding a personal "complex" they may incidentally be
shattering an "ideal." That American men and women
coarsen on a fare that seems to agree with the sophisticates
of the Old World is both a warning and a reason for optimism.
It points the way to a reaction of feeling that Europe will
not understand.

Americans tend, in the most disconcerting way, to be
both realistic and conservative in the matter of sex. That
psychological health demands sex satisfaction at a much
earlier period than the general postponement of marriage
makes possible is coming to be generally recognized. It is
clear, however, that a true tolerance for illicit relationships
of a promiscuous sort is not likely to become prevalent. Such
suggested institutions as the companionate marriage lead one
rather to suspect that America is feeling its way toward a
loosening of the institutional rigors and responsibilities of
marriage by the growth of new types of sex relationship.

It is difficult to say just what is likely to emerge from the
present period of unrest and experimentation, but one thing
seems certain. America will not be a docile pupil of Europe,
and the sophisticates of this country who are taken in by the
apparently easy solutions of their European brethren, whom
they so vainly admire, are likely to find themselves in a
strangely unsympathetic clime. That new institutions of an
erotic and marital nature are slowly maturing is obvious. It

is my belief that it is no less obvious that these institutions, whatever their forms may be, will not mean a surrender to license but will have for their object, however obscurely and indirectly, the saving of love and the perpetuation of romantic intimacy and of the ideal of fidelity by those who are capable of this intimacy. And it is more likely than not that the average American, for a long time to come, will have the delusion, if it is nothing else, that he is capable of just this experience.

THE NEW VIEW OF SEX [1]

By George Jean Nathan

THE doctrine that there is a very considerable humor in sex, long upheld by the small minority of men and women who were able to think with their emotions, has spread so rapidly and so widely in the last decade that it is difficult to find more than one man or woman out of every dozen who doesn't currently believe in it. It used to be thought pretty generally that sex was a grim, serious and ominous business, to be entered into only by those duly joined in holy wedlock or by those lost souls already in thrall to the devil. Sex was synonymous with danger, tragedy, woe or, at its best, with legalized baby carriages. This view of sex has gone out of style with such other contemporary delusions as French altruism, the making of the world safe for democracy and the evil of Bolshevist government. I do not argue, plainly enough, that back in the cow pastures of the land the old view of sex does not still prevail, for it does; but wherever lights are brighter and there are paving stones and so much as a single electric street car, wherever a band, however bad, plays on Saturday nights, there you will find a change in the old order. Sex, once wearing the tragic mask, wears now the mask of comedy. And whenever one laughs at a thing, one is no longer afraid of it.

I have alluded to the current prevalent looseness of conversation on sex matters. That conversation, as I have also indicated, generally takes on a humorous form, for one may be humorous about forbidden subjects with exemption, where a serious approach would be met with an offended air and

[1] From *Land of the Pilgrim's Pride*. New York: Alfred A. Knopf, Inc., 1927.

rebuff. Many years ago, in my university days, I had a friend who played left end on the football team. It was my friend's technique—he was gifted with an irresistible talent for low comedy—to tell funny stories to the end playing opposite him on a rival eleven, weaken the latter with laughter and thus easily dispose of him. Since sex has become the playing-ground of conversational humor, we may believe that the technique of my football friend is often adopted in other directions.

What has brought about this view of sex as a humorous business is problematical. It is possible that the altered view has come about in due course of time and nature, that all such things move in inscrutable cycles and that once again we are in the midst of a quasi-Restoration turn of the clock. However, I make a guess in another direction. After a long and uninterrupted period of serious regard of anything, the wind always changes and there is born a sudden and re-calcitrant laughter. Human nature is such that it cannot stand monotony; it demands relief. And history shows us that as surely as a period of high gayety is followed abruptly by one of desolation and as surely as a period of misery is followed by one of prosperity, so, too, does a psychically and philo-sophically glum period inevitably soon or late give way to one of psychic and philosophical revelry. Thus, it is proba-ble that the humorous view of sex has come about as a direct result of the long serious view of sex, that human nature simply demanded a change. As it deposed czars and kings and set up Yiddish pants-cutters and Wop soap-box bally-hoos in their places, so it deposed the tragedians and trage-diennes of sex and set up comedians and comediennes.

But the change in the approach to the sex question has not, as might be inferred, been an arbitrary one. It is based upon a thoroughly clear and intelligent view of sex. Sex, in the great majority of instances, is a much more casual and unimportant thing than it is customarily admitted to be. An idiotic conspiracy has sought, with almost uniform success, to make the world accept it as something of paramount consequence in the life of man, the ground of his happiness or unhappiness, of his triumph or defeat, of his joy or his affliction. Yet the reflective man has long known that it is nothing of the kind, that it is, as a matter of fact, of considerably less importance in his general scheme of life than, say, his tobacco or his wine-cellar. Sex is, purely and simply, the diversion of man, a pastime for his leisure hours and, as such, on the same plane with his other pleasures. The civilized man knows little difference between his bottle of vintage champagne, his Corona Corona, his seat at the *Follies* and the gratification of his sex impulse. They all fall much under the same heading. He takes sex no whit more seriously than he takes, to put it superlatively, a symphony concert. He sees in it simply something always amusing and sometimes beautiful, and lets it go at that.

Well, the world itself grows more and more civilized as century chases century down the alley of time and gradually it works itself up to the level of its more civilized inhabitants. And thus gradually the newer view of sex gains recruits And what men believe, women in due time also believe. I do not say that such beliefs are commendable, for I am no judge, but merely an historian. I simply say that so long as men and women merely *felt* about sex, it was what it was yesterday. The moment they began instead to *think* about it, it dropped its mourning and wove vine leaves about its head—and painted its nose red.

In the course of man's contemplation of sex, one phenomenon has gradually impressed itself upon his consciousness above all others, and it is this one phenomenon that, more than anything else, has influenced him in his present attitude toward the subject. That sex is a relatively trivial and inconsequential event in life, that it is of infinitely less permanent significance in his scheme of things than his work in the world, however humble the nature of that work, or than his material welfare or his physical comfort or, as I have hinted, even certain other of his diversions, is clearly borne in upon him after a meditation of the history of sex life as it has directly concerned him.

One of the first things that strikes such a reflective man is the manner in which the brain cells themselves peculiarly operate to demote sex to a plane of unimportance. Such is the curious functioning of the male cerebral centers that the sex act, once it is so much as twenty-four hours past, quite passes from the memory or, at all events, from the direct consciousness. Although the fact, so far as I know, has never been articulated, it remains as an actuality that nothing is so quickly erased from masculine tablets of memory as the sex act accomplished. It is a mental idiosyncrasy, indeed, that the association of the act with a specific woman vanishes within an unbelievably short space of time, that so evanescent is the recollection that the woman actually seems a physical stranger to the man. What remains in the masculine mind is not the consciousness of the sex act, but only what may have proceeded from it, to wit, affection, companionship, friendship or spiritual, as opposed to physical, love. It is not an easy matter to set down delicately in type the most incomprehensible degree to which this post-consciousness of sexual indulgence evaporates. Yet there is no man, if he will view himself honestly in the light of his experience, but will recall at once the peculiar sense of remoteness that has generally and quickly enveloped the woman with whom he has been on terms of physical intimacy. It would seem that nature, operating through the human mind, has contrived thus to make the world frequently a happier and more peaceful spot than it otherwise might be. In man's defective memory lies woman's symbol of chastity.

If sex were the important event in a man's life that some hold it to be, his mind would surely be influenced by it quite differently than it is. A woman, instead of so quickly and unintelligibly taking on the aspect of a complete physical stranger to him, would remain fixed in his sex consciousness. Sex would surely retain a vividness after its performance that it actually does not retain. Yet such is the baffling drollery of human nature that a man's wife ever seems to him a virgin.

II

THE PSYCHOLOGY OF SEX

THE SEX IMPULSE IN MAN [1]

By Jacques Fischer

EXAMPLES have shown us that in the animal kingdom the sex impulse is indeed, as we had foreseen, dependent upon external forces, acting either directly or by the agency of the internal organic environment.

The most elementary observation enables us to establish that the sex impulse in man is the sum of a sex impulse analogous to that of other living creatures, and of superadded phenomena peculiar to mankind alone. In man we may write it down mathematically that the sexual impulse, or cerebral reaction accompanying love = the sexual impulse of the animal + superadded phenomena.

We have to study the different terms of this equation separately, before trying to understand the problem as a whole.

In this paragraph we may marshal the whole of the impulses directly determined by bio-chemical reactions and cyclic influences.

We may recall that the very nature of our working method obliges us to dissociate, as far as we possibly can, all the facts which it is our intention to examine. It is only by application of this old Cartesian principle that it will be possible for us to find our way through this still badly explored chaos.

We at once see that these common sex impulses offer certain obvious points of almost perfect comparison, but that for the most part there are remarkable differences which make it difficult entirely to assimilate the general sex impulse to that of man, even if we only desire to examine

[1] From *Love and Morality*. New York: Alfred A. Knopf, Inc., 1927.

33

under this name that part of our impulses which seem at first sight to be in undoubted connection with what observation has enabled us to establish in the case of other living creatures.

Since man cannot be classified like any other animal, and presents individual characteristics which cannot be denied, we believe that in the interests of clear exposition it will be well first to examine in what respects our sex impulses differ from those of outer beings, and afterwards to make a study of the points common to both which consequently persist in us, as a store of "sex impulses."

The reasons for which it is impossible for man to be regarded as an animal obeying the usual laws of sex can be classified under several heads.

1) The cycle recurrence of sexual excitement has been practically abolished in man; and, side by side with this, the idea of reproduction has become separated in him from the idea of love.

2) The periods of generation in man are not divided in the same clear-cut fashion as in the case of animals.

3) The conditions of life are not analogous for all men, as they generally are for all animals of the same family.

4) Under the common term "man" we include a whole series of races which can probably be differentiated by the bio-chemical characters of their tissues.

5) Derangements of the sex impulse in man are the cause of the production in him of a peculiar phenomenon, which we shall call erotomania.

1. *Modification in the periodicity of the sex impulse in man.*

This difference at once forces itself upon our attention. In the animal the sex instinct is manifested in an overwhelmingly powerful form at well-defined periods, which are special to every kind. The force of this impulse is such that it may impel the animal to sacrifice its life without hesitation in order to obey this law, which has acquired the overwhelming force of an instinct.

In man, on the contrary, the sex impulse rarely occurs in such a violent form, but, on the other hand, it is apt to be set in motion at any moment. There are of course circumstances in which the sex impulse also occurs in the form of an irresistible wave of instinct. We will speak of these manifestations later. But it is undeniable that in many cases a clear-cut distinction may be established between the cyclic phenomena of sexual impulse in the animal, and the continually recurrent sex impulses of man. So that man has at his disposal two sources of reaction to sexual thoughts. Why is man not content with the law of instinct, the cyclic periods of sexual excitement, outside of which he would remain like the other animals, absolutely indifferent to all ideas of love?

In man there only subsist traces of a cyclic urge: The seasonal sexual excitement of the spring, and sometimes a complementary impulse in the autumn. But it is very probable that there were originally clearly determined periods during which the human being was under the influence of the sex impulse.

Physiological laws being the same for all animals, we may regard it as beyond dispute that these periods coincided with the lunar cycle and corresponded with the menstrual periods of the female. Consequently the period intended by the laws of nature for the exercise of the functions of human reproduction recurred every twenty-eight days, and lasted from two to four days.

This was the normal, regular law, that of all other animals, and the sole peculiarity which it offered in man was that of a comparatively frequent recurrence. Morever, we seem to find in woman supplementary phenomena of slight uteroovarian congestion returning at intervals which cut the lunar month almost in two. Under the influence of propitious external conditions, it ought to be possible to produce at that moment, in connection with a slight utero-ovarian internal hypersecretion, a momentary upset of the endocrine equilibrium of the individual, which might bring about a result identical with that of the menstrual flow—that is to say, a short slight supplementary period of sexual excitement.

We know that the biological laws of a species never apply to all its members in a strictly and brutally identical manner; there are always individual differences. Consequently, while sex impulses were exactly subject to the lunar cycle, we can observe a certain upsetting of this in the females of the human race. In most races of animals this individual disturbance, this sort of oscillation around the fixed period at which sexual excitement ought to take place, was only of small importance. Whereas in a herd of animals subject to a seasonal sexual excitement, occurring yearly or twice yearly, a period of a fortnight might be found necessary for the sex impulse to make itself felt in all the females in succession, this simply obliges the males to devote themselves almost completely during this fortnight to the functions of reproduction. But during all the rest of the year, normal life was resumed, entirely independent of any sexual disturbance, and on the whole, the disturbance in the social life of the herd had been as small as possible.

We can easily understand why the same was not the case with man. Individual variations, which were insignificant in the case of species having the period of sexual excitement recurring at long intervals, assumed, on the contrary, the highest importance in man, an animal with frequently recurring periods of love. In the primitive tribe, the females were under the influence of menstrual excitement, not all at once, but at intervals preceding or following by a few days the fateful date of the return of the lunar month; the total period during which sexual excitement prevailed among the women of the tribe encroached to a noticeable extent upon the interval of twenty-eight days. This disturbance was automatically transferred to the intermediate phenomenon of ovarian congestion, and here again a sort of minor period of sexual excitement extended both before and after the intermediate fourteenth day. So that in consequence of these encroachments which tended to meet, the periods during which the females of our first ancestral tribe were capable of experiencing the sex impulse ended by forming an almost uninterrupted succession during the whole month. Every female, it is obvious, was only under the influence of sex during a short period, which did not coincide with that of her sisters. But the male or males of the tribe were constantly surrounded with females in a state of sexual excitement.

The male was in a different position. He had preserved the physiological traditions of his ancestors—monkey or reptile—much better. In him the sexual flow manifested its chief activity in the springtime, in accordance with a great natural law; and a secondary activity of less importance in the autumn, according to the generally accepted rule of seasonal equipoise. It is extremely probable that if the female had been subject to physiological influences of an equally absolute nature, the sex impulse in man would have followed rules analogous to that of other animals.

But a new complication arose, due to the actual composition of this primitive tribe, which generally consisted of a single male living in polygamy with a certain number of females. It seems indeed to be admitted—though this is only a hypothesis which cannot be tested—that a few couples were at once formed. The father made a selection from among the children born of every union: he killed or drove out the sons, in order to avoid all subsequent sexual competition, and kept the girls, who constituted his harem. The operation continued with the new-born sons of the second generation, until the head of the tribe was abandoned by both virility and life.

During this time the sons who had been driven out banded together in hordes, satisfying their sex impulses by homosexualism or the common possession of some female who had fallen into their power by chance. This lasted until the sons could surprise and kill the father, share the females, who were their mothers and sisters, and found a new social order, which has lasted down to our time.

We can understand how many strange consequences may have arisen from the compulsory polygamy reigning in the primitive horde which only possessed one male, the chief of the tribe. The only male in the horde was obliged to renounce his primitive habits of cyclic sexual practices, in order to adapt himself to his numerous females; and this meant that he was obliged to respond to feminine solicitations during almost the whole time between two menstrual periods. So that, during the process of development of the race, the male was accustomed to being in a state of constant sexual excitement, and the primitive cyclic influences, which had at first been the rule, only continued in him as an additional stimulation, the influence of which only appears in very peculiar cases: as, for instance, in that of males deprived of females, or that of seasonal influences, a sort of chemical menstruation, which may be compared to the fermentation set up in wine when vintage time comes round again.

This new tradition of the species became gradually fixed by insensible changes. It was transmitted by heredity, and took on the characteristics, first of a habit, then of an instinct; and thus it became the rule, or rather the cause of the absence of a rule, controlling sexual excitement in the male human being.

For their part, the females did not long remain subject to a well-defined cyclic impulse. The fact that none of them happened to be at the same degree of sexual excitement at the same time was the reason why they did not observe any well-defined and incontrovertible laws of the species. Moreover, the excessive closeness of the possible sexual periods coincided with the fact that the menstruation of women is subject to individual variations, and can occur several days earlier or later. In these circumstances, the periods of sexual excitement were themselves disorganized, and a species of zones of physiological interference were set up, answering to a sort of intermediate sexual stage which was neither that of sexual excitement nor of dormant sexuality, but had some of the qualities of both. We may realize what must have been the influence in these cases of accessory external phenomena, such as the desire of the male (who was unable exactly to know the physiological state of the female, and made advances to her during one of these periods), jealousy of other females, or merely any other simple physiological cause: More abundant food, variation of temperature, etc.

It may be understood that in these conditions the brutal law of sex impulse in immediate relation with menstruation tended gradually to disappear. The sensitiveness of the utero-ovarian apparatus of the woman soon made it possible, as soon as human society and an embryonic civilization were constituted, to substitute a sort of psychological sexual excitement for the original physiological one, or at least to add to the latter supplementary ones destined to allow the sex impulse to develop during the intermenstrual periods.

These psychological excitations—thought, imagination, all those phenomena of which we have tried to demonstrate the purely physiological origin—succeeded in bringing about in the second place modifications in the internal secretions of the genito-ovarian organs, which are exquisitely sensitive to external reactions. As a result of this, substances analogous to those which are poured into the blood at periods of sexual excitation were able to be produced, and poured into the blood-stream, so as to create an endocrine equilibrium similar to that existing at the time of menstruation, and capable of bringing about the same cerebral reactions, that is to say, the sex impulse and the secondary idea of love.

We may begin to see how, by a sort of double and contradictory reaction, the man and the woman came to renounce the primitive physiological law common to all nature, that of a sexual urge occurring at regular cyclic periods and limited to a short space of time, outside of which the

animal, the plant, and perhaps even the mineral, are in a
state of sexual sleep. The human being, on the contrary, has
ended by suppressing the periodic character of the sex impulse, and only traces of primitive influences are found in
him; the seasonal sexual excitement taking place in man, in
the spring, the excessive development of sexuality in the
woman at the moment of menstruation. It may further be
noted that, as a result of the evolution of ideas, it is precisely
this menstrual period which has been eliminated from the
active period of human love.

It is as a result of these constant changes in the order existing primitively in our sex impulses that we have arrived at
that state of anarchy which characterizes the human species
with regard to the organization of its reproductive functions.
In animals, the fixing of the cycle of reproduction in an im-
mutable form is a law which nobody can or will disobey;
reproduction is the final act towards which all the activities
of the species converge; it seems to be the sole reason of the
life of individuals. Very often the sexual act is only accomplished once during the existence of the animal, and frequently coincides with its death, either because the exhaustion
caused by coition brings about such a rapid physical degeneration that the animal cannot survive, or because coition
is itself obligatorily accompanied by an enormous mutilation,
and brings about death (as in the drone, which leaves its
penis and genital glands in the sexual apparatus of the female), or because for some obscure reason the male cannot effect conjugation with the female without risking being
almost certainly put to death by her (the spider, praying
mantis, etc.).

In all animals the sex instinct is an absolute law which
is never disobeyed, whatever may be the results of accomplishment of this duty. And we may also note that in each
of these species the sex impulse is cyclic and only occupies
part of the animal's life. In man, on the contrary, the sex
impulse is continual, obeys no fixed law, and has no character

of inevitable necessity. Finally, and perhaps this is the most important point, the sex impulse is so separate from the idea of reproduction that this latter seems to be no more than a superadded phenomenon, occurring mostly by chance, and in most people only connected with the idea of the sex impulse in virtue of the ideas of duty or personal satisfaction. It is only in a few that it is due to the action of a fund of instinct which is not yet quite destroyed.

Man, then, is an animal who, in this particular point of reproduction, has freed himself from the laws of instinct, and lives on the outskirts of natural law.

For the time being, let us bear in mind that there are endocrine stimuli in men which give rise to sexual thoughts in him. But the part played by these bio-chemical excitants has been complicated by the revolt of man against the great cyclic law of sexual excitement in animals; and we very often have difficulty in evading this organic influence, which will, moreover, always be present, directing our thoughts and actions, no longer by the logic of animal instinct, but by an individual fancy which is sometimes regrettable.

2. *Disturbances of the sex impulse brought about by the continuous succession of births in the human race, and secondarily, by different conditions of life for different individuals.*

This breach of the natural cyclic law of sexual excitement not only shows us the possibility of individualism in sexual thought and, it goes without saying, the hesitation which we may now feel with regard to precise value of a morality applied to ideas whose formation is brought about by uniformly individual reactions; but it enables us to foresee another inevitable consequence: the physiological fulfillment of the sex impulse, reproduction, will not take place in man at clearly defined periods; his young will not all be born in successive batches, in one or more annual broods; but fertilization may, on the contrary, take place at any time; man is not an animal living together. like the others, in groups of individuals of the same age, and likely to react in an identical manner to the internal influences of organs formed under the same conditions. His sex impulse will differ from the general laws for a whole group of reasons.

In the first place, physical reasons:

Unlike other animals the new generations of mankind will not arrive in compact series, born and dying at about the same time. The scattering of the sex impulse over the whole course of the year will involve constant fertilization, and, in a group of some size, daily births.

In mankind there will, consequently, not be a series of young ones, subject simultaneously to influences at once hereditary and rhythmical, which will bring on the period of sexual excitement at the same time. Moreover, the constitution of human society will be such that the family or tribe containing but few individuals will no longer be the social rule.

Among the insects, society will be composed of one, two or three generations at the outside, the oldest members of which all disappear together almost contemporaneously with the birth of a new generation.

Among the animals, whose life is longer, there are, so to speak, autonomous generations, that is to say, the young ones belonging to the same litter, or born at the same time, will not continue to live with their parents for very long, and will soon separate from them to form a new family or tribe composed of individuals of the same age.

In man, on the contrary, the successive generations will all live together, a society will at one and the same time include individuals ninety years of age and sucklings; there will not, as among a society of animals, be four or five distinct generations, but there will be, on the contrary, an almost infinite series of individuals born at intervals of a few days or months.

We can understand that the division of a society of animals into four or five generations, consisting of identical individuals, will have a strong influence upon the possibility of four or five waves of sex impulse, resembling one another in their instinctive element, and only differing as regards the part due to external influences, which is proper to the development of each generation.

We should have here four or five completely analogous, or almost identical, waves of sex impulse, and we might say four or five sexual moralities, which might differ slightly, but which, in the probable case of the external causes of life being identical, would approach one another so closely, that in practice, we may fuse them, and be led to see one single, mighty sex impulse characteristic of the species, and applying to the animal tribe as a whole.

Conditions are different in a human society, and an uninterrupted series of births will break the animal harmony. The most serious result of this state of things, from the physiological point of view, will be that, from the point of view of sexual maturity, in the first case, man will not be at the stage of a mass development of the sex impulse, brought about by a vast, mighty current, such as that which provokes the physiological reflexes of love at the same moment in a whole generation of animals. Lost in the midst of a mass of individuals, not of his own age, having relations with only a small number of other organisms at the same stage of functional development, man will not be very favorably circumstanced for the accomplishment of his sexual evolution together with those individuals of his generation, in physical, physiological and rhythmical harmony with whom he ought logically to make love.

The idea of instinct will here be dimmed and masked by psychological impulses deriving, indeed, from the sex impulse, but often distorted and transposed by extraneous ideas and associated phenomena of thought; the law of rhythm and instinct ought irresistibly to impel the individuals of a generation to make love only with the other members of this generation; but it is often deranged by social considerations, or even by what are called moral questions.

Other causes intervene, of which we have already spoken: there ceases to be a seasonal recurrence of sexual excitement, there is a partial forgetting or at least a vitiation of the function of reproduction, the supreme and only object of the sex impulse in other animals.

Man likewise manifests some morphological differences, some particularly important variations in outward appearance. In a whole section of the animal kingdom (insects, crustacea, etc.), the formation of an outer shell may have reduced these differences to a minimum. They are generally inconsiderable among the vertebrata, and it is only in man that they acquire a very noticeable importance, of such a nature that its repercussion upon the sex impulse may have consequences into which it is useless to enter.

In a beehive, all the individuals are brothers and sisters, and consequently, their physiological constitution is likely to be as similar as possible. In man, on the contrary, the individuality of the tissues and internal organs is carried very far. Moreover, hereditary ailments (various diatheses, syphilis, etc.) may also intervene to increase this individuality of the tissues. Our sex impulse will, then, be subject to extraneous influences unknown to the other species. Here we shall have a probable fresh cause of disorders proper to man, which lead us naturally to the conception of another of those dissociations of thought which are necessary for our study: man, *homo sapiens*, is a collective term, under which are included species which are different from the point of view of physiological reactions, and will consequently have a dissimilar psychological activity.

All these differences, working upon the constitution of the tissues and the chemical composition of the blood, end by creating individuals who hardly resemble one another in anything save their outer envelope. A whole body of external influences, food and clothing, still further aggravates these

differences. The conditions of life have a profound repercussion upon these organisms, which have ceased to be perfectly similar.

In a beehive, all the inhabitants are born at the same time,
and react in an identical manner to outward influences, cold,
heat, abundance or lack of food: there is only one sex impulse
for one and the same race. But in man there may be many
reasons which prevent this simultaneity of sensations:

1) Though the conditions of life are the same for a whole
race, it is composed of individuals of different ages, that is to
say, in effect, of tissues at more or less advanced stages of
development, and organs either embryonic or at the height
of their activity, or perhaps, in the end hardened by old
age.

The action of external influences, however identical, may
be manifested in these individuals by different organic reactions; and the secondary result will be that even their
psychological reactions will have no resemblance. In the particular case which interests us, we can conceive of the existence of an infinite number of sex impulses, varying almost
with every creature. In practice, to render our classification
clear, we may group certain of these impulses together, and
collect those which are not too different in the same class.
It is the age of the organs and the state of their activity
which we shall use in order to make these distinctions, and
we may already foresee that, from the bio-chemical point of
view, we shall no longer have to regard the human race as a
well-defined species, but as a collection of sub-species characterized in accordance with their histological or glandular
coefficient.

2) A second cause of differentiation between the individuals composing the human race arises from the fact that we
must pursue our argument still further, and establish the
fact that these sub-species themselves, grouped according to
age, are not homogeneous. The same tissue, the same colloidal
jelly, will have variable reactions according to the modifica-

tions of its external environment. Subjects of the same age, though analogous to one another in their glandular functions, will manifest considerable variations in the composition of their blood (and, in consequence, of their psychology and sex impulses) according as they are exposed to cold or heat, or as they are well or badly nourished.

An infinite number of sub-species will thus be constantly created and destroyed. These individual variations, due to external reactions, will be of small importance in those animals which, like the insects, develop inside an armor of chitin. This separates them fairly well from the outer world, and withdraws them from most of its influences, and this almost indestructible rigidity of the external covering of their body ensures them a certain autonomy, which explains why, as experience shows us, the sex impulse will be almost constant for all the members of the same generation.

The case is different for those animals which build up their soft, plastic outward covering, which separates them from the outer world, upon the solid framework of a skeleton running through the interior of the body. It is curious to note that of the membranes enclosing the embryo, the endoderm and mesoderm go to make up the internal part of the creature, while the ectoderm serves to form both the superficial region, which separates the individual from the outer world, and that unit which is formed by the brain and the nervous system.

The part of the creature, then, which reacts directly to outside influences has the same origin as the brain. The plastic differences in the corporeal envelope will correspond to similar variations in weight, and in the chemical constitution of the brains of the series of human beings, and this may also explain to us why a sex impulse which is automic in an insect, which wears its skeleton outside it, becomes autonomous in man, who has an inner skeleton.

The possible repercussion of the bio-chemical properties of a being upon its sexual character may be illustrated by phenomena observable in plants and animals during the act of reproduction, which constitutes in them the very basis of the sex impulse.

By effecting cross-fertilization between an Aramon and a Teinturier vine-stock, Armand Gautier produced a new sort of vine, the Petit Bouschet. Now in studying a coloring pigment contained in the leaf of the latter—a substance belonging to the pyrocatechin family—he ascertained that its formula was made up precisely by the addition of the formulæ of the catechins in the two original plants. A new race, then, can be created under the direct influence of a chemical combination, in the same way as the formation of animal hybrids can be almost mathematically controlled. As we know that for this reproduction it is not necessary to take into account the somatic cells of the animal, that is to say, those which constitute its body, but only its germinative cells, we can see that here again experimental bio-chemistry will play a preponderating part in the formation of the new being, the hybrid, which will, in short, be the result of unexpected chemical interactions between the substances composing the two original germs, between the male and female germ plasms.

We can see what a powerful influence these different reactions may have upon the human race, which we have already regarded as split up into sub-species, according to the age or conditions of life of its members. Personal chemical influences will further step in to complete this splitting-up of the race. In the end we shall be a long way from the physiological and chemical homogeneity which is manifested by a colony of bees; so we need not be surprised if in the latter the sex impulse is an instinctive, collective manifestation, whereas in man there are various forms of sex instinct corresponding to the sub-races of mankind which can almost be distinguished. Experience will easily disclose to us the existence of these special, peculiar races in the great tribe of mankind; differences of country or color will no longer serve as the basis of this classification, but rather a particular physiological condition, a certain bio-chemical make-up of the organism. Our unreasoning sympathies, attractions or repulsions show us that we really act as if, among the vast human flock, we only felt a physiological kinship with a few individuals. It is very probable that to an observer possessed of vision of a kind unlike that of man, a collection of men— for instance, the population of a city—would be distinguishable into a certain number of well-differentiated kinds; just as we are enabled to classify in separate families the ants which we may by chance come upon mingled together.

Each of these human races will have a sex impulse corresponding to its histological and bio-chemical characteristics. The species as a whole will obey certain great general common laws, which we shall try to bring out later. But we have still to examine a last element of discord: it is only in man that the sex impulse is capable of undergoing derangements which may go to the lengths of erotomania.

We have seen that it has been possible to establish a vague classification of the human races, and to attribute to certain groups sex impulses which are almost similar for the whole of their members: it is this, indeed, which is the very foundation of various kinds of sexual morality. But man, viewed as an animal, revolted at the outset against the great cyclic law of the sex impulse: these very classifications which we are bound to make show how impossible it was to admit a single and universally valid law.

This revolt will be renewed in the sub-species which we have considered. Each of them has a peculiar impulse which seems to govern its sexual life. But these are only approximations: in these smaller groups represented by the sub-species, certain individuals, under a complication of influences, may revolt, and reject the sexual law. The causes of this insubordination may be many: modification of external conditions, reminiscences of the habits of ancestors—or even of the animals which are doubtless the creators of our race—a return to the morals of some old totem animal, etc. All this may suddenly bring about an occurrence which generally presents itself in the following form: individuals who have lived for many years a life in which the sex impulses have been rigidly under the control of psycho-moral influences find themselves suddenly and irresistibly carried away as though by a sort of sexual ground swell. All control becomes impossible to them, and they are bound to obey an all-powerful command coming from the depths of their unconscious self. These facts afford a good characterization for defining the human race. A bee will never disobey the sex impulse of the race; though we may sometimes notice some aberrations (for example, an excessive number of male eggs), which appear at first sight to approximate to those of man, a more careful examination will at once show us that we are here concerned not with individual acts, but with a collective disorder, definitely determined by a modification of outward conditions. In the case we have cited all the bees in a hive, under the influence of insufficient nourishment, will begin to modify the feeding of the larvæ, and bring about the hatching of a far more considerable number of males. It is never an unexpected, or, as we might say, fanciful aberration, such as is often produced in man by attacks of erotomania.

The study of this form of mania is important, for it enables us to arrive at an idea as to how individual physiological reactions may be reflected in the formation of thoughts, and we must attempt to solve this problem on a bio-chemical basis.

THE FREUDIAN EMPHASIS ON SEX [1]

By Samuel D. Schmalhausen

No criticism has been more often hurled at Freud than that he has stressed sex too much. The very insistence and universality of the criticism make one feel as if it were reasonably true. But, in another sense, the criticism is a dodge, sheer evasion. The dramatist uses a method of theatric condensation of experience which is intended to secure effective attention to a segment of experience. Not only is the dramatist not censured for this literal falsification of reality, he is, on the contrary, hailed as ingenious and creative if he is really able to make reality more vividly real by his dramatic exaggeration and theatric intensity. Freud as an artist in the subtle field of new ideas has indulged the luxury of dramatic falsification for the sake of imparting to the reluctant and resistant conventional mind the profound truth about the rôle of sex in civilization.

At any rate, Freud's high-power emphasis on sex has persuaded a whole world to pay attention to obscure realities long denied as non-existent (or at least unworthy of existence) and now more easily confronted as too important to be neglected by those who would call themselves enlightened. In this amazing sense, the Freudian emphasis on sex may almost be said to have created a new psychology of attention. No one possessed of a flexible mind can longer evade the truths first probed and published by Sigmund Freud, latterly acknowledged to be one of the world's great geniuses. Part of his genius lay in his knowledge of how to impart to a squeamish and shamefaced mankind those fundamental in-

[1] From *Why We Misbehave*. New York: The Macaulay Company, 1928.

sights into "the buried life" which a hypocritical morality, a humorlessly puritanic Weltanschauung, had completely ostracized as beneath the dignity of the conscious rational mind.

What new knowledge may be attributed to Freudian psychoanalysis? It is foolish to assert that any man, however great, can create a whole body of knowledge all by himself. There are always speculations and findings, delvings and procedures that form a kind of prelude to any apparently new branch of learning. In short, a true perspective can always discover a history of flowing facts in which the novel insights will be imbedded. So with the Freudian wisdom. Acknowledging as much, one may permissibly insist that certain psycho-sexual discoveries are Freudian in the momentous sense of having been given a powerful status in the world of thought only with the enunciation of psychoanalytic principles and procedures.

For example, who had ever heard of infantile sexuality as a widespread reality of the utmost significance for the evolution of the erotic life? Who had ever even begun dimly to realize the amount of auto-erotic behavior there is in childhood? Though a phrase like "polymorphous perverse" sounds grotesque enough to be humorous, the humor is somewhat abated in the presence of the sexual realties underlying. The interest of little children in urinating and defecating has frequently enough sexual contexts and complications that may drag with them into maturity obsessions, anxieties, compulsions, that plague the psychoneurotic of a certain species.

How many persons, before the Freudian ascendancy, possessed the keenness to perceive in "crushes" a form of homosexuality, albeit rather innocent in the milder cases, and anything but innocent in certain other cases? How does it happen that the world has suddenly awakened to the startlingly wide existence among persons of high and low degree of homosexual attachments? Whatever is scientific and sane in our new attitude toward masturbation is almost wholly traceable to the courageous insistence of the psychoanalysts that auto-erotic practices constitute an inevitable phase of normal sex life.

What generations of young men and young women have suffered in private humiliation and remorse and shame and anxiety amounting to torture, it is difficult to visualize now that the life of youth has been freed from the horrible burden of self-accusation, of unclean conscience pangs, in the presence of a sexual behavior that is, under certain conditions of stress and strain, as natural and inevitable as breathing, exercising, dreaming, and kissing. The psychoanalysts are wise in simply having removed auto-erotism from the superstitious background of private self-indulgence, shameful and painful, and given it a simple unworried status of biologic urgency under certain perfectly human conditions of stimulation and tension. The light of publicity that has been shed upon this universal habit of the sexes has helped to ventilate the matter and to give it a scientific status at once wholesome and sane. The evil of masturbation could certainly not arise from the physical relief consequent upon unbearable tension; it must have resulted from the anxiety and brooding shame accompanying such self-conscious behavior, by its nature sneaky, awkward, and rather humiliating to one's personal sense of free will and self-control which were being so obviously put in jeopardy.

As an American poet and philosopher, Max Eastman, has generously written: "Freud has made himself a wise and wonderful scientist of sex, and has given a gift of illumination to the world not second to that which Hobbes gave, and so we can forgive him if he somewhat overstrains the generalization, and tends to carry us back to a contemplation of oneness almost as bad as that of the sickly mystics whom he knows how to cure. He has at least lifted a great incubus of shame from the shoulders of humanity, and given the boon of candor to a poor animal desperately endeavoring to become a man."

THE FREUDIAN EMPHASIS ON SEX

The concepts introduced by the psychoanalytic way of thinking have not only given a new lease of life to psychiatry and psychopathology, but have insidiously undermined the abstractionist foundations of academic psychology with the utterly wholesome result that psychology nowadays, to be treated seriously, must be drastically dynamic. The *psychiatrizing* of academic psychology constitutes a revolution in itself, in the sedate halls of learning. No significant psychology written within the past ten years by an academical has failed to pay tribute (honorable or dishonorable) to Freudian insights. Illuminating concepts like infantile sexuality, mother fixation, narcissism, homosexual attachment, rationalization, complex, libido, compulsion, psychoneurotic, dream interpretation, the unconscious, have shed a wonderful light on the obscurer motivations of men, revealing layers of desire in the troubled deeps of the subconscious mind to which the classic psychologists were for the most part gravel-blind.

Is it not inappropriate to ask why so dramatic and vital a reality as sex had been evaded so successfully by generations of philosophers, psychologists, medical men, thinkers in general? In retrospect the omission seems incredible. On the reasonable assumption that philosophers as a class were sexually a feeble brood, that psychologists were impotent or at least squeamish and repressed, that medical men labored under a theologic burden of shame and fear, that thinkers in general lacked the courage to confront their own human nature realistically, only on some such assumptions is it at all possible to understand the long neglect of a field of human reality more significant and interesting than any to which these experts had been giving their brilliant and often quite sterile devotion.

Another point of approach is the realization of man's childish delight in make-believe which he refers to as idealism. Man does not find it easy to absorb reality. The reason is clear at length. Reality represents disharmony, imperfection, evil. His infantile imagination creates a private universe in which harmony, perfection, good, rule as the holy trinity of the inner life. When confronted with the contradiction between his private imaginary universe and the public realistic world, his first tendency is to deny objective reality and to slide back into the comfort and reaffirmation of subjectivism. The ancient dualism between idealism and realism resolves itself into the conflict between infantile make-believe and mature disillusionment. Once we perceive how deeply rooted in his childish theatric nature is the disposition to accept illusion and to deny or flee from disillusion, we shall be close to the heart of the matter: pretense soothes the mind of man, reality disturbs it.

In relation to professional thinkers,—the professors and the academicians,—a special selective tendency is at work to assign positions of importance in our institutions of learning to those persons whose human nature is not richly endowed emotionally. No man has ever been selected for a university job on the ground of his exceeding compassion for his fellow men. No woman has ever been honored with a professorship because of her loyalty to love. Men and women whose human nature is intense, emotionally sincere, erotically lyrical, sympathetically deep, are simply déclassé. Our institutions of learning are houses of refuge for men and women who are emotionally unfit for any of the more vigorous and realistic burdens of life: chalk-laden pedagogues, peddlers of anæmic platitudes, sterile grammarians, cowardly passionless humans all.

The point of interest is to observe how these anæmic professors are flirting with the realistic sexual interpretations of Freud and gradually, by the indirection and left-handedness congenial to academicals, are becoming the interested victims of the psychoanalytical ways of thinking. Evil, that is, life, always ill at ease in the academic groves, has of late begun to feel surprisingly at home in that make-believe environment. Freud (quite innocently) has made evil so fascinating that the more sprightly of the professors find his subject-matter as attractive as the forbidden passages in Shakespeare which as sophomores they had no moral right to read, and therefore, digested with an almost indecent avidity, on the sly. Psychology, even academic psychology, has had color and vivacity and galvanic shock imparted to it by the vital impulse of psychoanalysis. Freud has *humanized* psychology.

Why were we all so loath to believe that sex manifests itself in earliest infancy? Why was it more congenial to believe that the sex instinct is non-existent until puberty arrives? Why in general did we find it consoling to think that sex belongs to maturity and can be safely neglected in infancy and in childhood and possibly in early adolescence? I suppose our unclean attitude toward sex is in large part responsible for our blindness and psychologic obtuseness. Then, too, our ignorant assumption that sex behavior cannot occur until a certain stage in physiologic maturity has been attained was somewhat responsible for our silly philosophy of innocence. Nor must we neglect the influence upon our make-believe thinking of the moralistic conception of children (in particular, our own) as little angels, innocent darlings sprung from the chaste head of God, incapable of evil, that is, of sexuality. It was refreshing to believe that we were innocent once, in our infancy, however guilty we might feel now in our corrupt maturity!

Thanks to the evil influence of Christian morality (that is, of hypocrisy), we all surrendered to the foolish belief that sex was something to be ashamed of. What could be more natural, in view of this belief, than to falsify the simple lustful reality of conception, to cleanse childbirth of its sinful origin, to think of children as sexless (the compensation for our unforgettable knowledge of their sexual begetting). Thanks to Freud, we have become more vigorous, more honest, more intelligent, and best of all, more humble. If Freudianism had done nothing else than cleanse our hypocritical and prurient minds of the poison ethics of shame, all mankind (and even more truly, all womankind) would be Freud's eternal debtor. We are no longer ashamed of sensuality, appreciating in a new and exhilarating sense the marvelous meanings resident in sexual potency.

Recently some experiments in the field of animal psychology have added surprising bits of new knowledge to our store. It had been taken for granted that nature once for all had laid down certain enduring reaction patterns which deserved, because of their universality and stability, to be called instincts. Instincts appeared to be modes of behavior beyond the power of man to tamper with, as he might with habits, for example. Instincts were assumed to be wholly unlearned reactions and therefore fundamental in the organism. Among these stable ingredients of the organism, none was conceived to be more eternal and reliable than the so-called sex instinct. All the activities centering around the impulse that leads to mating and offspring were envisaged as purely instinctive reactions. Thus, nothing seemed more natural than the assumption of an instinctive sex attraction between male and female. The surprising bit of new knowledge referred to above consists in the demonstration (by scientific experiment) of the essentially undifferentiated and far from fixed nature of the sex instinct.

Animals, for example monkeys, show no decided and inevitable preference for the opposite sex. Succinctly summarized, said animals enjoy (we'll call it that) the practices of masturbation and homosexuality, even as they appear to enjoy heterosexual relations. We discover no overwhelming evidence in favor of the traditional hypothesis that sex expression unquestionably implies the presence of both sexes, at least, so it had been argued, among the higher animals. The primary fact seems to be sheer undifferentiated sex tension. What mode of relief this tension shall take depends, not upon eternally fixed patterns of response called instinctive, but rather upon the opportunities of the environment at the given moment. In the animal experiments, in the absence of the opposite sex, a male monkey had no hesitancy in mating with a small and youthful male of the species. Or, for lack of either male or female cohabitant, our lust-laden monkey will content himself with any object close by as a point of contact for the sheer mechanics of coitus. These unfamiliar facts reopen the whole problem of the nature of instinct.

Increasingly we must prepare our reluctant minds for the knowledge of the spreading cult of sexual behavior once looked upon as definitely pathologic and monstrous, latterly surveyed as within the field of human nature's true preferences. We are all becoming acquainted with abnormal sex practices. Whether we have in mind boarding schools, seminaries, college dorms, army life, reformatories, prisons, art colonies, monasteries, camps, in fine, any human center where one sex predominates, we are no longer shocked to learn of the existence of homosexuality, sometimes tentative and playful, sometimes deliberate and overt, not to mention more innocent sex behavior that would until the day before yesterday have been called even by sexologists, abnormal, in fact, pathologic. The big question confronting sexologists of the psychoanalytic school is this: Is there any form of sex behavior that may be called abnormal in the pathologic sense, and if so, from whose point of view? This troubling query introduces the expert at once into the more perturbing subject of perversions. One thing seems perfectly clear: it is no longer permissible for an enlightened person to be horrified by perversion.

Strangely enough, even Freud who has, in the face of the most humiliating opposition from the respectable folk, habituated our reasonable minds to the wide permissible variety of sex expression, takes as his point of departure for sexual normality the ancient fact of reproduction. In such a view, the use of one's sex in ways that sidetrack libidinous desire from the true goal of mating drags in its train the possibility of perversion. In the most naturalistic view, perversion is sexual behavior that thwarts the aim of reproduction. Thus the true indictment of the "polymorphous perverse" sexual practices of children is the danger resident in them for infantile fixations that distort the evolution of erotic desire toward uninhibited heterosexuality. On the basis of such a logic, auto-erotism, homosexual fixations, narcissistic sexuality, are all undesirable forms of sex expression because of the danger of arrested development at one of these immature levels. These are literally perversions in the sense that such behaviors sidetrack libidinous desire from "object love" which in a normal maturity means love of the opposite sex.

There are tendencies of a sociological and psycho-sexual nature in our age that make abundantly clear the subordination of the goal of reproduction to that of self-indulgence. Expressed more graphically, the contemporary cultural situation is subordinating procreation to recreation. If this be true, —no tendency in modernity appears to be more emphatically in the ascendant,—it is incumbent upon us to realize that what used to be called perversion has become the new normality. Sex is no longer being primarily used for purposes of reproduction. This singular fact must be our starting point for whatever enlightened thinking we are preparing to do in the attempt to enrich the life of the sexes in whatever ways seem conducive to such enrichment. The old criteria of normality are no longer tenable. The new criteria are in the process of creation. Toward the creation of the new norms the variety of human nature and the potentialities of sex expression will make their significant contribution. What we of the puritanic tradition must courageously confront is the nature and extent of the sexual revolution that unfolds itself fascinatingly before our affrighted eyes.

Once we clearly envisage the sheer inevitability of the sexual revolution, the social and psycho-sexual forces that were predetermining the shift of the center of gravity from procreation to recreation, we shall be in a calmer mood to understand some of the eccentric by-products of so vast a change in sex fulfillment. Sex as duty (a theologic ethic) has gone the way of all wearisome and life-denying superstitions. Sex as delight (an æsthetic and psychoanalytic ethic) has captured the minds of men and women eager for felicity. With the bankruptcy of the older ethic as latterly manifested in the growing phenomena of experimental marriage, freedom in love, adultery, divorce, the candid acceptance of auto-erotism, the distinguished pleas for the rights of homo-sexuals, goes quite inevitably the emergence of a sexual ethics that *must* seem by antithesis the very quintessence of ab-normality: what some would call pathology and perversion.

No theme is more deserving of our sincere and unfrightened attention than the new freedom in sex expression based upon the triumph of recreation over procreation as the goal of sex love.

The rediscovery of passion is the shining novelty of an age which has simultaneously discovered that woman pos-sesses sexual personality. Henceforth, it is woman who will be setting the patterns of permissible sex behavior. Her emancipation from the bondage of fecundity has left her with a fund of erotic energy that must seek outlets in non-reproductive fashions. The speed and ease with which this newly emancipated female has taken to varietism in sex hints at the supersession of ancient norms by ultra-modern ones. If the accumulating evidence in the case should plainly show that what men and women of another time had agreed, out of the depths of their sweet sexual reticence, to call modesty, has disappeared from the bosoms of respectable females (an unreality that had never been more than a metaphysical pretense honored in a world of make-believe), we can the more serenely approach the new woman as the child of candor and life, the sworn enemy of sham and shame. The vital essence of the quite new morality is its reputable shamelessness. This contribution to the higher ethics is un-challengeably woman's.

Freud's brilliant conceptions of the mechanisms under-

lying psychoneurotic behavior were in considerable part
provoked by his study of women suffering from various kinds
of compulsions, anxieties, obsessions, which he traced to
infantile traumatic occurrences and to fixations and distor-
tions of the sexual impulse. It is not necessary to enter here
into a critical discussion of the Freudian theory of the
psychoneuroses. For our purposes it is enough to point out
that the undeniable rôle of sexual frustration in the development of various of the psychoneurotic states has been illuminated most impressively by the Freudian technique.
The vast amount of sexual suffering engendered in marriage
by the intrusion of memories and attachments and traumatic
experiences traceable to childhood has been clarified by psychoanalysis. The repressive power of conventional morality,
the inhibiting force of parental fixation, the disturbing influence of unconscious homosexual trends, the doubts and
anxieties engendered by fear and shame, the compulsions and
obsessions that act as a screen for immoral desires, the rôle
of oral and anal eroticism, the strange tenacity of certain
sexual episodes having their dark roots in childhood,—all
these matters, of the first importance to a realistic insight
into the variety of sex behavior, are the patient contribution
of the Freudian analysts. Such a contribution could never
have been made except by a group of experts in whom candor
and clarity had definitely triumphed over pretense and
evasion.

The vivid concepts of sadism and masochism enrich our
comprehension of human nature in a striking way. One need
not point to pathologic cases of sadistic and masochistic behavior sprung from sexual perversion to realize that these
components are widely distributed among so-called normal
people whose erotic life is considerably influenced by one or
the other of them. It is legitimate to supplement this notion
with the rôle played by sheer ego-dominance which is quite
as often responsible for these sexually perverse attitudes.
The sadistic lover is evidently expressing his will-to-supe-

riority quite as emphatically as his sheer exuberance of un-controllable sex desire. Perhaps the imposing of pain is the most fundamental device at the disposal of humans for putting their personalities across at all costs. Even in the less plausible instance of masochism, of the desire to suffer pain, we may be witnessing a cowardly and abnormal form of the will-to-power embodying itself in a kind of wretched martyrdom. At any rate, in the play of such powerful tendencies as sadism and masochism, we behold remarkable instances of the interrelation and overlapping of the fundamental factors of ego and sex, sometimes with the ego riding the situation, sometimes with sex in charge of affairs. There is a kind of egotism which is primarily sexual. There is a kind of sexuality which is fundamentally egotistic. This truth, which is somewhat wider and therefore more adequate than the Freudian or the Adlerian emphasis, deserves a more analytic study.

What is civilization? From a psychoanalytic point of view, civilization is a complicated device of repression and concealment, having as its major purpose the subordination of passion to social conformity, by means of the definite prohibition of free and easy sex expression in youth, and correlatively, by the sublimation of instinctive desire in socially useful modes. Civilization spells repression. To be perfectly accurate, let us say that conventional civilization spells repression. Perhaps men and women can build a new unconventional civilization which will not rest upon the props of repression and concealment. We shall see.

If we survey traditional civilization, we are impressed by one fact as always conspicuously present; the vast array of machinery of intimidation (physical, emotional, intellectual, spiritual) used by the authoritative elders to prevent the free and easy expression of sex desire. The times waited for a Freud to come along and make clear to a blind mankind how tragic the costs of this civilized machinery of intimidation. This exposé of the staggering human cost of sexual frustration I look upon as the ultimately important contribution of

Freud. Why were the authoritative elders so concerned with preventing nature from being natural?

One explanation leans on ego-dominance, the other explanation belongs to the life of sex. Can you imagine a more reliable source of self-importance than playing at the rôle of moral censor? The melodramatic thrill of moral superiority is the most exquisite kind of sadistic delight. To sit in judgment: that pose suits human nature beautifully. To find scapegoats for one's moralistic viciousness is the most interesting of pastimes. Those who have suffered deprivation and frustration cannot be counted on to be generous. Their only source of compensatory satisfaction lies in a malicious kill-joy attitude that seeks to prevent others from enjoyment. In the field of sex, the kill-joy attitude is too familiar to leave us in any doubt of its evil potency. The elders of the tribe are in a holy-holy conspiracy to deny to the young the prerogatives of sex love because they themselves are debarred (by natural limitation or social taboo) from a similar happy indulgence. What they miss in sex fulfillment they seek to wrest from ego-dominance. Then, too, their dwarfish and tainted attitudes toward the spontaneity and adventurousness of passion and love have for so long marred their own capacity for highly evaluating romance and mating that they are really quite incapable of understanding why illuminated young bodies should yearn toward one another so madly. The virtue of the old is the virtue of impotence. The wisdom of the old is the wisdom of frustration. Deprivation from the experimental felicities of sex prompts the ego to make a last brave stand for compensatory status by brandishing the will-to-power over the heads of lawless youth who are too preoccupied in the quest of happiness to be impressed with the vicious demands of frustrated egotists for a place in the sun.

If conventional civilization has insisted on putting a strait-jacket on the live passionate impulses of youth, the reason was by no means consistently rational. The fear of promiscuous parenthood played its inhibiting part, of course. But, psychologically, the essence of the true reason (obscured by rationalization) was simply the kill-joy jealousy of the young nestling poisonously in the hearts of the old. We cannot think graciously of a feast from which we are debarred.

Can civilization, under new psychoanalytic auspices, allow to sex the wide margins of pleasurable freedom it yearns for, without undermining those values deemed precious by men and women as *human* beings, sensitive, egotistic, willful, self-conscious? A subtle warfare is on between the ego and sex components in human nature. Can the ego and sex forces do as they please, under a régime of freedom of personal impulse, without eventually introducing more torture into the relation of the sexes than we are as yet more than dimly aware of, in our inevitably hectic pursuit of self-expression?

The most interesting and important movement in America for applying rational and humanistic techniques to the study of the complicated problems of sexual maladjustment is the mental hygiene movement. Recently, Dr. Frankwood E. Williams, its director, has emphasized as of paramount importance in youthtime two problems, viz., emancipation from the home and the attainment of heterosexuality. These propositions imply two antecedent situations: the obsessive and distorting influence of overemotional familial authority, and the existence of temptations and opportunities for sexual behavior that stand in the way of normal sex expression. The dependence of the child upon the parent; the dependence of the parent upon the child; the veiled incestuous bond that may exist between parent and child where the emotional relation is exceedingly intense; the evil after-effects upon a child's development of having come under the sway of an authoritative father or an indulgent mother; the untoward consequences for the love life of the young of having dwelt for the most impressionable years with loveless or unhappy parents; the obviously bad influence of parents who, having failed frankly to confront and to solve their own erotic problems, nevertheless proceed, in their haughty blindness, to impose negations and taboos and repressions upon their growing offspring whose animalism and natural candor so often outrage and shame them;—these momentous problems have been brought to public consciousness by the hopeful new science of mental hygiene which has been inspired by the brilliant discoveries of Freud, Jung, Adler and a host of psychoanalytic-minded psychologists.

Not so long ago even the most enlightened persons assumed the naturalness and therefore the inevitability of heterosexual attachment. The wise admonition of Dr. Williams gives us pause. Are there any forces in contemporary civilization that tend to thwart normal sexing? I believe so. The rhythm of the jazz age has infected our sex life: no doubt of that. We seek stimulation incessantly. No one can reasonably deny that the old-fashioned sobriety of marriage with its spiritless ritual and routine of all work and no play has lost its coercion over the consciences of young men and young women. For the younger generation, fecundity is out of the question. The new gospel is one of frank fun and happy-go-lucky pleasure seeking. This shift in psychological atmospheres has brought with it a jazzing of sexual eagerness, a call for more zest, an open-hearted invitation to sensual playful experience. When you consider how very easily normal sex behavior slides into a kind of monotonous ceremonial devoid of spontaneity or passional enthusiasm, you can catch the meaning of that flirting with the unusual, the forbidden, the immoral, which marks the new sexual regimen. We cannot evade the troubling fact that marriage and reproduction and normality and duty, whatever their status in heaven, are losing their ancient sanction on earth. The modern mad quest for stimulation is driving men and women into the arms of abnormality. Pathology promises novel sensations.

There are other vital points to be reckoned with. The physiological enlightenment that removes the mystery and the illusion surrounding sex; the general disrobing of the female in public that gradually habituates the male to a simple, athletic, and feebly erotic conception of the magic of sex (once dwelt upon by the race of man as the wonder of wonders); the all-pervading cult of contraception; the substitution of a mechanical deliberateness for a natural reckless spontaneity in the performance of the sex act; the disheartening simplicity, almost automaticity, of sexing in marriage; finally, the transformation of the very basis of life from one of sober duty and conscience pangs (for infringement) to that of drunken disregard and light-hearted self-indulgence;—these mutations in the philosophy and deportment of the sexes have contributed hugely to that search for recreation and playful erotic experience with which our neurotic age is acquainted.

What I want to stress is the inevitability of these changes. The older normality implied procreation as the goal of the sex life. The newer normality assumes recreation as the goal of the sex life. The difference is nothing if not revolutionary. The most radical by-product of the change in norms is the emergence of abnormal sexual experience with appropriate apologetic, rationalization, and reputable justification. Because these things are true, we must view heterosexual attachment as no longer the secure and sacred reality we were taught to believe it to be, in the nature of things, eternally. Homosexual attachment achieves increasingly a status of respectability. If normal sexual intercourse between men and women, shut off from the larger aim of reproduction, should find itself subject to the self-centered limitation of monotony and routine and passionlessness, as it is in danger of doing, what alternatives remain to the sexes for erotic zest and unique stimulation except those resident in playful experimental behaviors that approach by perilous degrees to abnormality and perversions? Doubt it not: pathology is woven into the very texture of contemporary civilization.

Matings should begin at puberty. Marriage, from a moralistic angle, should provide the responsible and sacred sanction for mating. *Apparently,* the simplest solution for sex desire would be marriage in earliest youth when puberty precipitates genital eagerness. What do we find? Sex desire begins as of old in puberty (much earlier, in fact, in many cases). Marriage, thanks to the unbearable demands of the economic and the cultural situation, what is blithely termed "the standard of living," has been deferred for men and for women until late maturity; between ages twenty-five and thirty-five for females, and between ages thirty and forty for males. The great gap between the arrival of puberty and the time of marriage constitutes the overwhelmingly big unsolved problem of the sexes. What, one may inquire, are the sexes doing with their stirred erotic energies during this enormous interval? Whatever they may be doing in intimate detail, we know very well that in general they are pursuing —or, if you will, being pursued by—*casual* sex experience. The old stability has given place to the new instability as the *normal* pattern of the love life. Casualness best expresses the nature of this transvaluation of values.

Marriage used to mean living together until death do us part. Marriage now means living apart until death do bring us together. Marriage no longer binds. Marriage no longer unites. Marriage as a sacred psycho-sexual union conceived in heaven and perpetrated on earth is no longer meaningful to us. The habit of marriage remains. The psychology of marriage has petered out. The custom of marriage is still with us. The familiar wistful sanctions of marriage are now a chapter in antiquarian lore. The new casual way of sexing has modified all our traditional thinking on the subject of holy matrimony.

We might put it this way and say that we have moved from an overvaluation to an undervaluation of the significance of the sex act. Even today there is a considerable body of religious and inspired opinion (which has its fountain head in the cult of the holy virgin) in favor of the chastity of marriage, i.e., the practice of abstinence except for those brief luminous moments when conception is being sweetly perpetrated. Sex at the service of reproduction, and for the rest of the time, religiously out of service. This point of view is what I allude to as overvaluation. Now we have moved, pendulum-like, to the other extreme. Reproduction has become a mere episode in the relations of the sexes. Procreation is not taken too seriously. But recreation in the sex life has been elevated to the status of a religion. This is what I referred to as undervaluation. The very casualness of modern sex life (we are only witnessing the first fevered beginnings of the new morality) makes for a kind of repudiation of the entire ethics and philosophy of procreation.

Family life as such is on the wane. Instability of marital ties is the outstanding fact. Infidelity is no longer deemed a violation of a sacred vow. A kind of loosening of the old erotic bonds is occurring among all strata of the population, among young and old, good and bad, male and female. This loosening of the old erotic bonds is what is technically called the new morality. The new morality is really new in the original sense that it assigns a status of reasonable reputability to behavior branded throughout the moralistic Christian centuries as immoral, disreputable: for example, auto-erotism, adultery, easy divorce, promiscuity, homosexual affection, casualness in the love life.

Casualness in the sex relation condenses it into such a simple, straightforward, unmysterious, candid, mechanistic and transitory experience that the vogue of sexual stimulation is inevitable.

What we witness in the history of thought, as our instruments of analysis and precision become more subtle, is the differentiation of unity into variety, the dismemberment of a reality into a number of realities. This pluralistic tendency in analytic thought has recently affected our most intimate conceptions of life, revealing a richness of possibility which had been hidden from sight when we gazed too steadfastly at unity, wholeness, concepts in their unanalyzed totality.

For example, in thinking of love we dwelt upon its universal quality, unaware of the varieties and levels, so to speak, that may dwell together within that original context. Only of late, as an echo of the Freudian candor in matters sexual, have psychologists found the courage to separate out from among the several ingredients the very significant element of lust. Thus in dynamic textbooks on psychology you will find lust as the term most appropriate for the quintessential attribute of love. In due time, a more perfect analysis will have been completed revealing other vital components in that once mystic conception of sex attraction romantically alluded to as love.

If we apply this analytic dismemberment to the love of the sexes, we shall discover an interesting difference between marital love and sexual love. Under the older morality, the only honorable love was what I have called marital love. The sexual revolution, transpiring in our very midst, has ruthlessly analyzed out the truth about marital love and discovered that its characteristic attribute is compassion. On the other hand, the essence of sexual love resides in its passion. Under the new morality, sanctions are fast being built up for sexual love that are competing very favorably with the traditional sanctions woven about marital love. A marvelous keen rivalry now exists between these two kinds of love. Such a telltale title as *Married Love*, which Marie Stopes wisely gives to her enlightening book, gives the secret away. The secret that marital love, whatever its title to honor, loyalty, self-sacrifice, chivalry, compassion, must not be confounded with that less reputable and more volcanic kind of sex attraction known as sexual love. *Married love* is a fine phrase for the splendidly new experiment in equating the magic turbulent passion of sex love with the responsible and dignified status of marriage. Can marriage give passion the lease of life it hungers for?

Many psychoanalytical studies demonstrate with a shocking clarity how marital disharmony may be linked with the absence or petering out of sexual love. In a sense never before dreamed of by the evasive and shame-ridden minds of men (and women!), marriage is coming to be construed as an empty ceremonial, sheer futile make-believe, unless buoyed up by the inspiration and stimulation of great passion. Under the older morality, the very mention of making love to one's wife as one might to a secret mistress seemed an unclean and shameful notion. Under the newer morality, the one disreputable behavior will be the denial to one's wife of audacious passion, once looked down upon as fit only for the "painted disasters of the street." Well, the astonishing fact is that our wives and sisters and daughters and sweethearts (a most respectable crew) have all taken to emulating and rivaling the said painted disasters of the street. And why this unseemly haste to model themselves after the pattern of the quondam disreputable daughters of joy? Because they have come to the realization of the quickening uses to which passion can be put. Thus, we witness incredible changes in personal deportment which defy explanation unless we are equipped with enough sympathy and wisdom to appreciate how desperately men and women are trying to save marriage by galvanizing it into a new lease of life by sexualizing it. Latter-day disreputability is merely a crude expression of a wonderful impulse on the part of our respectable females: to win for themselves the spontaneous passionate loyalty of men by weaning them from the moralistic absurdity that wives are too good for passion. As Freud sagely remarks: "We can prove to society mathematically that its code of ethics has exacted more sacrifices than it is worth, and that its procedure rests neither on veracity nor wisdom."

Owing to the penetrating discoveries of the psychoanalysts, we have been compelled to undergo a crisis in our lives which really marks the evolution of a mind from an infantile to a mature stage. The most powerful force in our human nature that makes for maturity is sex expression. We are gradually unlearning the abysmal superstitious dogmas of puritanic prudery, and with a surprising rapidity learning to live by the clarifying and courageous insights of a psychoanalytic philosophy of love. In the life of the sexes the beginning of wisdom is to cast out shame. There is in candor, scientifically illuminated, a dignity that is immeasurably superior in spiritual power to the moralistic shame that has served so poorly the deep human needs of men and women, ignorant of how to love one another bravely, beautifully.

The Freudian emphasis on sex, for all its exaggeration and grotesquerie, is one of the most wholesome contributions ever made to the liberation of the mind from the bondage of shame and fear.

"I cannot understand why Wisdom, which is, so to speak, the sediment of everyday experiences, should be denied admission among the acquisitions of knowledge." One must agree with the great Freud that wisdom is the most perfect fruit of knowledge.

SEX [1]

By Alfred Adler

WE have learned that two great tendencies dominate all psychic phenomena. These two tendencies, the social feeling, and the individual striving for power and domination, influence every human activity and color the attitude of every individual in his striving for security, in his fulfillment of the three great challenges of life: love, work, and society. We shall have to accustom ourselves, in judging psychic phenomena, to investigate the quantitative and the qualitative relationships of these two factors if we want to understand the human soul. The relationship of these factors to one another conditions the degree to which anyone is capable of comprehending the logic of communal life, and therefore, the degree to which he is capable of subordinating himself to the division of labor which grows out of the necessity of that communal life.

Division of labor is a factor in the maintenance of human society which must not be overlooked. Everyone at some time, or at some place, must contribute his quota. That man who does not deliver his quota, who denies the value of communal life, becomes an anti-social being, and resigns his fellowship in humanity. In simple cases of this sort we speak of egotism, of mischievousness, of self-centeredness, of nuisance. In the more complicated cases, we see the eccentrics, the hoboes, and the criminals. Public condemnation of these traits and characteristics grows out of an appreciation of their origins, an intuition of their incompatibility with the demands of social life. Any man's value, therefore, is determined by

[1] From *Understanding Human Nature.* New York: Greenberg, 1927.

his attitude toward his fellow men, and by the degree in which he partakes of the division of labor which communal life demands. His affirmation of this communal life makes him important to other human beings, makes him a link in the great chain which binds society, the chain which we cannot in any way disturb without also disturbing human society. A man's capabilities determine his place in the total production of human society. Much confusion has clouded this simple truth, because the striving for power and the lust for dominance have introduced false values into the normal division of labor. This striving for dominance has disturbed and thwarted the total production, and has given us a false basis for the judgment of human values.

Individuals have disturbed this division of labor by refusing to adapt themselves to the place that they must fill. Further, difficulties have arisen out of the false ambition and power wishes of individuals who have blocked communal life and the communal work for their own egoistic interests. Similarly, entanglements have been caused by class differences in our society. Personal power or economic interest have influenced the division of the field of labor by reserving all the better positions for individuals of certain classes, that is, those affording the greater power while other individuals, of other classes, have been excluded from them. The recognition of these numerous factors in the structure of society enables us to understand why the division of labor has never proceeded smoothly. Forces continually disturbing this division of labor have created privilege for one, and slavery for another.

The bisexuality of the human race conditions another division of labor. Woman, by virtue of her physical constitution, is excluded from some certain activities, while on the other hand, there are certain labors which are not given to man, because man could better be employed at other tasks. This division of labor should have been instituted according to an entirely unprejudiced standard, and all the movements for the emancipation of women in so far as they have not overstepped logical points in the heat of conflict, have taken up the logic of this point of view. A division of labor is far from robbing woman of her femininity, or disturbing the natural relationships between man and woman. Each acquires those opportunities of labor which are best fitted for him. In the course of human development this division of labor has so configured itself that woman has taken over a certain part of the world's work (which might otherwise occupy a man too), in return for which man is in the position to use his powers to greater effect. We cannot call this division of labor senseless so long as the powers for work are not misused, and so long as physical and mental powers are not deflected to a bad end.

As a consequence of the development of culture in the direction of personal power, especially through the efforts of certain individuals and certain classes of society, who wish to secure privileges for themselves, this division of labor has fallen into characteristic channels which have colored our entire civilization. The importance of the male in the culture of today is greatly emphasized as a result. The division of labor is such that the privileged group, men, are guaranteed certain advantages, and this as a result of their domination over women in the division of labor. Thus the dominant male assumes advantages and directs the activity of women to the end that the more agreeable forms of life shall appertain always to the males, whereas those activities are allowed women which men can advantageously avoid.

As things stand now there is a constant striving on the part of men to dominate women, and an appropriate dissatisfaction with masculine domination on the part of women. Since the two sexes are so narrowly connected it is easily conceivable that this constant tension leads to psychic dissonances and to far-reaching physical disturbances which must of necessity be extraordinarily painful to both sexes.

All our institutions, our traditional attitudes, our laws, our morals, our customs, give evidence of the fact that they are determined and maintained by privileged males for the glory of male domination. These institutions reach out into the very nurseries and have a great influence upon the child's soul. A child's understanding of these relationships need not be very great, but we must admit that his emotional life is immensely affected by them. These attitudes may well be investigated when for instance we see a young boy responding to the request to put on girls' clothes, with a terrific temper tantrum. Once let a boy's craving for power reach a certain degree, and you will surely find him showing a preference for the privileges of being a man which, he recognizes, guarantee his superiority everywhere. We have already mentioned the fact that the education in our families nowadays is only too well designed to overvalue the striving for power. The consequent tendency to maintain and exaggerate the masculine privilege follows naturally, for it is usually the father who stands as the family symbol of power His mysterious comings and goings arouse the interest of the child much more than the constant presence of a mother The child quickly recognizes the prominent rôle his father plays, and notes how he sets the pace, makes all arrangements, and appears everywhere as the leader. He sees how all obey his commands and how his mother asks him for his advice. From every angle, his father seems to be the one who is strong and powerful. There are children for whom the father is so much a standard that they believe that everything he says must be holy; they attest to the rightness of their views simply by saying that their father once said so Even in those cases in which the fatherly influence does not seem to be so well marked, children will get the idea of the domination of the father because the whole load of the family seems to rest upon him, whereas, as a matter of fact, it is only the division of labor which enables the father in the family to use his powers to better advantage.

So far as the history of the origin of masculine dominance is concerned, we must call attention to the fact that this is a phenomenon which does not occur as a natural thing. This is indicated by the numerous laws which are necessary legally to guarantee this domination to men. It is also an indication that previous to the legal enforcement of masculine domination there must have been other epochs in which the masculine privilege was not nearly so certain. History proves that such epochs actually existed in the days of the matriarchate, the age in which it was the mother, the woman, who played the important rôle in life, particularly so far as the child was concerned. At that time each man in the clan was in duty bound to respect the honored position of the mother. Certain customs and usages are still colored by this ancient institution, as for instance, the introduction of all strange men to a child with the title of "uncle" or "cousin." A terrific battle must have preceded the transition from matriarchate to masculine domination. Men who like to believe that their privileges and prerogatives are determined by nature will be surprised to learn that men did not possess these prerogatives from the beginning, but had to fight for them.[2] The triumph of man was simultaneous with the subjugation of women, and it is especially the evidence in the development of the law which bears witness to this long process of subjugation.

Masculine dominance is not a natural thing. There is evidence to prove that it occurred chiefly as a result of constant battles between primitive peoples, during the course of which man assumed the more prominent rôle as warrior, and finally used his newly won superiority in order to retain the leadership for himself and for his own ends. Hand in hand with this development was a development of property rights and inheritance rights which became a basis of mascu-

[2] A very good description of this development can be found in August Bebel's *Woman and Socialism* and in Mathias and Mathilde Vaerting's *The Dominant Sex*.

line domination, in so far as man usually was the acquirer and owner of property.

A growing child need not however read books on this theme. Despite the fact that he knows nothing of these archæological data he senses the fact that the male is the privileged member of the family. This occurs even when fathers and mothers with considerable insight are disposed to overlook those privileges which we have inherited from ancient days, in favor of a greater equality. It is very difficult to make it clear to a child that a mother who is engaged in household duties is as valuable as a father.

Think what it means to a young boy who sees the prevailing privilege of manhood before his eyes from his earliest days. From the day of his birth he is received with greater acclamation than a girl child. It is a well known and all too frequent occurrence that parents prefer to have boys as children. A boy senses at every step that, as a chip of the old block, he has certain privileges and a greater social value. Casual words directed toward him or taken up by him occasionally are constantly calling to his attention the fact of the greater importance of the masculine rôle.

The domination of the male also appears to him in the institution of female servants about the house who are used for menial tasks, and finally he is reënforced in his sentiments by the fact that the women in his environment are not at all convinced of their equality with men. That most important question which all women should ask their prospective husbands before marriage: "What is your attitude toward masculine domination, particularly in family life?" is usually never answered. In one case we find an expression of the striving for equality and in another case any of the various degrees of resignation. In contrast we see the father convinced from boyhood that as a man he has a more important rôle to play. He interprets this conviction as an implicit duty, and concerns himself solely with responding to the challenges of life and society in favor of masculine privilege.

Every situation which arises out of this relationship is experienced by the child. What he gets out of it is a number of pictures concerning the nature of woman, in which for the most part the woman plays a sorry figure. In this way the development of the boy has a distinct masculine color. What he believes to be the worth-while goals in his striving for power are exclusively masculine qualities and masculine attitudes. A typical masculine virtue grows out of these power relationships, which patently indicates its origins to us. Certain character traits count as masculine, others as feminine, albeit there is no basis to justify these valuations. If we compare the psychic state of boys and girls and seemingly find evidence in support of this classification, we do not deal with natural phenomena, but are describing the expressions of individuals who have been directed into a very specific channel, whose style of life and behavior pattern have been narrowed down by specific conceptions of power. These conceptions of power have indicated to them with compelling force the place where they must seek to develop. There is no justification for the differentiation of "manly" and "womanly" character traits. We shall see how both these traits are capable of being used to fulfill the striving for power. In other words, that one can express power with the so-called "feminine" traits, such as obedience and submission. The advantages which an obedient child enjoys can sometimes bring it much more into the lime-light than a disobedient child, though the striving for power is present in both cases. Our insight into psychic life is often made more difficult by the fact that striving for power expresses itself in the most complex fashion.

As a boy grows older his masculinity becomes a significant duty, his ambition, his desire for power and superiority is indisputably connected and identified with the duty to be masculine. For many children who desire power it is not sufficient to be simply aware of their masculinity; they must show a proof that they are men, and therefore they must have privileges. They accomplish this, on the one hand, by efforts to excel, thereby measuring their masculine traits; on the other hand they may succeed by tyrannizing their feminine environment in every possible way. According to the degree of resistance which they meet, these boys utilize either stubbornness and wild insurgency, or craft and cunning, to gain their ends.

Since every human being is measured according to the standard of the privileged male, it is no wonder that one always holds this standard before a boy. Finally he measures himself according to it, observing and asking whether his activities are sufficiently "masculine," whether he is "fully a man." What we consider "masculine" nowadays is common knowledge. Above all it is something purely egoistic, something which satisfies self-love, gives a feeling of superiority and domination over others, all with the aid of seemingly "active" characteristics such as courage, strength, duty, the winning of all manner of victories, especially those over women, the acquisition of positions, honors, titles, and the desire to harden himself against so-called "feminine" tendencies, and the like. There is a constant battle for personal superiority because it counts as a "masculine" virtue to be dominant.

In this manner every boy assumes characteristics which he sees in adult men, especially his father. We can trace the ramifications of this artificially nourished delusion of grandeur in the most diverse manifestations of our society. At an early age a boy is urged to secure for himself a reserve of power and privileges. This is what is called "manliness." In bad cases it degenerates into the well-known expressions of rudeness and brutality.

The advantages of being a man are, under such conditions, very alluring. We must not be astonished therefore when we see many girls who maintain a masculine ideal either as an unfulfillable desire, or as a standard for the judgment of their behavior; this ideal may evince itself as a pattern for action and appearance. It would seem that in our culture every woman wanted to be a man! In this class we find those girls particularly who have an uncontrollable desire to distinguish themselves in games and activities which are more appropriate to boys by virtue of their different physique. They climb up every tree, play rather with boys than with girls, and avoid every "womanly" activity as a shameful thing. Their satisfaction lies only in masculine activities. The preference for manliness makes all these phenomena understandable when we understand how the striving for superiority is more concerned with the symbols of things than with the activities of life.

Man has been wont to justify his domination not only by maintaining that his position is natural, but also that his dominance results from the inferiority of woman. This conception of the inferiority of woman is so widespread that it appears as the common property of all races. Linked with this prejudice is a certain unrest on the part of men which may well have originated in the time of the war against the matriarchate, when woman was a source of actual anxiety. We come upon indications of this constantly in literature and history. A Latin author writes "Mulier est hominis confusio," "Woman is the confusion of man." In the theological consilia the question was often argued whether a woman had a soul, and learned theses were written concerning the question whether woman was actually a human being. The century-long period of witch-persecution and witch-burning is a sorry witness of the errors, the tremendous uncertainty and confusion of that happily forgotten age concerning this question.

Woman was often held up as the source of all evil, as in the Biblical conception of the original sin, or as in the *Iliad* of Homer. The story of Helen demonstrated how one woman was capable of throwing whole peoples into misfortune.

Legends and fairy tales of all times contain indices of the moral inferiority of woman, of her wickedness, of her falsity, of her treachery and of her fickleness. "Womanly folly" has even been used as an argument in legal cases. Coincident with these prejudices is the degradation of woman's capability, industry, and ability. Figures of speech, anecdotes, mottoes, and jokes, in all literatures and among all peoples, are full of degrading critiques of woman. Woman is reproached with her spitefulness, her pettiness, her stupidity, and the like.

An extraordinary acuity is sometimes developed in order to bear witness to the inferiority of woman. The number of men like Strindberg, Moebius, Schopenhauer, and Weininger, who have upheld this thesis, has been enlarged by a not inconsiderable number of women whose resignation has caused them to subscribe to a belief in the inferiority of woman. They are the champions of woman's rôle of submission. The degradation of woman and womanly labor is further indicated by the fact that women are paid less than men, regardless of whether their work is of equal value.

In the comparison of the results of intelligence and talent tests it was actually found that for particular subjects, as for instance, mathematics, boys showed more talent, whereas girls showed more talent for other subjects, such as languages. Boys actually do show greater talent than girls for studies which are capable of preparing them for their masculine occupation but this is only a seemingly greater talent. If we investigate the situation of the girls more closely we learn that the story of the lesser capability of woman is a palpable fable.

A girl is daily subjected to the argument that girls are less capable than boys and are suitable only for unessential activities. It is not surprising then that a girl is firmly convinced of the unchangeable and bitter fate of a woman and sooner or later because of her lack of training in childhood, actually believes in her own incapability. Discouraged in this manner, a girl approaches "masculine" occupations if the opportunity to approach them ever presents, with a fore-gone conclusion that she will not have the necessary interest for them. Should she possess such interest, she soon loses it, and thus she is denied both an outer and an inner prepara-tion.

Under such circumstances proof of the incapability of woman seems valid. There are two causes for this. In the first place the error is accentuated by the fact that the value of a human being is frequently judged from purely business standpoints, or on one-sided and purely egoistic grounds. With such prejudices we can hardly be expected to under-stand how far performance and capability are coincident with psychic development. And this leads us to the second main factor to which the fallacy of the lesser capability of woman may thank its existence. It is a frequently overlooked fact that a girl comes into the world with a prejudice sounding in her ears which is designed only to rob her of her belief in her own value, to shatter her self-confidence and destroy her hope of ever doing anything worth while. If this prejudice is constantly being strengthened, if a girl sees again and again how women are given servile rôles to play, it is not hard to understand how she loses courage, fails to face her obliga-tions, and sinks back from the solution of her life's problems. Then indeed she is useless and incapable! Yet if we approach a human being, undermine his self-respect so far as his re-lationship to society is concerned, cause him to abandon all hope of ever accomplishing anything, ruin his courage, and then find that he actually never amounts to anything, then we dare not maintain that we were right, for we must admit that it is *we* who have caused all his sorrow!

It is easy enough for a girl to lose her courage and her self-confidence in our civilization, yet, as a matter of fact, certain intelligence tests proved the interesting fact that in a certain group of girls, aged from fourteen to eighteen, greater talent and capability were evinced than was shown by all other groups, boys included. Further researches show that these were all girls from families in which the mother was either the sole bread winner, or at least contributed largely to the family support. What this means is that these girls were in a situation at home in which the prejudice of the lesser capability of woman was either not present or existed only to a slight extent. They could see with their own eyes how their mother's industry had its rewards, and as a result they developed themselves much more freely and much more independently, entirely uninfluenced by those inhibitions which are inevitably associated with the belief in the lesser powers of a woman.

A further argument against this prejudice is the not inconsiderable number of women who have accomplished results in the most varied fields, particularly in literature, art, crafts, and medicine, of such remarkable value that they are quite capable of standing any comparison with the results of men in these fields. There are so many men furthermore who not only do not show any achievements but are possessed of such a high grade of incapability that we could easily find an equal number of proofs (of course falsely) that men were the inferior sex.

One of the bitter consequences of the prejudices concerning the inferiority of women is the sharp division and pigeonholing of concepts according to a scheme: thus "masculine" signifies worth while, powerful, victorious, capable, whereas "feminine" becomes identical with obedient, servile, subordinate. This type of thinking has become so deeply anchored in human thought processes that in our civilization everything laudable has a "masculine" color whereas everything less valuable or actually derogatory is designated "feminine." We all know men who could not be more insulted than if we told them that they were feminine, whereas if we say to a girl that she is masculine it need signify no insult. The accent always falls so that everything which is reminiscent of woman appears inferior.

Character traits which would seem to prove this fallacious

contention of the inferiority of woman prove themselves on closer observation nothing more than the manifestation of an inhibited psychic development. We do not maintain that we can make what is called a "talented" individual out of every child, but we can always make an "untalented" adult out of him. We have never done this fortunately. Others, however, we know have succeeded only too well. That such a fate overtakes girls more frequently than boys, in our day and age, is easily understood. We have often had the opportunity of seeing these "untalented" children suddenly become so talented that one might have spoken of a miracle!

The obvious advantages of being a man have caused severe disturbances in the psychic development of women as a consequence of which there is an almost universal dissatisfaction with the feminine rôle. The psychic life of woman moves in much the same channels, and under much the same rules, as that of any human beings who find themselves the possessors of a strong feeling of inferiority because of their situation in the scheme of things. The prejudice of her alleged inferiority as a woman signifies an additional aggravating complication. If a considerable number of girls find some sort of compensation, they owe it to their character development, to their intelligence, and sometimes to certain acquired privileges. This shows simply how one mistake may give rise to others. Such privileges are the special dispensations, exemptions from obligations, and the luxuries, which give a semblance of advantage in that they simulate what purports to be a high degree of respect for woman. There may be a certain degree of idealism in this, but finally this idealism is always an ideal which has been fashioned by men to the advantage of men. George Sand once described it very tellingly when she said: "The virtue of woman is a fine invention of man."

In general we can distinguish two types of women in the battle against the feminine rôle. One type has already been indicated: the girl who develops in an active, "masculine," direction. She becomes extraordinarily energetic and ambitious, and is constantly fighting for the prizes of life. She attempts to exceed her brothers and male comrades, chooses activities which are usually considered the privilege of men by preference, is interested in sports and the like. Very often she evades all the relationships of love and marriage. If she enters into such a relationship she may disturb its harmony by striving to be superior to her husband! She may have tremendous disinclination to any of the domestic activities. She may voice her disinclination directly, or indirectly by disavowing all talent for domestic duties, and constantly give evidence attempting to prove that she has never developed a talent for domesticity.

This is the type that seeks to compensate for the evil of the masculine attitude with a "masculine" response. The defense attitude toward womanhood is the foundation of her whole being. She has been designated "the boy-girl," "la garçonne," the "mannish" woman, and the like. This designation, however, is based upon a false conception. There are many people who believe that there is a congenital factor present in such girls, a certain "masculine" substance or secretion which causes their "masculine" attitude. The whole history of civilization, however, shows us that the pressure exerted upon woman, and the inhibitions to which she must submit today, are not to be borne by any human being; they always give rise to revolt. If this revolt now exhibits itself in the direction which we call "masculine," the reason for it is simply that there are only *two* sex rôles possible. One must orient oneself according to one of two models, either that of an ideal woman, or according to that of an ideal man. Desertion from the rôle of woman can therefore appear only as "masculine," and vice versa. This does not occur as the result of some mysterious secretion, but because in the given time and place, there is no other possibility. We must never lose sight of the difficulties under which the psychic development of a girl takes place. So long as we cannot guarantee every woman an absolute equality with man we cannot demand her complete reconciliation with life, with the facts of our civilization, and the forms of our social life.

The woman who goes through life with an attitude of resignation, who exhibits an almost unbelievable degree of adjustment, obedience, and humbleness, belongs to the second type. Seemingly she adjusts herself everywhere, takes root wherever placed, but demonstrates such a high degree of clumsiness and helplessness that she accomplishes nothing at all! She may produce nervous symptoms, which serve her in her weakness, to demonstrate her need for consideration to others; and she shows clearly thereby how the training she has undergone, how her misuse of life, is regularly accompanied by nervous diseases, and makes her totally unfit for social life. She belongs to the best people in the world, but unfortunately she is sick and cannot meet the challenge of existence to any satisfying degree. She cannot win the satisfaction of her environment for any time. Her submission, her humility, her self-repression, is founded on the same revolt as that of her sister of the first type, a revolt which says clearly enough: "This is no happy life!"

The woman who does not defend herself against the womanly rôle but carries in herself the torturing consciousness that she is condemned to be an inferior being and ordained to play a subordinate rôle in life, makes up the third type. She is fully convinced of the inferiority of women, just as she is convinced that man alone is called upon to do the worth-while things in life. As a consequence, she approves his privileged position. Thus she swells the chorus of voices which sound the praises of man as the doer and the achiever, and demands a special position for him. She shows her feeling of weakness as clearly as if she wanted recognition for it, and demanded additional support because of it; but this attitude is the beginning of a long prepared revolt. By way of revenge she will shift her marital responsibilities upon her husband with a light-hearted catchword to the effect that "Only a man could do these things!"

Although woman is considered an inferior being, the business of education is largely delegated to her. Let us now picture these three types of woman for ourselves with reference to this most important and difficult task. At this juncture we can differentiate the types even more clearly. Women of the first type, the "masculine" attitude, will tyrannize, will occupy themselves with punishment, and thus exercise a tremendous pressure upon children, which these children will, of course, attempt to avoid. When this type of education is effective, its best possible result is a sort of military training which is quite valueless. Children usually think that mothers of this kind are very bad educators. The noise, the great to-do, always has a bad effect, and there arises the danger that girls will be instigated to imitate them, whereas boys are frightened for the rest of their lives. Among men who have stood under the dominance of such mothers we shall find a number who avoid women as much as possible as though they had been inoculated with bitterness, and were incapable of bringing any sense of trust to a woman. What results is a definite division and separation between the sexes, whose pathology we can readily understand despite the fact that some investigators still exist who speak of a "faulty apportionment of the masculine and feminine elements."

Individuals of the other types are equally futile as educators. They may be so skeptical that the children soon discover their lack of self-confidence, and grow beyond them. In this case the mother renews her efforts, nags and scolds, and threatens to tell the father. The fact that she calls upon a masculine educator betrays her again, and shows her disbelief in the success of her educational activity. She deserts from the front in the matter of education just as though it were her duty to justify her standpoint that man alone is capable, and therefore, indispensable for education! Such women may simply avoid all educational efforts, and shift the responsibility therefor upon their husbands and governesses without compunction, since they feel they are incapable of any success.

Dissatisfaction with the womanly rôle is even more evident among girls who escape from life because of some so-called "higher" reasons. Nuns, or others who assume some occupation for which celibacy is an essential, are a case in point. Their lack of reconciliation with their rôle as women is clearly demonstrated in this gesture. Similarly, many girls go into business at an early age because the independence connected with employment seems a protection to them against the threatened necessity of marriage. Here again the driving power is the disinclination to assume the womanly rôle.

What of those cases in which marriage occurs, in which one could believe that the rôle of woman had been voluntarily assumed? We learn that marriage need not necessarily be an indication that a girl has reconciled herself with her womanly rôle. The example of a thirty-six-year-old woman is typical of this. She comes to the physician complaining of various nervous ills. She was the oldest child of a marriage between an aging man and a very domineering woman. The fact that her mother, a very beautiful young girl, had married an old man leads us to suspect that in the marriage of the parents the disinclination for the feminine rôle played some part. The marriage of the parents did not turn out happily. The mother ruled the house with clamor, and insisted upon having her will carried out at all costs, and regardless of anyone else's pleasure. The old man was forced into his corner at every opportunity. The daughter narrated how her mother would not even allow her father to lie down upon the sofa to rest. Her mother's whole activity consisted in maintaining certain "principles of domestic economy" which she felt were desirable to enforce. These were an absolute law to the family.

Our patient grew up a very capable child who was much pampered by the father. On the other hand, her mother was never satisfied with her and was always her enemy. Later, when a boy, toward whom the mother was far more favorable, was born, the relationship became unbearable. The little girl was conscious that she had a support in her father, who, no matter how modest and retiring he was in other things, could take up the cudgels when his daughter's interests were at stake. Thus she began to hate her mother cordially.

In this stubborn conflict the cleanliness of the mother became the daughter's favorite point of attack. The mother was so pedantic in her cleanliness that she did not even allow the servant girl to touch a door knob without wiping it off later. The child made it a point of special pleasure to go about as dirty and ill clad as possible, and to soil the house whenever the occasion offered.

She developed all those characteristics which were the exact opposite of that which her mother expected of her. This fact speaks very clearly against any inherited characteristics. If a child develops only those characteristics which must anger her mother almost to death, there is either a conscious or unconscious plan underlying them. The hate between mother and child has lasted until the present day, and a more bitter belligerency could not be imagined.

When this little girl was eight years old the following situation existed. The father was permanently on his daughter's side; her mother went about with a bitter face, making pointed remarks, enforcing her "rules," and reproaching the girl. The girl, embittered and belligerent, availed herself of an extraordinary sarcasm which crippled the activity of her mother. An additional complicating factor was the valvular heart disease of the younger brother who was his mother's favorite and a very much pampered child, who used his sickness to hold the attentions of his mother to an even more intensive degree. One could observe the constantly thwarted activities of the parents toward their children. Under such circumstances did this little girl grow up.

It then occurred that she fell sick of a nervous ailment which no one could explain. Her sickness consisted in the fact that she was tortured by evil thoughts which were directed against her mother, the consequence of which was that she felt herself hindered in all her activities. Finally she occupied herself very deeply, and suddenly, and without success, in religion. After some time these evil thoughts disappeared. Some medicine or other was given the credit for the disappearance, although it is more probable that her mother was forced into the defensive. A residue which expressed itself in a remarkable fear of thunder and lightning remained.

The little girl believed that the thunder and lightning came only as a result of her bad conscience, and would some day cause her death because she had such evil thoughts. One can see how the child was attempting to free itself of its hate for its mother at this time. The development of the child went further, and it seemed that a bright future was beckoning her. The statement of a teacher who said: "This little girl could do anything that she wanted to!" had a great effect on her. These words are unimportant in themselves but for this girl they meant, "I can accomplish something if I wish." This realization was followed by an even greater intensity in the combat against her mother.

Adolescence came, and she grew up into a beautiful young woman, became marriageable, and had many suitors; yet all opportunities of a relationship were broken off because of the peculiar sharpness of her tongue. She felt herself drawn only to one man, an elderly man who lived in her neighborhood, and everyone feared that some day she might marry him. But this man moved after some time and the girl remained, until she was twenty-six years old, without a suitor. In the circles in which she moved this was very remarkable, and no one could explain it because no one understood her history. In the bitter battle which she had been carrying on against her mother ever since her childhood, she had become unbearably quarrelsome. War was her victory. The behavior of her mother had constantly irritated this child and caused her to seek for fresh triumphs. A bitter word-battle was her greatest happiness; in this she showed her vanity. Her "masculine" attitude expressed itself also in that she desired such word battles only where she could conquer her opponent.

When she was twenty-six years old she made the acquaintance of a very honorable man who did not allow himself to be repulsed by her belligerent character and paid court to her very earnestly. He was very humble and submissive in his approach. Pressure from her relatives to marry this man led her to explain repeatedly that he was so very unpleasant to her that she could not think of marriage with him. This is not hard to understand when we know her character, yet after two years of resistance she finally accepted him in the deep conviction that she had made a slave of him, and that she could do with this man whatever she wished. She had hoped secretly that she would find in him a second edition of her father, who would give in to her whenever she wanted.

She soon learned that she had made a mistake. A few days after her marriage her husband was sitting in the room smoking his pipe and comfortably reading his paper. In the morning he left for his office, came home punctually for his meals, and grumbled a little if his meals were not ready. He demanded cleanliness, tenderness, punctuality, and all manner of unjustified requests which she was not prepared to fulfill. The relationship was not even remotely similar to that which she had experienced between herself and her father. She tumbled out of all her dreams. The more she demanded, the less her husband acceded to her wishes, and the more he indicated her domestic rôle to her, the less he saw of her domestic activity. She did not lose the opportunity to remind him daily that he really had no right to make these requests, as she had expressly told him that she did not like him. This made absolutely no impression upon him. He continued his demands with an inexorableness which caused her to have very unhappy prospects for the future. In an intoxication of self-effacement this righteous, dutiful man had wooed her, but no sooner did he have her in his possession, than his intoxication had disappeared.

No change in the lack of harmony which existed between them appeared when she became a mother. She was forced to assume new duties. In the meantime her relationship to her own mother, who was energetically taking up the cudgels for her son-in-law, became worse and worse. The constant warfare in her house was carried on with such heavy artillery that it is not to be wondered that her husband occasionally acted badly, and without consideration, and that occasionally the woman was right in her complaints. The behavior of her husband was the direct consequence of the fact that she was unapproachable, which, again, was a result of her lack of reconciliation with her womanliness. She had believed originally that she could play her rôle of empress forever, that she could wander through life surrounded by a slave who would carry out all her wishes. Life would have been possible for her only under these circumstances.

What could she do now? Should she divorce her husband and return to her mother and declare herself beaten? She was incapable of leading an independent life for she had never been prepared for it. A divorce would have been an insult to her pride and vanity. Life was misery for her; on the one hand her husband criticized her, and on the other side stood her mother with her heavy guns, preaching cleanliness and order.

Suddenly she, too, became cleanly and orderly! She did washing and polishing and cleaning the whole day. It seemed as though she had finally seen the light, and had acquired the teachings which her mother had drummed into her ears for so many years. In the beginning her mother must have smiled, and her husband must have been pleased at this sudden change of affairs, at the sight of this young woman emptying and cleaning bureaus, cabinets, and closets. But one can carry a thing like this too far. She washed and scoured so long, until there was not an unscrubbed shred in the house, and her zeal was so apparent that she was disturbed by everyone in her efforts; and in turn disturbed everyone else in her zeal. If she washed something and another touched it, then she would have to wash it again, and only she could do it.

The disease which manifests itself in continual washing and cleaning is an extraordinarily frequent occurrence in women who are belligerent against their womanliness and attempt in this fashion to elevate themselves by their complete virtue in cleanliness, over those who do not wash themselves so frequently. Unconsciously all these efforts are aimed solely at exploding the entire household. Few households were ever more disorderly than the household of this woman. Not cleanliness, but the discomfiture of her entire household, was her goal.

We could tell of very many cases in which a reconciliation with the rôle of being a woman was only *apparently* true. That our patient had no friends among women, could get along with no one, and knew no consideration for another human being, fits very well into the pattern which we might have expected in her life.

It will be necessary for us to evolve better methods of educating girls in the future, so that they shall be better prepared to reconcile themselves with life. Under the most favorable circumstances it is occasionally impossible to effect this reconciliation with life, as in this case. The alleged inferiority of woman is maintained in our age by law and tradition, though it is denied by anyone with a real psychological insight. We must therefore be on the watch to recognize and counter the whole technique of society's mistaken behavior in this connection. We must take up the battle not because we have some pathologically exaggerated respect for woman, but because the present fallacious attitude negates the logic of our whole social life.

Let us take this occasion to discuss another relationship which is often used in order to degrade woman: the so-called "dangerous age," that period which occurs about the fiftieth year, accompanied by the accentuation of certain character traits. Physical changes serve to indicate to woman in the menopause that the bitter time in which she must lose forever that little semblance of significance which she has so laboriously built up during the course of her life has come. Under these circumstances she searches with redoubled efforts for any instrument which will be useful in maintaining her position, now grown more precarious than ever before. Our civilization is dominated by a principle in which present performance alone is a source of value; every aging individual, but especially a woman who is growing old, experiences difficulties at this time. The damage which is done to an aging woman by entirely undermining her value affects every human being, in so far as we cannot count our worth solely from day to day in the prime of life. What one has accomplished at the height of his activities must be credited to him during the years in which his powers and activity are of necessity lessened. It is not right to exclude someone entirely from the spiritual and material relationships of society simply because he is growing old. In the case of a woman this amounts to a virtual degradation and enslavement. Imagine the anxiety of an adolescent girl who thinks of this epoch in her life which lies in her future. Womanliness is not extinguished with the fiftieth year. The honor and worth of a human being lasts unaltered beyond this age. And it must be guaranteed.

The foundations of all these unhappy manifestations are built upon the mistakes of our civilization. If our civilization is marked by a prejudice, then this prejudice reaches out and touches every aspect of that civilization, and is to be found in its every manifestation. The fallacy of the inferiority of woman, and its corollary, the superiority of man, constantly disturbs the harmony of the sexes. As a result, an unusual tension is introduced into all erotic relationships, thereby threatening, and often entirely annihilating, every chance for happiness between the sexes. Our whole love life is poisoned, distorted, and corroded by this tension. This explains why one so seldom finds a harmonious marriage, this is the reason so many children grow up in the feeling that marriage is something extremely difficult and dangerous.

Prejudices such as we have described above prevent children, to a large measure, from understanding life adequately. Think of the numerous young girls who consider marriage only as a sort of emergency exit out of life, and think of those men and women who see in marriage only a necessary evil! The difficulties which originally grew out of this tension between the sexes have assumed gigantic proportions today. They become greater and greater the more clearly a girl acquires the tendency to avoid the sexual rôle which society compels her to assume and the more, in the case of a man, there is a desire to play the privileged rôle despite all the false logic in such behavior.

Comradeship is the characteristic index of a true reconciliation with the sexual rôle, of a veritable equilibrium between the sexes. A subordination of one individual to another in sexual relationships is just as unbearable as in the life of nations. Everyone should consider this problem very attentively since the difficulties which may arise for each partner from a mistaken attitude are considerable. This is an aspect of our life which is so widespread and important that every one of us is involved in it. It becomes the more complicated since in our day a child is forced into a behavior pattern which is a depreciation and negation of the other sex.

A calm education certainly could overcome these difficulties, but the hurry of our days, the lack of really proved and tested educational methods, and particularly the competitive nature of our whole life which reaches even into the nursery, determine only too harshly the tendencies of later life. The fear which causes so many human beings to shrink from assuming any love relationships is caused largely by the useless pressure which forces every man to prove his masculinity under all circumstances, even though he must do it by treachery and malice or force.

That this serves to destroy all candor and trust in the love relationships is self-understood. The Don Juan is a man who doubts his own manliness, and is seeking constant additional evidence for it, in his conquests. The distrust which is so universal between the sexes prevents all frankness, and humanity as a whole suffers as a consequence. The exaggerated masculine ideal signifies a constant challenge, a constant spur, a restlessness whose results naturally are only vanity and self-enrichment, maintenance of the "privileged" attitude; and all these, of course, are contrary to a healthy communal life. We have no reason to combat the former purposes of the emancipation-for-women movements. It is our duty to support them in their efforts to gain freedom and equality, because finally the happiness of the whole of humanity depends upon effecting such conditions that a woman will be enabled to be reconciled with her womanly rôle, just as the possibility of a man's adequate solution of his relationship to woman likewise depends upon it.

Of all the institutions which have been developed to better the relationship between the sexes, coeducation is the most important. This institution is not universally accepted; it has its opponents, and its friends. Its friends maintain as their most powerful argument that, through coeducation, the two sexes have an opportunity to become acquainted with one another at an early date and that through this acquaintanceship the fallacious prejudices, and their disastrous consequences, can be prevented in a measure. The opponents usually counter that boys and girls are already so different at the time that they enter school that their coeducation results only in accentuating these differences, because the boys feel themselves under pressure. This occurs because the spiritual development of girls advances more quickly than that of boys during the school years. These boys, under the necessity of carrying their privilege and giving evidence of the fact that they are more capable, must suddenly recognize that their privilege is only a soap bubble which in reality bursts very easily. Other investigators have maintained that in coeducation boys become anxious in front of girls, and lose their self-esteem.

There is no doubt that some measure of truth lies in these arguments, but they hold water only when we consider coeducation in the sense of *competition* between the sexes for the prize of greater talent and capability. If that is what coeducation means to teachers and pupils, it is a damaging doctrine. If we cannot find any teachers who have a better notion of coeducation, that is, that it represents a training and preparation for future *coöperation* between the sexes in communal tasks, then every attempt at coeducation must fail. Its opponents will see but an affirmation of their attitude in its failure.

It would require the creative power of a poet to give an adequate picture of this whole situation. We must be content to indicate only the main points. An adolescent girl acts very much as though she were inferior, and what we have said concerning the compensation of organic inferiorities holds equally well for her. The difference is this: the belief in her inferiority is forced upon a girl by her environment. She is so irrevocably guided into this channel of behavior that even investigators with a great deal of insight have from time to time fallen into the fallacy of believing in her inferiority. The universal result of this fallacy is that both sexes have finally fallen into the hasty pudding of prestige politics, and each tries to play a rôle for which he is not suited. What happens? Both their lives become complicated, their relationships are robbed of all candor, they become surfeited with fallacies and prejudices, in the face of which all hope of happiness vanishes.

III

LOVE

THE PLAY-FUNCTION OF SEX [1]

By Havelock Ellis

WHEN we hear the sexual functions spoken of we commonly understand the performance of an act which normally tends to the propagation of the race. When we see the question of sexual abstinence discussed, when the desirability of sexual gratification is asserted or denied, when the idea arises of the erotic rights and needs of woman, it is always the same act with physical results that is chiefly in mind. Such a conception is quite adequate for practical working purposes in the social world. It enables us to deal with all our established human institutions in the sphere of sex, as arbitrary assumptions of Euclid enable us to traverse the field of elementary geometry. But beyond these useful purposes it is inadequate and even inexact. The functions of sex on the psychic and erotic side are of far greater extension than any act of procreation, they may even exclude it altogether, and when we are concerned with the welfare of the individual human being we must enlarge our outlook and deepen our insight.

There are, we know, two main functions in the sexual relationship, or what in the biological sense we term "marriage," among civilized human beings, the primary physiological function of begetting and bearing of offspring and the secondary spiritual function of furthering the higher mental and emotional processes. These are the main functions of the sexual impulse, and in order to understand any further object of the sexual relationship—or even in order to understand all that is involved in the secondary object of marriage—we must go beyond conscious motives and con-

[1] From *Little Essays of Love and Virtue*. Garden City: Doubleday, Doran and Company, 1922.

sider the nature of the sexual impulse, physical and psychic, as rooted in the human organism.

The human organism, as we know, is a machine on which excitations from without, streaming through the nerves and brain, effect internal work, and notably, stimulate the glandular system. In recent years the glandular system, and especially that of the ductless glands, has taken on an altogether new significance. These ductless glands, as we know, liberate into the blood what are termed "hormones," or chemical messengers, which have a complex but precise action in exciting and developing all those physical and psychic activities which make up a full life alike on the general side and the reproductive side, so that their balanced functions are essential to wholesome and complete existence. In a rudimentary form these functions may be traced back to our earliest ancestors who possessed brains. In those times the predominant sense for arousing the internal mental and emotional faculties was that of smell, the other senses being gradually evolved subsequently, and it is significant that the pituitary, one of the chief ductless glands active in ourselves today, was developed out of the nervous center for smell in conjunction with the membrane of the mouth. The energies of the whole organism were set in action through stimuli arising from the outside world by way of the sense of smell. In process of time the mechanism has become immensely elaborated, yet its healthy activity is ultimately dependent on a rich and varied action and reaction with the external world. It is becoming recognized that the tendency to pluri-glandular insufficiency with its resulting lack of organic harmony and equilibrium, can be counteracted by the physical and psychic stimuli of intimate contacts with the external world. In this action and reaction, moreover, we cannot distinguish between sexual ends and general ends. The activities of the ductless glands and their hormones equally serve both ends in ways that cannot be distinguished. "The individual metabolism," as a distinguished authority

in this field has expressed it, "is the reproductive metabolism." [2] Thus the establishment of our complete activities
as human beings in the world is aided by, if not indeed ultimately dependent upon, a perpetual and many-sided play
with our environment.

It is thus that we arrive at the importance of the play-
function, and thus, also, we realize that while it extends
beyond the sexual sphere it yet definitely includes that sphere.
There are at least three different ways of understanding the
biological function of play. There is the conception of play,
on which Groos has elaborately insisted, as education: the
cat "plays" with the mouse and is thereby educating itself
in the skill necessary to catch mice; all our human games
are a training in qualities that are required in life, and that
is why in England we continue to attribute to the Duke of
Wellington the saying that "the battle of Waterloo was won
on the playing fields of Eton." Then there is the conception
of play as the utilization in art of the superfluous energies
left unemployed in the practical work of life; this enlarging
and harmonizing function of play, while in the lower ranges
it may be spent trivially, leads in the higher ranges to the
production of the most magnificent human achievements. But
there is yet a third conception of play, according to which it
exerts a direct internal influence—health-giving, developmental, and balancing—on the whole organism of the player
himself. This conception is related to the other two, and yet
distinct, for it is not primarily a definite education in specific
kinds of life-conserving skill, although it may involve the
acquisition of such skill, and it is not concerned with the
construction of objective works of art, although—by means
of contact in human relationship—it attains the wholesome
organic effects which may be indirectly achieved by artistic

[2] W. Blair Bell, *The Sex-Complex*, 1920, p. 108. This book is a
cautious and precise statement of the present state of knowledge on
this subject, although some of the author's psychological deductions
must be treated with circumspection.

activities. It is in this sense that we are here concerned with what we may perhaps best call the play-function of sex.[3]

As thus understood, the play-function of sex is at once in an inseparable way both physical and psychic. It stimulates to wholesome activity all the complex and interrelated systems of the organism. At the same time it satisfies the most profound emotional impulses, controlling in harmonious poise the various mental instincts. Along these lines it necessarily tends in the end to go beyond its own sphere and to embrace and introduce into the sphere of sex the other two more objective fields of play, that of play as education, and that of play as artistic creation. It may not be true, as was said of old time, "most of our arts and sciences were invented for love's sake." But it is certainly true that, in proportion as we truly and wisely exercise the play-function of sex, we are at the same time training our personality on the erotic side and acquiring a mastery of the art of love.

The longer I live the more I realize the immense importance for the individual of the development through the play-function of erotic personality, and for human society of the acquirement of the art of love. At the same time I am ever more astonished at the rarity of erotic personality and the ignorance of the art of love even among those men and women, experienced in the exercise of procreation, in whom we might most confidently expect to find such development and such art. At times one feels hopeless at the thought that civilization in this supremely intimate field of life has yet achieved so little. For until it is generally possible to acquire erotic personality and to master the art of loving, the development of the individual man or woman is marred, the acquirement of human happiness and harmony remains impossible.

In entering this field, indeed, we not only have to gain

[3] The term seems to have been devised by Professor Maurice Parmelee, *Personality and Conduct,* 1918, pp. 104, 107, 113. But it is understood by Parmelee in a much vaguer and more extended sense than I have used it.

true knowledge but to cast off false knowledge, and above all to purify our hearts from superstitions which have no connection with any kind of existing knowledge. We have to cease to regard as admirable the man who regards the accomplishment of the procreative act, with the pleasurable relief it affords to himself, as the whole code of love. We have to treat with contempt the woman who abjectly accepts the act, and her own passivity therein, as the whole duty of love. We have to understand that the art of love has nothing to do with vice, and the acquirement of erotic personality nothing to do with sensuality. But we have also to realize that the art of love is far from being the attainment of a refined and luxurious self-indulgence, and the acquirement of erotic personality of little worth unless it fortifies and enlarges the whole personality in all its aspects. Now all this is difficult, and for some people even painful; to root up is a more serious matter than to sow; it cannot all be done in a day.

It is not easy to form a clear picture of the erotic life of the average man in our society. To the best informed among us knowledge in this field only comes slowly. Even when we have decided what may or may not be termed "average," the sources of approach to this intimate sphere remain few and misleading; at the best the women a man loves remain far more illuminating sources of information than the man himself. The more one knows about him, however, the more one is convinced that, quite independently of the place we may feel inclined to afford to him in the scale of virtue, his conception of erotic personality, his ideas on the art of love, if they have any existence at all, are of a humble character. As to the notion of play in the sphere of sex, even if he makes blundering attempts to practice it, that is for him something quite low down, something to be ashamed of, and he would not dream of associating it with anything he has been taught to regard as belonging to the spiritual sphere. The conception of "divine play" is meaningless to him. His fundamental ideas, his cherished ideals, in the erotic sphere, seem to be reducible to two: (1) He wishes to prove that he is "a man," and he experiences what seems to him the pride of virility in the successful attainment of that proof; (2) he finds in the same act the most satisfactory method of removing sexual tension and in the ensuing relief one of the chief pleasures of life. It cannot be said that either of these ideals is absolutely unsound; each is part of the truth; it is only as a complete statement of the truth that they become pathetically inadequate. It is to be noted that both of them are based solely on the physical act of sexual conjunction, and that they are both exclusively self-regarding. So that they are, after all, although the nearest approach to the erotic sphere he may be able to find, yet still not really erotic. For love is not primarily self-regarding. It is the intimate, harmonious, combined play—the play in the wide as well as in the more narrow sense we are here concerned with—of two personalities. It would not be love if it were primarily self-regarding, and the act of intercourse, however essential to secure the propagation of the race, is only an incident, and not an essential in love.

Let us turn to the average woman. Here the picture must usually be still more unsatisfactory. The man at least, crude as we may find his two fundamental notions to be, has at all events attained mental pride and physical satisfaction. The woman often attains neither, and since the man, by instinct or tradition, has maintained a self-regarding attitude, that is not surprising. The husband—by primitive instinct partly, certainly by ancient tradition—regards himself as the active partner in matters of love and his own pleasure as legitimately the prime motive for activity. His wife consequently falls into a complementary position, and regards herself as the passive partner and her pleasure as negligible, if not indeed as a thing to be rather ashamed of, should she by chance experience it. So that, while the husband is content with a mere simulacrum and pretense of the erotic life, the wife has often had none at all.

Few people realize—few indeed have the knowledge or the opportunity to realize—how much women thus lose, alike in the means to fulfill their own lives and in the power to help others. A woman has a husband, she has marital relationships, she has children, she has all the usual domestic troubles —it seems to the casual observer that she has everything that constitutes a fully developed matron fit to play her proper part in the home and in the world. Yet with all these experiences, which undoubtedly are an important part of life, she may yet remain on the emotional side—and, as a matter of fact, frequently remains—quite virginal, as immature as a schoolgirl. She has not acquired an erotic personality, she has not mastered the art of love, with the result that her whole nature remains ill-developed and unharmonized, and that she is incapable of bringing her personality—having indeed no achieved personality to bring—to bear effectively on the problems of society and the world around her.

That alone is a great misfortune, all the more tragic since under favorable conditions, which it should have been natural to attain, it might so easily be avoided. But there is this further result, full of the possibilities of domestic tragedy, that the wife so situated, however innocent, however virtuous, may at any time find her virginally sensitive emotional nature fertilized by the touch of some other man than her husband.

It happens so often. A girl who has been carefully guarded in the home, preserved from evil companions, preserved also from what her friends regarded as the contamination of sexual knowledge, a girl of high ideals, yet healthy and robust, is married to a man of whom she probably has little more than a conventional knowledge. Yet he may by good chance be the masculine counterpart of herself, well brought up, without sexual experience and ignorant of all but the elementary facts of sex, loyal and honorable, prepared to be, fitted to be, a devoted husband. The union seems to be of the happiest kind; no one detects that anything is lacking to this perfect marriage; in course of time one or more children are born. But during all this time the husband has never really made love to his wife; he has not even understood what court-ship in the intimate sense means; love as an art has no existence for him; he has loved his wife according to his imperfect knowledge, but he has never so much as realized that his knowledge was imperfect. She on her side loves her husband; she comes in time indeed to have a sort of tender maternal feeling for him. Possibly she feels a little pleasure in intercourse with him. But she has never once been pro-foundly aroused, and she has never once been utterly satis-fied. The deep fountains of her nature have never been unsealed; she has never been fertilized throughout her whole nature by their liberating influence; her erotic personality has never been developed. Then something happens. Perhaps the husband is called away, it may have been to take part in the Great War. The wife, whatever her tender solicitude for her absent partner, feels her solitude and is drawn nearer to friends, perhaps her husband's friends. Some man among them becomes congenial to her. There need be no conscious or overt love-making on either side, and if there were the wife's loyalty might be aroused and the friendship brought to an end. Love-making is not indeed necessary. The wife's latent erotic needs, while still remaining unconscious, have come nearer to the surface; now that she has grown mature and that they have been stimulated yet unsatisfied for so long, they have, unknown to herself, become insistent and sensitive to a sympathetic touch. The friends may indeed grow into lovers, and then some sort of solution, by divorce, or intrigue—scarcely, however, a desirable kind of solution—becomes possible. But we are here taking the highest ground and assuming that honorable feeling, domestic affection, or a stern sense of moral duty, renders such solution unac-ceptable. In due course the husband returns, and then, to her utter dismay, the wife discovers, if she has not discovered it before, that during his absence, and for the first time in her life, she has fallen in love. She loyally confesses the situation to her husband, for whom her affection and attachment remain the same as before, for what has happened to her is the coming of a totally new kind of love and not any change in her old love. The situation which arises is one of torturing anxiety for all concerned, and it is not less so when all concerned are animated by noble and self-sacrificing impulses. The husband in his devotion to his wife may even be willing that her new impulses should be gratified. She, on her side, will not think of yielding to desires which seem both unfair to her husband and opposed to all her moral traditions. We are not here concerned to consider the most likely, or the most desirable, exit from this unfortunate situation. The points to note are that it is a situation which today actually occurs; that it causes acute unhappiness to at least two people who may be of the finest physical and intellectual type and the noblest character, and that it might be avoided if there were at the outset a proper understanding of the married state and of the part which the art of love plays in married happiness and the development of personality.

A woman may have been married once, she may have been married twice, she may have had children by both husbands, and yet it may not be until she is past the age of thirty and is united to a third man that she attains the development of erotic personality and all that it involves in the full flowering of her whole nature. Up to then she had to all appearance had all the essential experiences of life. Yet she had remained spiritually virginal, with conventionally prim ideas of life, narrow in her sympathies, with the finest, noblest functions of her soul helpless and bound, at heart unhappy even if not clearly realizing that she was unhappy. Now she has become another person. The new liberated forces from within have not only enabled her to become sensitive to the rich complexities of intimate personal relationship, they have enlarged and harmonized her realization of all relationships. Her new erotic experience has not only stimulated all her energies, but her new knowledge has quickened all her sympathies. She feels, at the same time, more mentally alert, and she finds that she is more alive than before to the influences of nature and of art. Moreover, as others observe, however they may explain it, a new beauty has come into her face, a new radiancy into her expression, a new force into all her activities. Such is the exquisite flowering of love which some of us who may penetrate beneath the surface of life are now and then privileged to see. The sad part of it is that we see it so seldom and then often so late.

It must not be supposed that there is any direct or speedy way of introducing into life a wider and deeper conception of the erotic play-function, and all that it means for the development of the individual, the enrichment of the marriage relationship, and the moral harmony of society. Such a supposition would merely be to vulgarize and to stultify the divine and elusive mystery. It is only slowly and indirectly that we can bring about the revolution which in this direction would renew life. We may prepare the way for it by undermining and destroying those degrading traditional conceptions which have persisted so long that they are instilled into us almost from birth, to work like a virus in the heart, and to become almost a disease of the soul. To make way for the true and beautiful revelation, we can at least seek to cast out those ancient growths, which may once have been true and beautiful, but now are false and poisonous. By casting out from us the conception of love as vile and unclean we shall purify the chambers of our hearts for the reception of love as something unspeakably holy.

In this matter we may learn a lesson from the psychoanalysts of today without any implication that psychoanalysis is necessarily a desirable or even possible way of attaining the revelation of love. The wiser psychoanalysts insist that the process of liberating the individual from outer and inner influences that repress or deform his energies and impulses is effected by removing the inhibitions on the free-play of his nature. It is a process of education in the true sense, not of the suppression of natural impulses nor even of the instillation of sound rules and maxims for their control, not of the pressing in but of the leading out of the individual's special tendencies.[4] It removes inhibitions, even inhibitions that were placed upon the individual, or that he consciously or unconsciously placed upon himself, with the best moral intentions, and by so doing it allows a larger and freer and more natively spontaneous morality to come into play. It has this influence above all in the sphere of sex, where such inhibitions have been most powerfully laid on the native impulses, where the natural tendencies have been most surrounded by taboos and terrors, most tinged with artificial stains of impurity and degradation derived from alien and antiquated traditions. Thus the therapeutical experience of the psychoanalysts reënforces the lessons we learn from physiology and psychology and the intimate experiences of life.

Sexual activity, we see, is not merely a bald propagative act, nor, when propagation is put aside, is it merely the relief of distended vessels. It is something more even than the foundation of great social institutions. It is the function by which all the finer activities of the organism, physical and psychic, may be developed and satisfied. Nothing, it has been said, is so serious as lust—to use the beautiful term which has been degraded into the expression of the lowest forms of sensual pleasure—and we have now to add that nothing is so full of play as love. Play is primarily the instinctive work of the brain, but it is brain activity united in the subtlest way to bodily activity. In the play-function of sex two forms of activity, physical and psychic, are most exquisitely and variously and harmoniously blended. We here understand best how it is that the brain organs and the sexual organs are, from the physiological standpoint, of equal

---

[4] See, for instance, H. W. Frink, *Morbid Fears and Compulsions*, 1918, Chap. **X**.

importance and equal dignity. Thus the adrenal glands, among the most influential of all the ductless glands, are specially and intimately associated alike with the brain and the sex organs. As we rise in the animal series, brain and adrenal glands march side by side in developmental increase of size, and at the same time, sexual activity and adrenal activity equally correspond.

Lovers in their play—when they have been liberated from the traditions which bound them to the trivial or the gross conception of play in love—are thus moving amongst the highest human activities, alike of the body and of the soul. They are passing to each other the sacramental chalice of that wine which imparts the deepest joy that men and women can know. They are subtly weaving the invisible cords that bind husband and wife together more truly and more firmly than the priest of any church. And if in the end—as may or may not be—they attain the climax of free and complete union, then their human play has become one with that divine play of creation in which old poets fabled that, out of the dust of the ground and in his own image, some God of Chaos once created Man.

IS SEXUALITY LOVE? [1]

By Grace Potter

WHEN a subject is viewed psychoanalytically a peculiar difficulty arises. There is available for use in interpretation only that measure of psychoanalysis which one has put to active use in his own life.

Psychoanalysis deals with human relationships, especially the part played in them by the Unconscious. As one has been psychoanalyzed only in proportion as the Unconscious has been made conscious, it comes about that interpretation of psychic material is possible only in the light of the individual's own development by it. One speaks, it could be said, through the medium of that completeness and harmony of being which has been achieved in one's own life. So what I say in my effort at a Freudian inquiry about some questions of interest to the birth control movement is to be taken as that part of Freudian principles which I have been able to accept, in both thought and feeling.

When Professor Sigmund Freud who developed and discovered the science of psychoanalysis was faced with the problem of deciding whether he should use the word "sexuality" or "love" in giving his theories to the world, he chose the former because he felt that otherwise he would be making a concession to the very prejudice and ignorance which his discoveries aimed to lessen, and which cause much of the failure and painful shortcomings of our culture. He knew that he was bound to be misunderstood either way. But he chose the way that would finally provide a further understanding of the important fact that sexuality and love are

[1] From *Religious and Ethical Aspects of Birth Control* (edited by Margaret Sanger). The American Birth Control League, 1926.

in their completeness one and the same, and that they go hand in hand.

So accepting the findings of a German doctor, a previous worker in this field, that sexual life begins in infancy, Freud's research shows that the pattern of this early sexuality, happy or otherwise, becomes in a way the pattern for all future experience. Further, he found that it was to a failure in the sexual life that neurosis on the one hand and stupidity on the other were often due. Years then passed before the shock of these pronouncements subsided enough for the academic and scientific worlds to recognize that these truths held the germ for a more real culture and a greater humanity than any we had yet known.

You will understand that I am not attempting to prove anything in this brief paper. I shall only briefly suggest here some of the effects which a distinction between the two ideas of love and sexuality seems to have had. From the psychoanalytic point of view one may ask whether the wide difference between love and sexuality, which our culture tries to make, may not have some bearing on three strange anomalies of this sometimes-called "scientific" age. The first anomaly is that we permit a law against birth control to remain on our statute books and to be invoked against certain unfortunates, although birth control is a matter of course with almost everybody, and that to try anyone for an infringement of this law it would be impossible to assemble a court of those who are not guilty of habitually breaking the statute. The second is that we have no adequate method of birth control. By this let me explain that there has as yet been no scientific research to announce a method of birth control which satisfies both health and our æsthetic needs. The third is that a mother's pain at childbirth is regarded as sufficiently a part of the natural course of events, and even in some way "sacred" so that interference with that suffering might be thought of as thwarting both Nature and God, and surely therefore a questionable proceeding if not a sin.

We may throw some light on these three facts if we turn our attention to the query as to whether there is a difference between love and sexuality. Perhaps we may say there is a distinction which lies in the special aspect of a complex impulse which is being considered rather than in any inherent difference which divides them.

Love is sometimes spoken of as sacred and profane, or spiritual and physical. So sexuality might be spoken of as psychic and physical. Love in its development alternates, so to say, from the physical attributes of it which have their early beginnings in the youngest infant to the tender components which are well developed at seven years of age. Another maturing of physical components has taken place by puberty and again tenderness blooms before the final correlation of all these is achieved and a harmonious mating is possible. A union which is on a purely physical basis is not even physically complete to a human being. It is not a mating. Sexuality is often supposed to mean the merely physical aspect of love. But just as anyone who has been in love knows that love includes sexuality, so also does sexuality include love. Analytic examination of those who have tried to express a physical sexuality without any allied tenderness has shown that such people do not achieve even a complete physical result. We may speak of one aspect of the complex impulse as love, another aspect we may as correctly call sexuality. But these two aspects are so linked that we bring about better understanding to say that love and sexuality are really one and the same. With some of us the two impulses have been so divided by our education that we feel shocked at the suggestion that in the healthy harmonious individual they are inextricably interwoven. That is evidence of how mistaken so-called education can be. Those in whom the two aspects of the impulse have not been finally correlated suffer for it either in sickness or nervous symptoms or loss of power to work. They will make society suffer for it too by reflecting in all the social institutions they help to erect or support this split in the individual psyche.

Love is developed in the little child by the giving up of his early partial trends of sexuality, by sublimating we say. So he develops tenderness. When later sexual maturity has been achieved, tenderness or love is waiting ready to add its power to its delayed but now more forcible physical relative. Freud speaks of two streams of interest, the tender stream and the physical stream. He who is fortunate enough to have the two unite at maturity can love and fully mate. One in whom the two remain divided will not know complete mating. He will feel, whether he consciously thinks so or not, that the two ideas of sexuality and love are different and cannot be experienced simultaneously in a relation with one person. He will wonder why mating is a matter of continual difficulty to him, and either he will spend much time trying in vain to achieve satisfactory sexual expression, or he may taboo it altogether and try to live "for love alone," as he may say, or he may give up all conscious interest in either love or sex.

The child's early training has been, of course, accompanied by repression. Under the happiest circumstances, at the wise insistence of parents whose tenderness for him makes the sacrifice not too painful, the child gives up the early sexual interests which every normal child feels. This postponement develops tenderness in the child, increases his educability, lengthens his period of growth and provides a possibility for his development as an individual. Such a sublimation is the basis for all culture. Such a child grown to maturity will be capable of feeling love and sexuality for the same person.

But it does not always happen this way. Successfully achieved repressions are the exception, not the rule. The training of the child usually develops too painful repressions so that the very aim of repression is lost—the happiness and health of the child is not achieved and he can make little or no contribution to society. Indeed he often has to take from the world more than ever he gives to it.

Stupid or ignorant parents cause the child, through fear, to give up unwillingly what he would enjoy, or even by their attitude make it impossible for him to give up youthful trends which he learns to abhor and yet to which the too painful repressions bind him. It is this harsh or stupid training which leaves the impression in the child that he has no right to experience or knowledge of sexual matters, no right to satisfy his natural curiosity and that sexuality as such is somehow wicked. Denied a knowledge of sexual matters which would allow for the psychic relief which the child's curiosity seeks, his physical impulses are harder than ever to deny.

The normal child is, as we now know, curious about sexual matters. Unless his parents' attitude has prevented such questioning, he will begin to ask where children come from and what the differences in the bodies of brother and sister signify from the time he is about three years old. If his parents are painfully occupied (either consciously or unconsciously) in sexual matters, if they are either vulgar or prudish, as we say, the child may fear so to question. Either the vulgar or the prudish parent may inhibit the child from questioning or leave the child who does question with the impression that sexuality is wrong. With the feeling that sexual interest is wrong goes the second feeling that he has no right to sexual knowledge and the third feeling that one who feels sexual interest is to be punished. These three feelings, which have a painful bearing on the character and health of the individual, are often repressed completely out of consciousness. But in the unconscious they may do much harm. Nothing remains inactive in the unconscious. Feelings painfully repressed may rise to consciousness in a sort of childish disguise, years later. The child questioning about sex and made to feel very painfully that he is naughty so to question, or that sex knowledge is not for him, may grow up

into an adult still suffering from that pain. Its path to consciousness direct may be closed by repression. Then it may
find an indirect path and it may appear in a wish to keep
from all the world any knowledge about sex which can be
denied them, and a wish to impress upon the world in every
possible way that sexuality is wrong and to demand punishment for sexual experience.

Some of the first most violent repressions result from the
eager inquiries which the child from two to five makes as to
where babies come from. The reproofs or misinformation
given leave an indelible feeling that his inquiry was shameful.
So too when he asks about his sexual organs, a sense of guilt
is developed which may later darken and render painful
every sexual experience of maturity. These effects may be
unconscious to the individual but register themselves in the
development of his glands, which as we know are so strongly
affected by the emotional life, or they may register themselves on other parts of his body, and also determine his
psychic attitude toward life. Such unconscious ideas may
exert enough power at this level of the unconscious so that
they will somehow thwart every conscious, painfully con-
certed effort and interest of the individual to love and be
lovable.

Could these unconscious forces repressed so painfully in
our own childhood account for the fact that, as adults, we
make laws against contraceptive information? It seems possible. Repressed material does not stay "down." The child
who was harshly denied a right to knowledge may, when a
man, unconsciously react to that deprivation by a wish to
deny this knowledge to others. Even more, he may feel by
a compulsion from his own unconscious pain that it is his
sacred duty to deny it to them. In other words, a wish to
curtail the liberty of others to get knowledge is a reflection
of some especially painful curtailing of one's own childish
efforts in an allied field. But this is not yet generally enough

IS SEXUALITY LOVE?   117

known or understood, and therefore we find people who think and feel they are cultured and who are yet eager for laws against sexual knowledge such as contraception.

The same painful repressions might also be potent in keeping laws effective once they were made. All this would be a reaction to the painful experiences of childhood, still compelling actions in adult life because working at an unconscious level. Such a dominance by his own painfully developed fantasy life keeps an individual from ever truly considering reality. The real factors of every adult person's need and right to birth control information become powerless to assert themselves against the painfully repressed and now unconscious experiences of childhood.

We find here, however, a curious situation which illustrates the queer quirks of which the unconscious is capable and which makes us realize both how stupid and how cruel it can be. Few of us react to our unconscious compulsion to feel that sexual information is wrong by acting *always* as if it were wrong for us. Most of us are only quite sure it is wrong for other people. Thus it is that perhaps no one who works for laws against birth control information ever lacks such for himself, or ceases eagerly to look for all that is new in this way.

Now we come to the question as to why indeed we have no adequate information to give about contraception. No information that will enable intelligent mates to be confident that they may control birth without running the risk of sickness to one or the other, without any such disagreeable features as would make one or the other question whether deprivation itself were not less hard to bear. No information that does not tend to do violence to such harmony between lovers as is an accompaniment of tender love. For a method of control which fails in any such way cannot reasonably be called adequate.

To quote what Professor Sigmund Freud said some years

ago: "All the contraceptives available hitherto impair sexual enjoyment, disturb the finer susceptibilities of both partners, or even act as a direct cause of illness." Nevertheless, so far no research has announced an adequate means of prevention of conception. Much as we may regret this, it is undeniable to anyone who has earnestly followed the history of birth control all over the world that each preventive which has appeared has tended to injure health, or the rhythm of love itself, or in some way the æsthetic demands required of such methods. We know well enough that the scientists who do research believe in the grave necessity for adequate means of birth control. We know that those who have money to give for research believe in the necessity for it. We know that both groups by experience and education are aware that no such adequate means are available. We must feel then that it is remarkable that such research still remains to be made. How can it be that no philanthropist has felt it necessary to his own peace of mind or has had such a wish to contribute to our culture that he has given the necessary hundreds of thousands of dollars for a scientific research for an adequate method of birth control?

It seems that unsuccessful childhood repressions may account both for our laws against birth control and for our lack of adequate methods. Perhaps it is the same unconscious feeling of guilt about sexuality appearing in a different way and at a deeper psychic level. We may say surely at a deeper psychic level, for to have no really adequate information is something which harms everyone, including even oneself. It seems that the feeling engendered in long ago childhood may now act to cut us off from knowledge which would further a more complete and happy love. Such an unconscious feeling could dominate our acts, even when our conscious minds have accepted the fact that the love life needs the support of science as truly as always it has had the support of art.

If there were time it would be interesting here to go into

the question of why it is that this unconscious guilty feeling about sexual knowledge finds it possible to express itself in an inhibition of scientific research. Perhaps a thorough understanding of the forces working against what all of us interested in birth control greatly desire may result in making possible this very desired research for harmless and æsthetic methods of contraception.

It seems that there is a third effect of this same unconscious guilty feeling which is also a serious detriment to our civilization. Today women as a matter of course suffer pain at childbirth. We do not any longer glorify that pain as much as our fathers used to do. We do not any longer think it so essential a part of sacred motherhood. But we do still "feel" it to be somehow so necessary a part of the birth of a child that the practical result is that women usually suffer great agony in bringing a child into the world. If it could be prevented we have not yet discovered how.

We cannot quite account for this. But may we not perhaps see in it the working of the unconscious feeling, developed in childhood, that one who has had sexual experience has sinned and should suffer? Perhaps so. Few consciously believe today that mothers in bearing children should suffer. But perhaps unconsciously we have enough of that attitude so that really in effect such suffering is not very effectually prevented.

We have then three effects: our laws against contraceptives, our lack of adequate contraceptive measures, and the tolerance of the suffering of women in childbirth, all of which evidently may be traced partly at least to the neurotic sense of guilt in regard to sex which our culture has fostered. And that guilt is also expressed directly in our division of sexuality and love, so that there are those who cannot even discuss whether sexuality is possible without love and love without sexuality. The ceaseless searching after new sexual interests which is sure to ensue in those who try to experience sex without love we know can never be satisfied. Those who so search will always have starved hearts and often enough sick bodies. Psychoanalysis has yet to find anyone in whom sexuality exists without allied emotional needs, however deeply repressions have buried them. Not that the puritan ideal of love without sex is further from the truth than this vulgar ideal of sex without love. They are equally based on the too painful repressions of infancy.

Repressions are a necessary part of culture. On them, as Freud has said, all civilization is built. Successful repressions take a part of the energy of the sexual instincts, after allowing for what is necessary for individual health, happiness and harmony, and deflect it to the uses of society. Those who have developed unsuccessful or too painful repressions not only make no contribution to the world which needs every man's aid, but they use up in their living more than they can contribute. They are inefficient in work, or sick so that they must be cared for, or unharmonious in their relations with other individuals, or often all three together. Also, it may be noted, in whichever way these painful and unsuccessful repressions are made, whether according to the puritan dictates, a repression of sexuality, or, according to the vulgar dictates, a repression of tenderness, they result in the end in difficulties that are curiously alike. The puritan with his negation becomes ill with much the same diseases that afflict his vulgar brother. Both may become mentally disturbed or even helpless from their repressions. Or they may be just stupid, inefficient creatures—the sad world is full of them.

The findings of psychoanalysis show, then, that what the world divides into sexuality and love are different aspects of one diversely-directed impulse. For either to be really experienced in fullness they must be harmoniously allied. A poet who thought of love and sexuality as allied expresses what its result might be:

Love some day shall make
This world as sweet and right for life
As ever mother made her body for our birth,
A world wherein we'll know
Because we dare to feel
New curiosities and needs and pain,
Beside just maudlin groping up from slime
And we shall be
Not only what now we aim to be
But something else beside.
Love shall teach us
What this new being is
That Man and Woman may become.
Love that shall bring peace
And endless moments' ecstasy,
To make us brave enough
To dare the world again;
Love that forms the lovers
To visions and capacities
Remote as new.
This love can do.

SEX LOVE [1]

By Dora Russell

THERE is no instinct that has been so maligned, suppressed, abused, and distorted by religious teaching as the instinct of sex. Yet sex love is the most intense instinctive pleasure known to men and women, and starvation or thwarting of this instinct causes more acute unhappiness than poverty, disease, or ignorance. I said that no men, with the exception, of course, of priests and other people of curious ethical standards, deprived themselves completely, or were deprived by the community, of their use of sexual functions. But traditional morality and early teaching, combined with the subjection of women, have robbed men of the spontaneous delight and vigor which should come to them through sex love. A man is taught never to indulge it—the very word indulge is repulsive—until he has found a woman with whom he is prepared to spend the whole of his life, and has been to church for a special ceremony allowing him to possess her and forcing her to obey him. Receiving what is virtually a slave, he is then told to approach her only in the spirit of holy reverence. Never again must he look affectionately upon or approach another woman. Till recently no serious restrictions were laid upon men in regard to their lawful wives, but the improved position of women has led many religious people, including some Anglo-Catholics, to propose quite a new ruling, namely long periods of chastity within marriage, if it should be necessary for health, or other reasons, to limit the number of the family. The Roman Catholics openly advocate widespread celibacy for men and women, which is, for them,

[1] From *The Right to be Happy.* New York: Harper & Brothers, 1927.

the most holy life and the only legitimate escape from parental responsibility. This teaching therefore quite clearly denies that sex is either a necessity or a lawful pleasure to men or to women and allows its indulgence only when the perpetuation of the race is desired. This is a perfectly natural result of the worship of fertility associated with agricultural superstitions. Yet anyone capable of examining his or her instincts without regard to prejudice associated with past environments finds that there is a clear division between the impulse to sexual enjoyment and the desire to have children. The primary motive involved in relations between men and women is the simple impulse towards sexual pleasure. This in primitive and ignorant communities obviously had a natural result in the responsibility of parenthood. Parental delights were not foreseen, but followed on experience. Experience in turn established a conscious tradition that the lack of offspring was a curse and a sorrow, their presence a blessing and a delight. Thus the conscious desire for parenthood arose as something separate from the sexual impulse. That there is any unconscious drive towards parenthood—any paternal or maternal instinct—is disputed. I think that there is, but that it is related rather to the phenomena of organic growth than to sex. But this is a subject for later discussion.

Because parenthood involved responsibility and pain, it was seized upon by ascetic religion as the sole justification of sexual intercourse. The major errors of Christian teachers seem to me always to arise from the insistence on ends while suppressing and thwarting the natural and pleasant means to those ends. They are so intent on proving that human life is miserable, that they cause every result desired to be reached through pain. If it be possible to arrive by pleasure that route must be barred. This principle has been applied throughout government and education in Christian countries. Therefore our society has insisted on the duties of fathers and mothers, which were to many people the less pleasant part of the instinctive relations of men and women, and at the same time made every effort to poison and destroy the impulse to sexual pleasure. Expressions of parental feeling in a distorted form pervade our social customs and institutions, but it is important to notice that the impulse to sexual pleasure has never yet had its rightful place in shaping our society, because it has not been allowed recognition. The loss we have suffered is beyond measure, but happily not beyond repair. Sex is not only the source of some of the finest poetry and art, of heroisms, sacrifices, dreams; it is also the source of a very important human experience. In sex love, through physical sympathy and intimate union, we draw into ourselves as in no other way the understanding of another human personality, and the knowledge that two very different creatures can live together in exquisite harmony. Such an experience alone, widespread, would be worth ten million platforms blaring pacifism. It gives, as nothing else can, the beauty of human partnership in love, of mutual abandonment of distrust for mutual joy. Christianity, it is true, enjoins that the "twain become one flesh"; it has need to enjoin and enforce this, since all the rest of its teaching goes to prevent so miraculous a consummation. Yet supreme unions exist: they exist in spite, not because, of orthodox Christian doctrine.

More important for us all than even a fuller exercise of sex functions is to realize that these functions are neither wicked nor obscene. Every one of us, man or woman, has been warped and corrupted in our innermost being by such teaching. Even those who repudiate the Christian synthesis and imagine themselves free of all prejudice, are a mass of tormenting inhibitions, doubts, and inconsistencies when they approach sex. Their imaginations remain filled with false notions of restraint and refinement; they break free and alternate between coarseness and self-pitying disgust. Moralists persist in imagining that those who speak of sex above a whisper are concerned only to advocate free love and excess. It is something quite different, it is the abandonment of a pernicious mental attitude, that we are demanding. No amount of license can cure our *malaise* in sexual matters so long as those who break loose continue to pay even lip-service to the notions of naughtiness, bawdiness, and sin. For these are only the reverse of abstention and asceticism, and nobody can feel them who is not at heart a puritan still.[2] After the manner of repressed instincts set free sex is now stalking society seeking whom he may devour, and devouring many. You will not stay his ravages, any more than the ravages of hatred and fear, by chaining him up and giving him a good beating. Indeed, if you approach him without prejudice and menace you may find him neither so destructive in his antics nor so hideous in his physiognomy as you imagined. He is far less dangerous to the human structure than drunkenness. Mystic horror has led us to exaggerate the potency of sex and therefore to suppose that to leave a man and woman together in isolation is to ensure what our law so confidently and comically terms "misconduct." Yet in the early days of free developing youth that is the least likely thing to happen. And a right education of young people, together with the claims which work and the exercise of their other functions will make upon their energies, would ensure the postponement of full sex experience until an age at which it will not injure their development. By a right education I do not mean repression, but the imparting of many kinds of knowledge and the direction of all impulses to a happy life of varied activity. When men and women first embark upon sexual experience, I make no doubt that they will be occupied with it constantly and experiment freely. That stage does not last, for the selectiveness based upon experience very

---

[2] The French are commonly supposed to be free and civilized in sex matters. On the contrary, though their conduct may be free, the game is played according to rigid old-fashioned conventions, lover, wife, and husband feeling stereotyped emotions. Pleasure is deliberately enhanced by insistence on spiciness and sin. The purity of young girls and the chastity of their mothers are sacrosanct to Frenchmen, who are too conventional to understand freedom.

speedily sets in. In this, greater freedom for women will play an important part. For, just as the moralist thinks everybody is out for free love, so does he think that free love means that no man or woman will ever refuse sexual favors to a person of the opposite sex. Yet large numbers of men and women who have freedom to experiment are not only most selective in love, but ultimately marry and never look at another man or woman for the rest of their lives, especially if they do not feel themselves compelled to this course of conduct. Others seek occasional adventures outside a permanent partnership. Others again do find that any permanency is distasteful. I incline to think that these people would prove to be rarer than either the prudish or the prurient imagine. After all, there are other pleasures besides sex, though one might scarcely think so when one hears the puritans and the Freudians talking.

What is there in this suggested freedom that is so dangerous and wicked other than its opposition to our traditional prejudices? It would strengthen and broaden rather than weaken and damage character; it would add to our lives great variety and happiness. It would make the friendship of men and women a real thing rather than a strained relation forever hovering on the brink of an abyss towards which neither dare cast his eyes.

We have been taught that incurable disease is the penalty of freedom, even that it is the Divine punishment of mortal sin. This is another of those superstitions, now exploded, which ignorance has set up as a barrier to joy. Do we forbid our children to have playmates, because from one or other of them they may catch scarlet fever? Sexual diseases, however repulsive, are like any others, and are open to cure. Already science has mastered them, and but for our superstitious morals, we should by now have eradicated them completely. Obviously, where disease is present, our ethical code should enjoin honest avowal and temporary abstention. One may point out that neither the law nor the church of our

Christian state enjoins this even in marital relations. On the
contrary, our social ethics prescribe a conspiracy of silence
that protects husbands and treats the bodies of wives and
possible children as chattels of no account. It ought to be
an offense involving the indignation of the whole community
and possibly the penalty of the law for anyone to infect
another, man or woman. Private notification which would be
followed by private free treatment should certainly be compulsory. If this were so, it might be safe and just to make
it a punishable offense to infect another human being. But
all legal action in these matters is likely to lead to tyranny
and abuse, and our best safeguard lies in an enlightened
public opinion. It should, I think, continue to be an offense
to force actual sex experience on the very young, but an
offense usually calling for pathological treatment rather than
castigation. I would not legislate against literature and pictures; the minds of freely taught people are quite adequately
safeguarded. Repressive laws invariably lead to the prosecution of works of art and to the free circulation of cunning
suggestiveness.

*   *   *   *   *

I do not think people realize, or will ever do so without
changing their whole idea of what constitutes a woman, what
sex starvation means in the ordinary lives of hundreds of
thousands of men and women who earn their living.[3] The
richer and more varied the personality the worse the effects

[3] In a report from Birmingham on unemployment pay (*Times,*
July 30, 1925) the following passage occurs: "A more serious aspect
of the case is the apparent readiness of both men and women to
undertake the responsibility of the married state on the flimsy security of the 'extended' benefit. . . . *The peculiar frame of mind*
(my italics) which will enable a girl to leave her employment and to
become the bride of a man in receipt of 'standard' or 'extended' benefit is difficult to understand." I see nothing either peculiar or difficult
to understand in a woman who takes the only road society allows
her to the satisfaction of her two most vital instincts. Nor would
anybody who had not been warped by two thousand years of
Christianity, and the later superstition that economic security alone
is the basis of happiness.

of repression. Most of the trouble flows from our absolute
refusal to separate the instincts of sex and parenthood in our
social and economic structure. Thus a young man dare not
marry until he has a good enough position to support a wife
and a family. The more skilled and brilliant he is the less
will he wish to hamper himself by these claims and anxieties.
Therefore for many years he is balked and starved—as all
virtuous single women are—or else he must go to a special
type of woman whom society for convenience sake forces to
sell her physical wares by direct barter. Yet men are hungry
for a fuller companionship with women than a mere sex
relation provides and they cannot get this from casual prostitutes. Rich men may find prostitutes as accomplished as
the *hetæra* of ancient Greece, but poor men rarely. All use
of sex outside marriage between men and young women
reared to virtue means clandestine meetings and elaborate
arrangements for secrecy. The penalties are still heavier for
the women than the men. What can the woman worker do?
She also must look upon marriage as parenthood with responsibility and suffering. She has perhaps a bare livelihood.
To marry a man of similar position means real hardship because she must not continue at work. When children are
added, she sees by the example of other women that she will
have to starve herself to feed them and her husband. Like
the man, the more valuable she is as an individual, the less
will she wish to relinquish her other activities. The incentive
to continue earning and lead a secret sexual life is obvious.
Yet that solution may bring misery. There is the sense of
social disapproval which enforces secrecy and the perpetual
dread of discovery or an accidental pregnancy. A woman may
feel that in sex she is merely claiming, as indeed she is, a
right and need of her nature, but guilt, disaster, difficulty lie
in wait for her on every side. What hinders us from establishing a social system in which young men and women who are
out in the world earning may enter into open temporary sex

partnerships without harm to the work and legitimate ambitions of either? Nothing whatever except our false picture of woman and our ingrained ascetic belief that sex is wicked if enjoyed and not immediately succeeded by the pains, anxieties, and penalties of parenthood. Yet such companionship, not despised and concealed, would work great changes in the character of individuals. There would be fewer lonely, hard, and envious men and women, less anger and jealousy, more generosity and love—the one kind of love that is really worth having, love based on understanding. The woman would not be primarily a sex creature, the man not there only to buy her favors. There would be holidays of mutual enjoyment, mutual discussion of all the problems of existence in which young and eager people delight. The day's work would be enlivened by the thought of the free and lovely companionship to come when it was over, of the other personality ready to sympathize and discuss. Such companionship arises between people of the same sex, but it is from each other that men and women draw the deepest sense of peace and self-completion. The idea of sin must be banished, as must any demand for special service or sacrifice by the woman. (Men sometimes tend to regard free love as a means to getting their socks darned cheaply.) There would be passionate griefs, disappointments and broken ideals, but none of this is so damaging to human personality as atrophy. We must have freedom and courage to learn if we are to be worth anything as human beings. And when these struggles are surmounted men and women often find they have been but the prelude to a symphony, a preparation for the most vital sex experience of their lives, which bears fruit in a union in which soul and body cry aloud: "For this, for this was I born!"

To such a union each partner brings a knowledge of his own temperament and needs and a willingness and ability to understand the needs of the other, to such a union are added loved and wanted children. I want both freedom and honesty for men and women because I believe that neither spasmodic sex experience nor a strict marriage entered into in ignorance or frivolity can give men and women the poise and harmony which should come to them through sex. Hot-headed choice is often at fault and experience is the only trustworthy guide. Similarly impatience and egotism frequently break off a union that promises well, because the two people concerned are not able to live the open common life which might weld them into harmony. Presenting a spontaneous psychological unity to the world is a quality which distinguishes perfect sex unions. It is not always achieved at first even by people who are well matched and passionate lovers. Yet it should not involve an effort or it is unreal.

In the minds of very many people who are not conventionally moral or religious lingers the notion that since a supreme union between man and woman is possible, physical and emotional energies should be reserved until that union is found. Men frequently regret what the moralist calls pre-marital indiscretions, and pre-marital experience for women is definitely still thought a crime. In books on marriage and child-rearing by good doctors, intended for the average middle-class man and woman, one is astonished to find how traditional prejudice will prevent the authors from drawing the moral and political conclusions which flow quite obviously from their medical diagnosis.

A doctor, for instance, will follow materialistic scientific psychology, and discount original sin in the rearing of young children, but he would not apply the same principles when it comes to labor troubles, or international rivalry. An expert spinster nurse will write pages of excellent advice on the feeding of children, and sheer dogmatic idiocy when she touches upon sex teaching. Books on marriage echo and re-echo with the sensitive delicacy of woman and the necessity of avoiding shocks to her nerves.[4] I cannot but feel that something quite blunt must be said on the subject of male and female chastity and this alleged delicacy of women. Over and over again these books tell us how marriages go wrong through the ignorance of women and the brutality of men, and yet go on preaching the conventional doctrine of planting down two people of complete inexperience in a marriage from which neither must seek to escape. It is admitted by these moralists that physical dissatisfaction will render such a marriage miserable, and that, when the complicated physical and psychical factors are all considered, the chances of success between two utterly inexperienced persons are very remote. A happy sexual life is, in fact, in a developed personality, the product not only of strong instinct but of art and science in its use.

It is not impossible that a time may come when pre-marital experience will no longer be regarded as a crime, or even as an indiscretion. People may come to think it better for the ultimate happiness of men and women if the affections and emotions are not too deeply entangled in their first experiences of sex. The idea that we fritter away our emotions and energy does not hold good of people whose training has not led to too great concentration on the sexual aspect of their lives. On the contrary, the maladjustments which may come at first and cause angry reactions against the person with whom they are associated, disappear as we grow more fully awake to the technique of sex, and we become more capable of an important, deep and happy sex union. The "superstition of chastity" is a part of that same false psychology which makes moral virtue consist in emptiness and abstention. Chastity for women has been a part of ethical teaching in nearly all societies where men were dominant.

[4] The books here referred to are: *Health in Children*, 1925; *Mothercraft*, Miss Liddiard, of the Truby King Institute at Earl's Court; *Hygiene in Marriage*, Dr. Isabel Emslie Hutton, 1923. See also *The Child, His Nature and His Needs*, Children's Foundation, Valparaiso, 1925.

It is associated primarily with property and children, and the desire to make sure of descent when it is traced through the male line. This has led to the caging of women both before and after marriage under the patriarchal system. Alike in Greece, China, Mohammedan and Christian countries insistence on female chastity has prevailed. It has become dissociated from its original purpose and has been valued for its own sake, with serious and far-reaching results. In Greece we find that the goddess of chastity is associated in men's minds with the pursuit of hunting. Artemis herself is a huntress, pure and boyish in her athletic integrity. But she suggests also the fleet doe which she hunts, and the pleasure of man in the primitive pursuit of a woman to conquer her virginity.

Sex love thus acquires, as in Christian countries, the aspect of a chase, which ends when the woman is finally caught and subdued. The refinements of chivalrous love in medieval times express the same feeling tempered to a more exquisite sensation by ascetic delicacy. The lady is adored by her lover from afar, and to possess her would spoil the refinement of emotion. This much lauded chivalrous love is really no more than the play of vanity in man and woman and the pleasure of gloating anticipation. The same thing appears in eighteenth century intrigue. The gallant strings conquered women on to his vanity as a Red Indian strings scalps to his girdle. Love is sought, not because the woman will be a prized and honored companion, but because it has a tang of wickedness, and a delight to vanity like that of the hunter who returns with a big bag from his day's sport. Comparisons between pursued and charming women and wounded birds or terrified wild creatures appear in the talk and writings of gallant old gentlemen of the Victorian age. The theory of woman's delicacy, her distaste for sex, her horror and dread in capture, all of them reënforced by mediæval asceticism, make this pursuit peculiarly delightful and brutalizing to the male. Women have played the horrible game till they are sick of it, or so obsessed by it that they feel it to be a reality. Even those who claim to enlighten them on sex are teaching them to play it still. The psychological results are deplorable. Enormous numbers of middle-class and working women apparently still despise their husbands as people of an inferior animal nature, whose desires a woman may condone in loving-kindness but can never share. Married life is a series of shocks to delicate nerves, against which the woman erects barriers of artificial separations and refinements, continuing to play the game of coyness which she has been taught to regard as necessary to retain a man's affections.[5] For this is the lamentable consequence of the superstition of chastity, that it leads people to look on marriage as the end rather than the beginning of happiness. The hunt is over, the quarry run to earth. Woman perhaps in modern times has been the huntress. The effect is the same, excitement dies and emptiness lays a cold hand on lovers' ardors. As we have learnt not to seek happiness in this world, but to wait for it till we reach heaven, so do we dream of that perfect wife or perfect husband whom in our folly we believe the world of real men and women cannot provide. Valuing chastity above love, and the chase above its ending, we come to believe that there is no happiness which, when we hold it close and clasp it to our hungry hearts, will not turn to dust and ashes in our hands. Therefore men and women flee from deep love as from a prison and dread marriage as a snare set for their unwary feet. Therefore not only in sex love, but in every activity of life men and women develop an attitude of dissatisfaction, waiting and longing, which blinds them to the fullness and beauty which even now may be theirs.

If women really desire an individual life, freedom and a part in the cultural development of the race, they must not only fight for the right to do any man's work of which they

[5] Cf. the early days of marriage between Rousseau's Sophie and Emile.

are mentally and physically capable, they must also be more honest and frank about their instinctive nature and its functions. Why should they seek only the traditional life of a woman or the traditional life of a man? Why try to combine these two, whose traditional philosophies are quite separate and mutually exclusive? Because men have so long ruled the world, it does not follow that the philosophy by which they have ruled it is the correct one. Nor does it follow that if woman rules she should do so in accordance with a picture of her nature almost wholly drawn by the religion and philosophy of men. Why all this feminine delicacy? If we are hysterical and timid about our animal desires and functions and cannot have the courage to be honest, that is a thing to be ashamed of, not a reason for boasting and special consideration. Men have pushed on to us all the reticence and virtue, we in turn push on to them all the brutality and vice. We incite them to brutality by the pretense of coldness, that we may escape the sin of the flesh by escaping the responsibility for aggression. Strength and health of body and honesty of mind would soon show that the modesty and sensitiveness of woman associated with this "shock" of marriage and her bodily changes, is as much a hysteria as the Victorian swoon at a man's declaration of love.

Clearly, in a society which assumes in woman a dislike of physical love, women can reap a great economic advantage by keeping up the pretense. They get paid for sex, because they are deemed to dislike it. Formerly the plea was just, because sex in marriage involved unlimited childbearing, and sex outside degradation and misery, for which no amount of riches and fine clothes could compensate. Now, however, women can make men and society reward them for what is their pleasure, and on the plea of delicacy, escape even the pains of maternity. Everybody except the society butterfly and her imitators stands to gain by dropping this pretense about woman's ethereal nature and her hypocritical assumption of sole guardianship over what is civilized and moral. Women should be paid, not for sex, which, if they were honest and robust, they would admit as a pleasure, but for maternity, which, though it, too, is a pleasure, is also a responsibility and a communal service. What women from their instinctive nature can bring to civilization is a warm physical and mental companionship in place of cold and genteel condescension, and a clear and scientific statement —not moralizing and sentimental—of the claims of maternity and child life on the political and economic system.

In sex life I believe that women who were free and honest would find that they did not differ very greatly from men. They would feel strong impulses towards some men, others they would feel to be sexually tolerable, others would suggest indifference or repulsion. Women are, I believe, more selective than men, but it is less easy for them to be selective without experience. They are not, as is commonly supposed, invariably entangled emotionally and hysterically in love; like men, they have great and small passions, and can learn by experience to choose a partner for permanence and parenthood. It is said that the sex impulse in women can flourish only at the expense of maternity. I think this view derives from past times when large families completely absorbed a woman's physical strength and emotional energy, so much so that the husband frequently felt himself cheated of the love he sought in mating. This led to the painful division between maternal women and the childless women sought by men for sexual love. In actual fact a woman is as capable as a man of combining love of a mate, parenthood and physical or intellectual work. Like so many things which people insist upon treating as matters of principle, this is purely a quantitative question. It depends on the physical and mental energy of the woman concerned, the number of her children, the economic status of the family. When opponents of birth control argue that it makes of marriage legalized prostitution, they mean simply that it might enable a man and woman to continue enjoying holy wedlock because they would retain health and a freedom from too great anxiety. It is alleged by many people, who profess to speak not ethically but from science, that but for the fear of children men would be savage and brutal and exhaust their wives, and even themselves, by excess. I do not believe this is possible for healthy, hard-working people within marriage, and birth control aims above all at conserving the physical and emotional energy of the wife. Apart from this, it is psychologically true that brutality is the reaction to coldness. A real sex union does not perpetuate the emotions of the chase, and a warm and physical love from a woman in some way stills the hunger of a man for the blunt sexual experience. Somehow two people who are really one flesh have less need to be constantly proving it. If the delicate woman really desires to diminish the dreaded masculine rapacity, her artificial barriers and niceties are a gross error in psychology. The civilizing of sex, as of everything else, lies in the thought and emotion which give varied and supple expression to primitive passion, not in checks and suppressions of the passion itself.

IV
MARRIAGE

SEX AND MARRIAGE [1]

By Robert H. Lowie

PRIMITIVE society does not allow its members to gratify their lust at will; hence there is no such thing as real promiscuity. Parent and child are never permitted to mate; brother and sister, very rarely. Often the rules are stricter than with us: fifth cousins are prohibited, and by sheer fiction even unrelated individuals rate as kin. About some unforbidden forms of sexual intercourse savage society is merely indifferent; others are positively approved, and stable unions of this sort may be called marriages.

An Australian was killed if he cohabited with a woman of the wrong group. No one cared if he slept with a woman of the right group. From the latter the elders of the tribe allotted to him a girl he *married*.

Western civilization also approves, tolerates, and condemns, but profession and practice do not tally so well as among savages. Until recently cohabitation was sanctioned only by a religious ceremony, which normally created a lifelong bond. However, bachelors were not outlawed for sowing their wild oats; and Dr. Samuel Johnson, devout churchman and moralist that he was, considered a married man's amours mere peccadilloes. On the other hand, single women became outcasts by losing their virginity, and so did wives by unfaithfulness to their husbands. That natural children should be regarded as bastards was a foregone conclusion. In practice, only those suffered who were without influence. A king's mistress was not treated as a streetwalker: the virtuous Empress Maria Theresa stooped to write polite

[1] From *Are We Civilized?* New York: Harcourt, Brace and Company, 1929.

letters to Madame de Pompadour and admonished Marie Antoinette to be nice to Madame du Barry. Humane sentiments also tempered behavior towards the bastards of princes.

Present custom in civilized countries varies and is in a flux; hence no general statement can be made to hold for all. Some substitute a legal for the religious rite. Divorce and remarriage are common. There are European states which ignore the difference between legitimate and natural children. In some circles equal freedom for both sexes is preached and practiced; others in the same countries cling to the old standards. What we nowadays call conservative and radical positions as to sex both occur in different primitive societies.

Among the Northern Plains Indians the double standard of conservatism held sway. Parents encouraged their sons to be gay young blades and bade their daughters beware of philanderers from other families. In a woman chastity was highly prized, though hardly expected. Girls who fell were not beyond the pale. But they would not fetch large offers of horses from a suitor, and some rites in the Sun Dance could be performed only by absolutely pure married women. There was surely more illicit intercourse than in the middle-class homes of Victorian Europe; there was perhaps less if we take into account the customs of the countryside and the prostitution of the cities. Real differences existed: a Crow or Blackfoot might be legal husband to two or more wives, and divorce was common, being in no wise hindered by authority. But in the *ideals* of sexual behavior there was much similarity: men were to be red-blooded Lotharios, and women saints; and stable unions ranked higher than loose ones.

But in other regions we find the radical pattern of free love. Off the coast of New Guinea lie the Trobriands where a girl is never a virgin at marriage. From a child she plays at the sex game; when older she sleeps with the youths of the village in the bachelors' hall; she becomes a particular boy's sweetheart; and finally the two set up a permanent household. Similarly, among the Masai of East Africa the young braves, to the number of fifty or a hundred, sleep in a dormitory of their own, the hut being shared by the young girls. Each warrior has his own mistress, who remains loyal so long as he is about. Should he go off for a single day, she takes up with another lover. Pregnancy, however, is a disgrace, which is staved off by artificial means.

Is this not promiscuity? It is not. For even this free and easy life has its limitations. One of them is not less quaint than the recently abolished British law forbidding a widower to marry his wife's sister. Though a girl mates with almost any other bachelor in the neighborhood, with her fiancé she must *not* sleep, and to prevent that she is sent to another dormitory. Further, both in youth and later there are fixed limits to license. Blood-relatives do not consort with each other, nor do people in the same subdivision of the tribe. A man may not mate with his foster-sister or wed two women in the same clan. He is further restricted to his own age-class and must not stoop to the daughter of a blacksmith.

In short, there is no promiscuity. But there *is* license, before, in, and outside of marriage. For the Masai are not like some other tribes that allow free love in youth, yet limit it in wedlock. Husbands exchange bedfellows; a host turns over his wife and hut to a guest; widows and divorcées live out of wedlock, but uncensured, with men of their husbands' age.

However, the Masai clearly distinguish between marriage and licensed fornication. Here, as elsewhere, the object of marriage is not indulgence of the flesh but a home and children. Of this, more anon; let us first see how one gets a spouse.

Primitive tribes generally dispose of their daughters at puberty. This explains why girls are often not consulted as to their marriages. At fourteen or thereabouts they do not know what is good for them. (Their parents do not either, but they can hardly be expected to realize that.) When it was the European custom to marry off daughters young, their inclinations counted for little. Experience shows that neither arrangement by parents nor free choice guarantees happiness, but that is immaterial for everyone but the couple in question.

With us and with savages what counted was other considerations, in some respects alike. Marriage took care of the daughter's sex life; it gave the husband the children he coveted; and it cemented a bond between two families. There was a difference, however, imposed by economic conditions. Primitive woman was an economic asset; why then give her up gratis? Compensation could be secured in several ways. In Australia and New Guinea two households having each a son and a daughter swap girls; each youth is thus provided with a wife in the least troublesome way. Elsewhere the suitor goes to live with his parents-in-law and for a year or more plays the part of servant to them. Or instead of such service he may offer a bride-price.

On the primitive level there is nothing degrading about the purchase of a woman. It was the highest form of marriage recognized by the Crow—the one most honorable for a girl. In a love match the man was trying to get something for nothing, he was "stealing" his sweetheart. Such unions were not likely to last long. But when a man paid ten horses for a girl, it was proof that he esteemed her for not being a spitfire or a gadabout; and then the marriage was likely to be stable. Northwest Californians stressed purchase even more, for the offspring of an unbought woman were reckoned bastards and excluded from the men's club.

Because marriage was a contract of *families*, certain customs naturally sprang up. When a man in north central California got his bride, his brothers and cousins usually chipped in to make up the "purse" required. Nothing more natural, then, than that if the husband died, one of his kinsmen should inherit the widow. On the other hand, if a woman died, her family would send a sister or cousin to take her place. Often two or more sisters might be wives at the same time: a Plains Indian paid for the eldest and married others as they came of age.

Interesting consequences flow from the idea of women as economic goods. They come to form the main part of a Negro's estate, so that his eldest son will inherit all wives except his own mother. Divorce logically implies return of the price paid. Adultery becomes trespass on property rights, calling for indemnification. Again, there is a logical development of the ruder Australian system of exchange, by which a youth obtained a wife through a trade of sisters. In the more complex African conditions, the same result is achieved by storing the amount "pocketed" for a daughter in order to pay for a son's spouse. Finally, though there is no end to legal possibilities, a father can get a loan on the security of a small daughter. He can borrow a heifer and a bull even on the merest prospect of having his wife bear a girl.

Marriage, then, is a contract. But the conditions implied in it vary. When a Kai in New Guinea pays for his wife, she becomes his property, to be inherited by his heirs and punishable for infidelity. But he gains control neither over her chattels nor over her issue: both belong to her and her kin. Contrast with this the common Negro idea of purchase. Here what the husband craves and secures is progeny. When he has paid the full price, he is entitled to children, and barrenness becomes the chief cause of divorce. The views of the Lango on the upper Nile are typical: "Infecundity brings more shame and disrepute on a woman than the most riotous living." But it is the recipients of the bride-price that are responsible, having failed in the implied contractual obligation. Hence the payment is returned, or a sister of the wife's is given to the husband gratis. Further, the price paid for a wife entitles the husband to *all* her offspring thereafter. Hence, in flat contradiction to our ideas, the results of adulterous matings are legally children of their mother's purchaser. Their blood-father has no claims upon them whatsoever. This is a common principle of African law. The Masai, for example, cannot always know who begot a particular infant. That, however, does not matter, for its legal relationship is fixed by payment for the mother.

Where women are bought, a rich man naturally buys two or more wives. Polygamy is hardly ever founded on masculine lechery, which can be satisfied outside of wedlock. But a Siberian with several herds of reindeer needs a wife for each, and a Negro with large tracts of land to till can put several women to hoeing. Sometimes a sexual reason also occurs: a Lango is forbidden to sleep with his wife until her child is weaned, and since it is nursed for nearly three years he turns to other wives. In no case do the natives consider the practice degrading. Generally the first wife herself twits a man with being a miser if he fails to buy her an assistant, and thus goads him into getting a second spouse.

However, considering that about an equal number of male and female children are born into this world, polygamy can never be common in a community unless there has been tampering with the normal ratio. For instance, if men are regularly killed off in war or on dangerous seal-hunting expeditions, an excess of women results. Or, as in Africa, the chiefs and wealthy men may seize an undue share of the females, letting the rest of the men go hang. These others prefer, however, to seduce the married women of the land. In most savage societies polygamy is not forbidden; yet most unions are monogamous. For wherever people are more or less on a level of equality, the tendency will be to follow the natural ratio of the sexes.

A rarer form of polygamy develops when infant girls are killed in large numbers—usually because of the hard struggle for existence. Then there results an excess of men, as in southern India; hence a woman will have several husbands. But since blood-fatherhood matters as little here as elsewhere, it is easy to assign children to their *social* fathers.

Primitive monogamy need not be any more "moral" than

polygamy. Marriage is rarely sacramental; hence divorce is easy and frequent. The Greenlanders, though not forbidding polygamy, are mostly content with one husband or wife; but Captain Holm found a girl barely twenty years old who had just left her sixth mate. The Hopi prescribe a single wife, but the partners are constantly shifting: it is "progressive" or "brittle" monogamy. Characteristically, however, unions always become more stable after the birth of children.

To sum up. The sex life of all civilized and all savage peoples is at bottom amazingly similar. What varies quite as remarkably is the emphasis on this or that feature, the appraisal of the same behavior. Modern prostitution enables a man to cohabit with an indefinite number of women, each having a similar range of partners. This, then, combines the two forms of polygamy that occur among savages. How does the Masai plan differ? It differs in that *all* the girls of a community share the experience of multiple sex relations, that accordingly none of them is outlawed, and that their favors are not for sale. Here it is the legal wife that is bought, and not mainly for sexual purposes. The traditional European father spurns the bastard foisted upon him by an adulterous wife; the African insists that all her children, begotten by whomsoever, shall be his.

There is not a single custom, a single sentiment, connected with Western marriage that cannot be paralleled from some savage people; and not one that is not proved conventional by the practice of other societies. Some tribes sanction male jealousy: a Blackfoot had the right to slice off his wife's nose to punish adultery. But the Masai share wives with agemates, and some tribes regard infidelity as irrelevant to divorce. There are always prohibited degrees, but the lines are differently drawn. The Lango forbid marriage with anyone no matter how remotely related on either the father's or the mother's side. Some West Australians, on the other hand, insist on a man's marrying his maternal uncle's daughter. So there is endless diversity on the basis of the selfsame instinct of reproduction. Yet again there is likeness, not in the concrete sex behavior or philosophy, but in that everywhere without exception some modes of intercourse are lifted above the rest as more dignified because bound up with the maintenance of society.

But what of love among savages? Can it flourish in the midst of such looseness and prudential considerations? Passion, of course, is taken for granted; affection, which many travelers vouch for, might be conceded; but Love? Well, the romantic sentiment occurs in simpler conditions—as with us—in fiction. A Plains Indian story shows the Sun himself smitten with the beauty of a maiden and luring her to the sky. Heroes set out to achieve deeds of derring-do "all for the love of a lady." Orpheus-like, a husband follows his beloved wife to the land of spirits; and even in historical tradition a young woman braves a long trip through hostile country to rescue her crippled lover. In frigid Siberia a lovesick Yukaghir maiden scratches her desires on a sheet of birchbark: it is the only outlet society allows. The symbols are oddly conventional: a figure like a folded umbrella represents the youth; a wider sample of the same design, the artist herself; crossing stripes above her betoken grief, connecting bars indicate love; and an incomplete house means desertion. So the girl can utter her plaint—"Thou goest hence, and I bide alone. For thy sake I weep and moan."

Yukaghir women are no better than they should be, but there is more than fleshly lust in these birchbark letters faithfully transcribed for us by Dr. Jochelson. They breathe the same wistful longing one meets now and then in the primitive tales that register the teller's outlook on life. So Love exists for the savage as it does for ourselves—in adolescence, in fiction, among the poetically minded.

THE BREAKDOWN OF MARRIAGE [1]

By Will Durant

AND so we come to marriage.

It was Bernard Shaw, presumably, who said that more nonsense had been uttered on the subject of marriage than on any other topic in the world. It is as simple to be foolish about love as in it, and with less excuse. Approaching the problem, even the most disembodied intellectual perceives that ideas have only a modest (though this is hardly the word) influence upon the relations of the sexes; that economic changes override philosophies and morals; and that the best that thought can do is to analyze the changes, foresee their development and result, and find some intelligent adjustment of behavior that may protect the individual and the race. In these affairs it is useless to preach, and helpful to understand.

In the midst of our machines, we have lost sight of the fact that the basic reality in life is not politics, nor industry, but human relationships—the associations of a man with a woman, and of parents with a child. About these two foci of love—mate-love and mother-love—all life revolves. Recall the story of the rebel lass who, when her lover (killed in the Moscow uprising of December, 1917) was buried at the "Red Funeral," leaped into the grave, flung herself prostrate upon the coffin that held him and cried out: "Bury me, too; what do I care about the revolution now that *he* is dead?" She may have been deluded in thinking him irreplaceably unique —we are so similar that broken hearts and broken vows are alike unreasonable; but she knew, with a wisdom born in

[1] From *The Mansions of Philosophy*. New York: Simon and Schuster, Inc., 1929.

the blood of woman, that this tremendous revolution was a transitory trifle compared with that Mississippi of mating, parentage, and death which is the central stream of human life. She understood, though she might never have found a phrase for it, that the family is greater than the state, that devotion and despair sink deeper into the heart than economic strife, and that in the end our happiness lies not in possessions, place, or power, but in the gift and return of love.

What is the meaning of marriage? Perhaps if we can uncover its origin, we shall better realize its significance.

Picture a starfish, among the lowliest of animals, stretching out her rays or arms over her fertilized eggs and her hatched young. It is the beginning of one of the central phenomena in nature—parental care. In the plant and animal world generally, the species is preserved not by maternal solicitude but by lavish and wasteful procreation. A flower must fill the air with pollen and allure some insect that will serve as messenger to the mate it will never see. The little blood-red *Hœmatococcus* has been known to turn an arctic landscape from snow white into scarlet by its reproductive energies in a single night. The oyster, with *Mayflower*-like fertility, deposits millions of eggs, and then with characteristic nonchalance, leaves them to their fate; a few of them develop, but most of them serve as food or are lost as just plain waste.

Slowly nature, as we have seen, discovered and developed parental care as a substitute for this reckless extravagance. From the lowest vertebræ to the highest tribe of men the size of the litter, the brood, or the family decreases, and parental care increases, with every stage of development in the genus, the species, the variety, the race, the nation, the class, and the individual. Marriage came not to license love, but to improve the quality of life by binding mates in permanence to care for the offspring they produce.

It is not an exclusively human phenomenon. Some species

of birds are more monogamous than man. De Crespigny writes of the orang-utangs of Borneo: "They live in families. They build commodious nests in the trees; and so far as I could observe, the nests are occupied only by the female and the young, the male passing the night in the fork of the same or a neighboring tree." Westermarck describes the gorilla as "living in families, the male parent building the nest and protecting the family; and the same is the case with the chimpanzee." "It is not unusual," says Savage, "to see the 'old folks' in a gorilla family sitting under a tree regaling themselves with fruit and friendly chat, while their children are leaping around them and swinging from branch to branch in boisterous merriment." [2]

Gradually selection weeds out those species that take little care of their offspring, and develops in the survivors that instinct of parental care which slowly raises the individual and the race. Ape mothers have been known to die of grief upon the death of their young. In one species of ape the mother carries her babe clasped in one arm uninterruptedly for several months.[3] In man the impulse becomes almost the ruling passion, stronger even than love; what woman loves her husband as she loves her child? Savage mothers nurse their children sometimes for twelve years; and among some tribes, as in the New Hebrides, it is no rarity that a mother should kill herself to take care of her dead child beyond the grave.[4] There are few things more marvelous in human history than the almost complete (though passing) transference of a woman's egotism to her child.

Along with this powerful impulse of parental care rose a central and dominating institution—the family. The origin of the family lay in the invaluable helplessness of the child, in its increasing susceptibility to development and training after birth. Evolution in animals is biological chiefly—it concerns

---

[2] Edward Westermarck, *History of Human Marriage*, p. 14.
[3] William McDougall, *Social Psychology*, p. 70.
[4] Prince Kropotkin, *Mutual Aid*, pp. 101, 89.

the increasing transmission of an accumulating heritage of technology and culture from generation to generation. The family was invented by nature to bind the male in service to the female whom nature had bound in service to the child. Men are by nature slaves to women, and women are by nature slaves to children and the race; in that natural slavery is the secret of their deepest and most durable content.

Let us understand, then, that marriage is not a relation between a man and a woman, designed to legalize desire; it is a relation between parents and children, designed to preserve and strengthen the race. If it had been a personal instead of a racial matter, it would not have been made the first concern of human custom and laws. Why have states legislated so carefully and spent so lavishly to regulate the love of a man for a maid? Why all this paraphernalia of license bureaus, marriage ceremonies, divorce courts, moral exhortations and taboos, if not for the reason that marriage is the most fundamental of all institutions, the one which guards and replenishes the stream of life? It is clear enough, God knows, that marriage was never intended for the happiness of the mates, but for the mating and rearing of children.[5] The average tenure of human existence in primitive days was so pitifully brief that no one seems to have bothered about the individual. Only with the modern lengthening of life, the superabundance of humanity (the one commodity that violates the law of supply and demand), and the reduction of parentage to a phase rather than the sole content of marriage, has the individual raised the query whether his own happiness in mating is not to be considered along with the continuance and elevation of the race. It is in the Age of the Individual that the revolt against marriage has risen to its present irresistible tide.

The evolution of marriage has followed the broadening

[5] Cf. Shelley: "A system could not well have been devised more studiously hostile to human happiness than marriage."—Notes to *Queen Mab*.

lines of racial interest. As far back as the eye of history can see, the freedom of the individual in choosing a mate was strictly limited by social need. The first sexual taboos seem to have aimed at preventing the mating of parents and children, then of brothers and sisters; gradually the prohibitions spread to "exogamy," which forbade the marriage of a man with a woman of his own tribe. Early sociologists like Lewis Morgan were inclined to attribute these restrictions to the primitive mind's perception of the disadvantages of inbreeding; later students, like Westermarck and Ellis, rather cynically ascribed it to the contempt which comes of familiarity. But it will not do to exaggerate the inability of our savage forebears to put two and two together and make their own systems of sociology; probably they also had the race in mind when they limited the individual.

Marriage evolved as economic relations changed. In the nomad stage, the male, a mighty hunter before the Lord, took his club and perhaps a friend, stole into another tribe, snatched some fair maiden from her tent, and carried her away after the manner of the Sabine rape. Then, through the growth of wealth and peace, morals improved, and the man took not a club, but a valuable present or an offer of long service to the father of the woman he desired; marriage by purchase replaced marriage by capture. Today the institution is a strange mixture of capture and purchase.

In those early days war was frequent and perils were many; death came upon the male with less procrastination than upon the female; and polygamy was a crude attempt of the surviving men to take care of the women who so outnumbered them. As women nursed their children for many years, and abstained from marital relations until the child was weaned, the male found it convenient to have a variety of partners to meet his perennial demands. Besides, polygamy produced more children than monogamy; and abundant offspring came as a blessing to a people forever harassed with accident, disease, and war.

But as war decreased in frequency, and life and health became more secure, the numerical superiority of women was reduced, and monogamy began. It was an advantage to the children, who had now a united care, a concentrated love, and more food to eat since there were fewer mouths to feed. It was an advantage to the man, for it enabled him to center his bequests, to found a family instead of scattering his wealth, like his seed, among a horde of progeny. He found himself still free to satisfy his variegated appetites in secret, while he could surround his wife's fidelity with all the guards of custom and power, and so secure the transmission of his property to children probably his own. Above all, and despite this double standard (so rooted in the institution of bequest), monogamy was an advantage to the woman. It solved some part of that problem of jealousy which must have made polygamy a bedlam; it gave woman at least a biological equality with man; and it made it possible for her, from that modest leverage, to move and raise the world.

The rest of the history of marriage has been a struggle between woman and property, between wealth and love. One might have supposed that as riches grew they would dominate unchallenged the choice and rule of mates, and that the subordination of woman as a mechanism for producing heirs, and an economical substitute for a slave, would become ineradicably established among the customs of the race. But it was the other way. Wealth brought education, education soothed the savage breast of the male, and after centuries of evolution the simple lust of body for body was replaced, over widening areas, by romantic love.

The marriage of convenience remained, and in many countries the girl was still mated by her parents to some potential millionaire; but in England and America, and here and there in every nation, the proprietary marriage yielded, and the troubadours triumphed. Slowly woman, who had been made gentle by the brutality of the male, softened his brutality by her gentleness; slowly by her tenderness and her maternal sacrifice she lifted him from his proximity to the brute, and taught him to see and to seek in her some qualities less tangible and corporeal than those which had lured him to her lair. Gradually upon the physical basis of desire civilization built the frail and precious superstructure of poetic love.

We have studied elsewhere the remarkable and picturesque development of spiritual love from the roundelays of the medieval singers, through the monumental sentiment of *Clarissa Harlowe* and *La Nouvelle Héloïse,* to the novels that struggled to meet the nineteenth century appetite for romance. Who can say how far this ocean of fiction cleansed away something of the coarser aspects of modern love, making incipiently real that hunger of soul for soul which had been at first, perhaps, the consolatory fancy of aging virgins and imaginative males? Certainly romantic love became real: youth burst forth at puberty into sonnets and madrigals dripping with sincerity; men knelt to women, bowed to kiss their hands, and loved them for something more than the cozy softness of their flesh. They killed themselves in jousts to win a smile; they created literatures in the ecstasy of their devotion; and gradually they brought all their proud wealth to lay at the feet of frail creatures who had no power over them except through their beauty and their subtlety. When, in many hearts, desire became devotion rather than possession, and a man, wooing a maid with limitless loyalty, pledged his faith to her through every trial until death, marriage reached the climax of its long development, the zenith of its slow ascent from brutality to love. Perhaps we shall never know it in all its fullness again.

For now is the day of the machine, and everything must change. Individual security has lessened even as social security has grown; physical life is safer than it was, but economic life is harassed with a thousand intricacies that make every day a peril. Youth, which is braver and more conceited than before, is materially helpless and economically ignorant beyond anything in the past. Love comes, and youth, finding its pockets empty, dares not marry: love comes again, more weakly (years have passed), and yet the pockets do not bulge enough for marriage; love comes once more, with half of its early freshness and power (years have passed), and now the pockets are full, and marriage celebrates the death of love.

Tired of waiting so long, the urban girl, as like as not, plunges into maturity, a frail, adventurous thing. The terrific compulsion is on her, she feels, of getting attention, entertainment, stockings, and champagne—everything except a wedding-ring—through sexual favors or display. Sometimes her freedom of behavior is the outcome and reflex of her economic freedom; she is no longer dependent on the male and may therefore risk the male's decreasing distaste for marrying a lady as learned as himself in the arts of love. Her very capacity to earn a good income makes the possible suitor hesitate; how can his modest wage suffice to keep both at their present standard?

At last she finds a mate who offers her his hand in marriage. They marry. Not in a church, for they are sophisticated people; they have no more religion, and the moral code which rested so largely on their abandoned faith has lost its hold upon their hearts. They marry in the basement of some city hall (perfumed with the aroma of politicians), to the melody of an alderman's incantations; they are making not a vow of honor but a business contract, which they shall feel free at any time to end. There is no solemnity of ritual, no majesty of speech, no glory of music, no depths or ecstasy of emotion to burn the words of their promise into their memories. They kiss with a laugh, and frolic home.

Not home. There is no cottage waiting to greet them, bowered amid fragrant grass and shady trees, no garden that shall grow for them flowers and food made fairer and sweeter because they have planted them. They must hide themselves timidly as if in prison cells; in narrow rooms which cannot hold them long, and which they will not care to improve and ornament into an expression of their personalities. This dwelling is no spiritual entity, like the home that has taken form and soul under the care of a score of years; rather it is a merely material thing, as hard and cold as an asylum. It stands amid noise and stone and steel, where spring will have no entrance, and will give them not growing things, but only rain; where autumn will bring no rainbows in the skies nor any colors on the leaves, but only lassitude and somber memories.

The woman is disappointed; she finds nothing here that can make these walls bearable night and day; soon she runs from them at every chance, and creeps into them only towards the dawn. The man is disappointed; he cannot putter about here, solacing his hammered thumbs with the sense of building or rebuilding his own home; slowly it comes to him that these rooms are precisely like those in which he had brooded as a lonely bachelor, that his relations with his wife are prosaically like those which he has had for years with women of undiscriminating receptivity. There is nothing new here, and nothing grows; no infant's voice disturbs the night, no merriness of children brightens the day, no chubby arms sanction toil with a prattling welcome home. For where could the child play?—and how could they afford another room, and the long years of care and education required of children in the city? Discretion, they think, is the better part of love; they resolve to have no children until—until they are divorced.

Their marriage being no marriage—being a sexual instead of a parental association—it decays for lack of root and sustenance; it dies because it is detached from the life of the race. They shrink into themselves, single and separate fragments; the altruism of love sinks into individualism irritated by the compulsion of masquerade. The natural varietism of the man reappears; familiarity has bred contempt; through her very generosity the woman has nothing new to give.

Childless, they find a thousand reasons for discord. The

word "dear," that had thrilled them in hearing and in utterance, becomes the cheapest syllable in the language, facile
and meaningless. The wife mourns the departed tenderness
of early days; and therefore, in the home, she neglects that
care of body, dress, action and speech which had drawn the
man to her as to something brighter and higher than himself.
If there is any sexual incompatibility between them it becomes an insuperable barrier, because they conceive of marriage as a purely sexual relation. If they are poor, the man
regrets the burdens he has assumed, and the woman dotes on
the Prince of Wales. If they are rich, the pretended com-
munism of love and marriage conflicts with the individualism
of greed and fear; quarrels about money begin as soon as
the delirium of love subsides. If they are modern, they play
at equality; and a tug of war ensues, till one or the other
has established an irritating mastery. If the woman works,
she resents her continued slavery; if she is idle, time hangs
heavy on her hands until Satan finds something for them to
do. They thought they could not afford a child; but they
discover, like Balzac, that "a vice costs less than a family."
If either has friends, the other is jealous of them; if neither
has friends, the two are forced back upon themselves, into
an inescapable intimacy too monotonous to be borne. The
freedom indispensable to personality disappears before the
passions of ownership and curiosity; the soul finds no sanc-
tuary in which it can heal itself with peace and solitude.
Love, which had always been a combat and a chase, becomes
a war, in which the night's embrace is but a passing armistice.

For meanwhile anatomical disillusionment sets in. Man
and woman alike discover that love's fitful fever burned not
primarily for their joy, but for the continuance of the race.
The woman finds herself changed from a goddess into a cook
—unless, perchance, she has found one of those gentle husbands who change a cook into a goddess. She senses the
polygamous propensities of the male, and watches him jeal-
ously because she knows that she cannot trust him far. She

observes that his attentions become less frequent and thought-ful, that he makes love, if at all, with absentminded punc-tuality. He lacks the imagination to see his wife as a stranger sees her, or to see a stranger's wife as she will appear at nine o'clock the next morning; in all his thinking (and in hers) distance lends enchantment to the view, and the new is mistaken for the beautiful. Add childlessness or idleness on the part of the woman, and she too begins to hunger for some unfamiliar face or scene that they may restore the charming flatteries of desire. Neither premeditates adultery; they only long for "life." Suddenly the senses conquer sense, loyalty slips away, suspicion comes on feline feet, and the final fury of detection is welcomed as simplifying a situation too complex for successful pretense and mastery.

And so they are divorced. See them, first, in the domestic relations court; waiting sadly while other tragedies are aired; exaggerating each other's cruelties, and flinging hot names into faces once idealized by desires; reconciled, perhaps, but only for awhile; hating each other now as only those can hate who remember the promises of love. Soon they are free, as the desert is free; they are divorced, and can experiment again. But the conditions are as before; how can the end be different?

Year by year marriage comes later, separation earlier; and fidelity finds few so simple as to do it honor. Soon no man will go down the hill of life with a woman who has climbed it with him, and a divorceless marriage will be as rare as a maiden bride. And the divorced are but a fraction of those who are unhappy in marriage. Let us not inquire how many long to be separated, but dare not ask; how many have asked and were denied. Do not look into the hearts of these others—there is no telling what we might find there: instead of separation, fear of shame; instead of love, indifference; instead of faithfulness, deceit. Perhaps it were as well that they too were torn apart, and that the breakdown of mar-riage should stand out naked and startling before our eyes, challenging every statesman who thinks in generations, and every lover who honors love enough to wish that it might not die so young.

To describe is easy; to prescribe is hard. What can we say that has not been said a thousand times before? What nostrum can we recommend that has not been tried and found wanting? What counsel can we give that will not be an insult to the wounds that we would heal?

Perhaps we should abandon the problem and say, with the oldest of the Christian religions: Close every door of escape, and the prisoners will forget that they are in jail. If marriage is for children and the race, and not for individuals and mates, then for the children's sake let marriage be irrevocable, and what God has joined together let no man part. There is, after all, so little difference between one of us and the next, that if we cannot get along with the mate we have, we shall soon find like difficulties with another. Man was not made for happiness; he is born for suffering; let him marry then, and hold his peace.

But shall we call indissoluble the vows that immature youth has made? Shall we shackle two souls for life though their love has fallen over into hate? Here is no tempting choice; the devil and the deep sea incite us. But now that children are fewer, and the career of the parents does not end as soon after the birth or maturing of the offspring as reckless nature arranged in the lower realms of life, we can afford to consider the mates a little more; it would be ridiculous to sacrifice a career of three score years and ten to considerations that arose when women had children whole-sale, and were worn out at forty-five. The very growth of the race in quality depends upon reducing the sacrifice which it requires of its members; the race is greater than the individual only because it may produce greater individuals. Beyond that it is a name and an abstraction; and the medieval theory of marriage belongs to pre-nominalist days.

Out of our individualistic age comes an opposite theory,

more interesting and as extreme; and how attractively it is
named!—"Free Love." Since vows are made to be broken,
why make any vows at all? Since marriages are now made
to be dissolved, why bother a thousand courts with a million matings and separations? If love is the best motive for
marriage, its death is sufficient reason for divorce; how can
love be real if it is not free? Let us then release these pompous
judges who pretend to solder our souls; let lovers wed with
only their mutual pledge of honesty and honor; and when
love is gone let them without hindrance seek other mates,
and recreate their love and their youth.

This solution of the marriage problem is gathering new
popularity every year. Judge Lindsey, reporting that marriage licenses fell 25 per cent from 1921 to 1922, explains
the decrease as due to the spread of unlicensed ménages.
These free unions would offer an admirable exit from the
difficulties of our current code were it not for the continued
economic dependence of woman upon man, and her psychological dependence upon him before marriage binds him to
her whims. Periodic disabilities, and the possibility of pregnancy, reduce the woman's earning power; unless she can
secure a home and some fairly permanent protection in return for the risks she runs, the advantage of "freedom" is
all on the side of the male. At present—though this feeling
too is in flux, and tends to grow weaker day by day—a
woman is lowered in the eyes of a man by her surrender;
the male is a fighter, or likes to conceive himself so, and
relishes at least a pretense of resistance to dignify his victory;
when he has quite won he seeks new fields of glory. At present, but again subject to change without notice, the male
likes to think that the woman whom he chooses as his permanent mate has never belonged to any other man; he will
readily agree to a temporary union with an experienced
woman, but he seldom desires her for his legal wife. It is as if
he accepted Weininger's brutal statement, that every woman
is by temperament either a mother or a rake; and as if he

suspected that a woman who has loved her neighbors as herself will revert to that promiscuity as soon as the novelty of marriage, or the burden of motherhood, disappears. The male never dreams of applying the same scrutiny or judgment to himself; he assumes his ability to pass from variety to monotony without any likelihood of deviation from uxorious fidelity. What actuates him is not reason, but the proprietary sense; his feelings go back to the ancient and almost universal custom of marriage by purchase; he is buying something on the market, and does not want to pay a good price for second-hand material. He thinks of woman as the author of the tenth commandment thought of her.

All that will change; and perhaps when woman's economic independence is complete, and contraceptives have quite differentiated mating from parentage, men will apply to women the same lenient standard by which they judge themselves, and our ancient moral code will come definitely to an end. But during the long transition woman will suffer through the reckless egoism and irresponsibility of man. Free love is love free for the male; it is a trap into which emancipated woman falls with a very emancipated man. Some day woman may be master of her own life, and motherhood may not leave her at the mercy of a naturally promiscuous male; some day, far distant, we may find a way of caring for children without binding the man to the woman who has borne them by him. Then free love will be a boon to all, and the ideal state of a finally liberated race. Till then we had better obey the law.

Confused with free love in the popular mind is companionate marriage. Hysteria conceives this in various shocking ways; but when we discover that its doughty protagonist defines it as "legal marriage with legalized birth control, and with the right to divorce by mutual consent for childless couples, usually without payment of alimony," it does not seem so very terrible; there is nothing in it (except for that bitter line about alimony) which does not already exist in the practice of presumably respectable families; and divorce by mutual consent, where there are no children, is preferable to divorce by collusion or "desertion." What people fear in the plan is the thoroughness with which it establishes the equality of the sexes. Very rapidly the luxurious ladies of the bourgeoisie are bringing down upon all their sex the revenge of the tired male; marriage is changing to a form that will not tolerate the unproductive women who are the ornament and horror of so many expensive homes; the men are inviting their modern wives to earn for themselves the money which they are to spend. For companionate marriage provides that until maternity is in the offing, the wife shall go to work. Here hides the joker by which the liberation of woman shall be made complete: she shall be privileged henceforth to pay her fare from A to Z. The industrial revolution is to be carried out to its logical and merciless conclusion; woman is to join her husband in the factory; instead of remaining idle in her bower, compelling the man to produce doubly as a balance to her economic sterility, she shall become his honored equal in toil as in reward, in obligations as in rights. Such is emancipation.

Much credit is due the man who has dared all the devils of orthodoxy to propose a specific cure for the sickness of modern marriage. But there is something hard and ruthless in the plan which a lingering gallantry will consider unfair so long as woman's economic and moral equality with man is incomplete. For man, as we have said, is secretly and ravenously polygamous. Give him a form of marriage in which he shall be free to leave his mate as soon as she has lost for him the lure of novelty and the pleasure of resistance, and he will itch for alien charms and uncaptured citadels; and sooner or later he will say adieu. It does not help to answer that the consent of both parties would be required for divorce; the modern woman will grant consent when it is asked. And then? Then she will find herself "free and independent" again, flung back upon the thorns and spikes of industry, immeasurably more depreciated than the male.

These are minor difficulties, and presumably the plan is offered as subject to amendment by experience. What is most constructive in it is the encouragement which it offers to early marriage. For here, after all, is the heart of our moral problem: if we could find a way to restore marriage to its natural age we should at one stroke reduce by half the prostitution, the venereal disease, the fruitless celibacy, the morbid chastity, and the experimental perversions that stigmatize our contemporary life.

Consider again how few are the men or the women who marry the one whom they love best. The bright passion of youth comes too soon for our finances; we shrink from the great adventure, and let love die away. And yet the earlier the love, the fresher and deeper it must be; no man can love after thirty with the ardor and self-abandonment of youth.[6] The devotion which first love evokes in the soul is too profound to be worn away with a year of intimacy and trial; this new tenderness of the boy, this clear-eyed trust of the girl, must carry them on happily through years whose memories will be like a fragrance in their lives.

Picture a marriage of first love. See the newlyweds, in ideal, choosing not a cell in a box, but a separate little home where nature has not yet been utterly dispossessed; furnishing it to the tune of a hundred merry debates as to what should be bought and where it should stand; planting flowers and growing with their growth; filling the home with color and music and books and friends; making it more lovable than the glare and blare of the street; and completing it at last with the turbulence and jollity of a child. Many times we have revenged ourselves with wit upon the hard restraints of marriage; and yet, in our secret hearts we shall always

[6] This is the harmless remark which, abbreviated in caption, by a hurried editor, was broadcast throughout the country as "No man can love after thirty." Publicity makes us and breaks us.

look back with longing to those sentimental days when love was young.[7]

There are many objections to early marriage. First it is useless to offer counsels of perfection; we cannot conquer the economic caution of youth with moral exhortations and real-estate poetry. But it is the parents, not the children, that advise, and financially enforce, delayed marriage; there is nothing further to be asked of the recklessness of youth. Let us persuade the mistaken parents that by compelling the deferment of marriage they are inviting an endless chain of coarsening substitutes and demoralizing perversions; that wisdom would lie not in making impediments to the marriage of true minds, but in providing for sons, as well as daughters, a substantial dowry that would balance their economic immaturity and strengthen their courage to face the world. It would be a debt of honor, which the children would repay to the next generation; no one would lose, everyone would gain. There was a time when fathers were generous enough for that.

With such assistance even a cautious lad might surrender to the call of love. And any lad, marrying, will find a grain of truth in the old proverb, "God will take care of you"; pride will stiffen his vertebræ, add power to his arm, and persistence to his courage; the compulsion of responsibility will deepen him; marriage will make him a man. If nothing else will serve, let the little goddess go forth to her daily labors as before, until she envisages motherhood. It is better that she should have something for her hands to do than pose as a bit of fragile ornament; and better that they should delay parentage, than fret in the irritability of mating unnaturally postponed: we must permit the separation of marriage from reproduction in order to diminish the separation of sex from marriage. Should the man relax under this aid,

[7] For a strong endorsement of early marriage from the biological standpoint, cf. S. J. Holmes, *Studies in Evolution and Genetics*, pp. 177-8.

the only remedy for him is fatherhood; the child will stir him on to manhood, or there is no man in him at all.

The second difficulty adduces the ignorance of youth. "At a time when a man is in love," said Nietzsche, "he should not be allowed to come to a decision about his life and to determine once for all the character of his society on account of a whim. We ought publicly to declare invalid the vows of lovers, and to refuse them permission to marry." [8] It is true that youth is blind, and cannot judge; but age is old, and cannot love. Perhaps at no time should we be permitted or required to make irrevocable decisions. It is not shown that men choose more wisely at thirty than at twenty in the matter of taking wives; and as all wives and all husbands are substantially alike, it does not make all the difference in the world. If a man cannot find some mode of concord with his wife it is, in a great majority of cases, because of some defect in his own behavior and philosophy, which would operate to the same result if he could exchange his neighbor's wife for his own. Divorce is like travel: it is useless if we cannot change ourselves.

Nevertheless the ignorance of youth is real; indeed, when, in these matters, do we cease to be ignorant? Which of us men yet understands women, and how many of us can manage them? To reduce the area of the unknown let us restore the old custom of requiring a public betrothal six months before marriage. During that pleasant half year the lovers would discover each other mentally; perhaps they would even begin to quarrel like man and wife; and there would be an opportunity for separation before the bonds of matrimony had made them one. Those six months would add to our marriage institutions a moral fiber and beauty which they sadly need; they would provide a lyric interlude amid the prose of economic life.

The last and greatest difficulty is the absurdity of encouraging youth, before experience has sobered sense, to enter a

[8] *Dawn of Day*, sect. 151.

house which at any moment may become a prison, incarcerating one for life. If early marriage is to be a reasonable arrangement, matrimony must have an exit as well as an entrance, and divorce must be obtainable by mutual consent. It may appear ridiculous, having argued that divorce is a regrettable thing, and that marriage exists for the care of children rather than for the happiness of mates, to urge the extension of divorce at the apparent cost of the family and the child. But who knows that the acceptance of mutual consent as a sufficient reason would multiply divorce? Or that the compulsory association of distrustful and alienated mates is any better for their children than the allotment or alteration of the children between two households separate and at peace? If we refuse divorce to a man and a woman merely because they unite in asking for it, we invite them to some form of collusion which will satisfy our irrational demands. Doubtless some delay is salutary; it would serve wisdom and order to require a trial separation for some considerable time before granting a definite decree; for in that interval the constant warriors might discover that solitude is worse than strife, and distance might reveal virtues which nearness had concealed.

In a Middle Western city recently a congressman and his wife joined in asking for a divorce; it was refused them on the ground that they had not violated a sufficient number of divine commandments and human laws. The fact that they agreed in desiring liberty was considered irrelevant, and they were "handcuffed for life." Such conditions are a provocation to adultery; there is nothing for a gentleman to do, under these circumstances, except to supply the law with its pound of flesh. For many years now Japan has given divorce for mutual consent, and yet its divorce rate is lower than our own. Russia has had such a law since the respectable days of 1907. Rome had it. Bonaparte put it into the Napoleonic Code; but the Bourbons, having learned nothing, struck it out. It is highly probable that an amendment of this kind would add little if at all to the number of separations; it would merely add to the honorableness of our conduct and the decency of our courts.

What the conclusion of our experiments will be let others tell who know. Probably it will be nothing that we shall wish or will; we are caught in a current of change, and shall doubtless be borne along to fated and unchosen ends. In this rushing flux of customs, habits, and institutions, anything at all may come. Now that the home, in our large cities, is disappearing, monogamy has lost its chief attraction. Without doubt, companionate marriage will be more and more condoned where there is no intent to reproduce. Free unions, sanctioned or not, will multiply; and though their freedom will be chiefly for the male, women will take them as a lesser evil than the sterile loneliness of uncourted days. The "double standard" will be broken down, and woman, having imitated man in all things else, will emulate his premarital experience. Divorce will grow, and every city will be crowded with the derelicts of shipwrecked unions. The entire institution of marriage will be recast into newer and looser forms. When the industrialization of woman is complete, and birth control is the secret of every class, motherhood will be an incident in woman's life, and state institutions for the care of children will replace the home. *Panta rei.*

The last word, however, must be for monogamy. The lifelong union remains the loftiest conception of human marriage; and it is still the goal which the complete lover will set himself when he pledges his troth. There is something cowardly in divorce, like flight from the field of war; and something unstable and superficial in one who flits from mate to mate. Men and women of character will solve these difficulties as they arise, knowing that difficulties as great would meet them on any other battleground. Their reward comes when the hard years of mutual readjustment are over, and a steady affection tenoned and mortised in the care of children and the sharing of a thousand vicissitudes has supplanted the transitory ardor of physical desire, and made two minds and two hearts one. Only when that test of the soul has been passed will they know the fullness of love.

That fullness cannot come without children. It is, again, for children that marriage was invented; it was designed not to unite mate with mate so much as to perpetuate the species by uniting parents with children in loyalty and care. Emancipate as we will, free ourselves as much as we can from the prejudices of our past, the voluntarily childless woman still fills us with a sense of something abnormal and disagreeable. Objective beauty, like subjective happiness, lies in the easy fulfillment of natural purposes and functions, so that those women who remain to the end without children seem a little ridiculous, and never quite convince us that they know content. If a woman has found another function than motherhood to absorb her energy and fill her life, it is passing well, and nature will bear with her; but if she wanders about aimless and dissatisfied, moving from one place, one man, or one amusement to another, and finding no interest anywhere, it is because she has turned her back on the natural purpose of love. A woman, as Nietzsche said, is a riddle, whose solution is a child.

The modern girl will laugh at this old-fashioned suggestion, and will remind the world that the day is gone when she can be used as a maternity machine. So we refute one another's extremes, and life moves roughshod over our arguments. No one with a sense of history, or a perception of irreversible economic developments, could think of asking a woman for the large family which was her lot on the farm; everyone understands (except the rural assemblymen who still rule our state legislatures) that the multiplication of machines and the reduction of the death rate have put an end to the need for the mass-production of children. If community good seems to require a large population it is because we delude ourselves by thinking in terms of quantity, or aspire to imperial and militaristic expansion, or vision a fertile China overflowing upon the West. But quantity never won a battle; it is brains and tools that win. And by the time the Chinese equal us in tools they will also have taken over from us those methods of controlling population which are the modern substitute for infanticide and abortion. There is no communal need, no moral claim, for large families any more; and if one suggests that women should still retain, in moderate measure, the function of motherhood, it is rather with a view to their own self-fulfillment and happiness than for the sake of the group.

It is remarkable how marriage withers when children stay away, and how it blossoms when they come. Before, marriage was a business contract for the mutual provision of physiological conveniences; now it recovers its natural meaning, it lifts little egos into a larger whole, and the union sprouts and flowers like a watered plant. The woman finds, in the midst of turmoil, trouble, worry and pain, a strange content that is like a quiet ecstasy; never in her idleness and luxury was she as happy as in these tasks and obligations that develop and complete her even while seeming to sacrifice her to the race. And the man, looking at her, falls in love with her anew; this is another woman than before, with new resources and abilities, with a patience and tenderness never felt in the violence of love; and though her face may be pale now, and her form for a time disfigured for corrupt and abnormal eyes, to him it seems as if she had come back out of the jaws of death with a gift absurdly precious; a gift for which he can never sufficiently repay her. Work that was bitter toil becomes now as natural and cheerful as the honey-seeking of the bee; and the house, that was but walls and a bed, becomes a home, filled with the laughter of rejuvenated life. For the first time in his career the man feels himself complete.

For through parentage (unless he is a genius, whose passion and completeness lie in intellectual maternity) he does not merely fulfill his function as a member of society, and as an individual in a species; he fulfills *himself*—he accepts the responsibilities that mature and widen him, he enjoys the satisfaction of an unsuspectedly profound instinct of parental love, he lays up the comradeship of children as a solace for his age, and in some measure eludes the searching scythe of Death. That ruthless scavenger takes of us only the decaying flesh and bones; he must clear them away to make room for youth; but in the youth which he protects is our own blood, our own life, and our own souls. We but surrender a part of ourselves to the grave that another part, generated from our substance, fed by our hands, and reared with our care, may survive as our reincarnation in the flow of life. Our children will bring us daily tribulation, and bitter pain, and perhaps in the end heartbreaking disillusionment; but they will bring us, just as surely, a fathomless delight that will surpass even the ecstasies of love. Let a man be complete. Not as a fragment, not as a ruthlessly competitive and narrowly separate individual, can he fulfill himself and be made whole; but as a sharer in a larger self, as a lover giving more than he receives, as a father gladly caught in the toils of the species, willingly consumed in the continuity and immortality of life. For in that coöperation of the part with the whole he shall find the essence of all morals, the secret of all living things, and a quiet lane of happiness for many years.

LEGISLATING FOR THE COMPANIONATE MARRIAGE [1]

By Ben B. Lindsey and Wainwright Evans

I HAVE been asked many times what specific measures I would take if it were in my power, by passing a law or a group of laws, to establish companionate marriage in the state of Colorado.

My answer is that there is no need for a bill to establish companionate marriage as a separate thing, either in Colorado or in any other state, because we already have the companionate as one of the privileges of present-day marriage —a privilege which merely needs to be recognized and made legal. The fact that contraception and divorce by mutual consent (collusion) are illegal does not particularly matter so long as people have the good sense to practice them anyway. But having them illegal does undoubtedly make needless difficulties and tragedies in marriage which could readily be avoided if these two remedies were within the easy reach of all persons. The present prohibitions on birth control impose ignorance or *half-knowledge* on thousands; and thus they have the evil effect of leading to the practice of much contraception that is unscientific, ineffective, risky, and often dangerous; and when such contraception fails, then abortion follows, not occasionally but in literally *millions* of cases.

Society *must* find relief from the population problem. The pressure is terrific. And if it cannot find it in humane ways, then it will find it in inhumane ways, and by the murder of unborn children if necessary. I know many very excellent persons who have been driven by their fears to this mur-

[1] From *The Companionate Marriage*. New York: Horace Liveright, 1927.

derous extreme.—The poor, the ignorant, the economically inefficient—in a word, the very persons who most need to know how to practice birth control, are the very ones who find it most difficult to obtain effective scientific knowledge of the subject. Thus they are tricked, as it were, by society into furnishing its unwanted progeny, while the more intelligent regulate their families by their individual preferences and economic necessities.

There is no need, I repeat, for any separate law that would change the present status of marriage or alter its fundamentals. It would not even be necessary to change the method of getting married. Companionate marriage *is* present marriage. What is needed is a law to legalize the already existing privileges and practices of marriage, and place them and their social benefits within the reach of all—even of the poor and the ignorant, who most need them.

Here is a brief outline of the three essential legislative enactments or bills I have in mind:

1. A bill for an act to repeal the present stupid laws against birth control, and to legalize and regulate the right of birth control clinics to carry on and give advice to married women, who might make use of the information or not, as they chose; leaving it to their personal judgment as to whether they should remain childless or not, and if so, how long.

This would not be the grudging permission which at present allows a physician or the Birth Control League to impart birth control knowledge to a woman when it would endanger her health, psychologically or physically, to have a child. Such information, imparted under such conditions, is a mere subterfuge which enables the physician to remain safe from prosecution on the charge of breaking the laws against the imparting of contraceptive information. It is an absolutely necessary and justifiable dodge for avoiding persecution by busybodies who are not content to abstain from the use of birth control themselves, and who insist on foisting their personal opinions on everybody else.

Let me say again in this connection that I haven't the slightest objection to Roman Catholics and others abstaining from birth control themselves, if they think it sinful. What I cannot understand is their fixed determination to force this fanaticism on the American nation. This government is not a theocracy. They have no right to try to read their theology into laws intended to govern people who do not subscribe to that theology, and who cannot legally—under the Constitution—be forced to do so. These opinions regarding the supposedly evil results of birth control are opinions, nothing more; and they are *minority* opinions at that. This country has too long been ruled by organized and fanatical minorities; and it is time to call a halt. It is not so much a question of my being for or against the use of birth control as it is the right of people to their freedom of choice as to whether they will or will not use it.

2. A second bill to amend the laws relating to divorce. This bill would add a clause providing that "where couples are childless, and where the efforts of the magistrate to bring about a reconcilement have failed, and where the couple mutually desire a divorce, the divorce shall be granted without further expense or needless delay." This would require no lawyer, any more than getting married requires a lawyer. A judge can marry people, and by this law he could, under the prescribed conditions, unmarry them.

3. A third bill to regulate the property status of the divorce. It would deal with the right of the wife to support and alimony. It would withhold or grant such support and alimony according to the conditions of the case. For instance, if a woman were in good health, and able to work, and to support herself, there would ordinarily be no alimony.—*Such a bill might provide that the property rights of childless couples should, at the discretion of the court, ordinarily be the same as the property rights of single persons.*

In this connection let me emphasize what I have already pointed out, that one very common condition in companionate marriage would be that both the husband and wife would go on earning a livelihood, exactly as before marriage. Naturally, however, this would not always be the case. It would depend on the inclination and desire of the couple, on the temperament and capabilities of the woman, etc. Some women find their most effective place in life in making a really happy and lovely home for the man they love. Such a home increases the man's economic efficiency and his value to society. The arrangements in marriage must depend on the situation and on the people; and so must the question of property and alimony. Equity and common sense would have to be the determining factor so far as the court decision was concerned. Rigid applications of rigid laws could have no place in such a system—and "legal minded" judges ought to keep out of, or be kept out of, such work. They would merely throw a monkey-wrench into the machine.

The passing of three such bills, as roughly sketched here, would establish the companionate, *as we now illegally have it*, on a legal basis. It would mark it off sharply from the procreative marriage, and it would justify us in calling childless marriage "The Companionate" and procreative marriage "The Family." This nomenclature has long been used by sociologists to distinguish the two—"*The Companionate*" and "*The Family*." I suggest these terms for general use.

Since the passage of these bills would in no way change the fundamental status and practice of marriage as we have it, and would merely make the institution flexible and better adapted to the needs of society, the only objections that could be made to these bills would be the already operative objections on the part of a minority of our population, to birth control and divorce by mutual consent. If this minority continued not to believe in these two things, they have the inalienable right not to practice them. If it would make them feel any better, we could pass a law giving them that liberty.

I propose that these three laws would be *immediately practicable,* if not in Colorado, then surely in some other state or states. The legislature of Nevada, for example, has recently passed a law reducing the time necessary for establishing residence in Nevada to three months. Why three months? It's a mere camouflage, in line with other hypocrisies of our marriage code. Why not call it a day? And why not at the same time establish the companionate in Nevada by passing three such bills as I am here suggesting? It would be a social experiment of the utmost importance; and it should be undertaken at once by at least three progressive states, one in the Far West, one in the Middle West and one in the East—so that the companionate would be within easy reach of all who want it.

I have a letter from a Chicago attorney who suggests that a practicable way to legislate for companionate marriage would be to alter certain already existing laws. I quote:

"The childless marriage, such by prenuptial agreement, is here. The dissolution of this by mutual consent is here for all who are willing to 'frame' the evidence. The evidence is rarely 'framed' until all property questions are settled by agreement. The 'framing' ordinarily gets the divorce and eliminates the alimony.

"If the law makes this divorce more respectable by making it more honest, and puts the truth-teller upon at least an equal footing with the perjurer, is not this about all it can do for this situation?

"And is not this done by two relatively simple statutory changes, i.e.: (1) Make the divorce easier by shortening the 'abandonment' where there are no children,—say, first to one year and, as public opinion permits, to, say, six months; and (2) abolish alimony where the wife has never borne children, or perhaps leave alimony to the discretion of the court, where marriage has lasted, say, three or five years?"

To these very interesting suggestions my correspondent adds, "Must not social usage evolve any further betterment of present conditions? And can it not be trusted to do so?"—To which I answer Yes to both questions. It would seem evident, however, that such changes can be hastened if their desirability can be pointed out to the public. That is one of my objects in the writing of this book.

No provision is made in the above suggestions for legalized *scientific* birth control. This would be an unfortunate omission, so far as the companionate is concerned, because the methods of contraception in present general use are often ineffective, dangerous to health, and psychologically unsatisfactory. Bootleg birth control would never meet the requirements of companionate marriage.

I understand that a bill for the establishment of companionate marriage was recently proposed in the California legislature. A bill for the establishing of the companionate on a separate basis from other marriage would be likely to fail in any legislature; but three such bills as I have outlined, for the modification of marriage as we have it, might, I think, readily appeal to the common sense of any progressive and courageous legislature. It has been my hope that the legislature of Colorado might lead the way in this, as it did long ago in the establishing of the Juvenile and Family Court of Denver—a pioneer step; but as the political issue is rather acute where I am concerned, I fear such a result would be impossible for the present. At this writing the Colorado legislature, many members of which were largely chosen and elected by the Ku Klux Klan, has before it a bill, sponsored by the Klan and by certain of the Roman Catholic clergy, for the abolition of the Juvenile Court; and it is now a question, not of whether this legislature would adopt the companionate, but of whether its Klan influences will so much as permit my official work in Colorado to continue on any basis. It is possible that by the time these words are in print, I shall be cut adrift by these forces from the work I founded.

—And so, as I say, I hope the proposed measures will appeal to the common sense of other legislatures.

Once such laws were passed, that would by no means be the end of the changes to be made. The companionate, once established on such a foundation, would grow and perfect itself as an institution along the lines I have indicated in earlier chapters of this book. For example, there should, in time, be a law requiring medical examination for all persons who marry, whether for the companionate or the family. There are persons who, by reason of infectious disease, should not be permitted even the companionate relationship till fully cured—much less procreative marriage, into which they can now enter without let or hindrance. There are still others who might properly enter the companionate, but who should never undertake to bring children into the world.

Under such a system of medical examination, I think it might some day become perfectly practicable for society to expect people to confine themselves to the companionate unless pronounced by a magistrate to be both *hygienically* and *economically* fit to undertake the family. *I do not say that there should necessarily be a coercive law to this effect.* I think the fewer laws we have the better. But I do believe public opinion would establish at least an unwritten custom of decency and right living in this matter which would be effective in most cases. A coercive law would be objectionable if only because people it restrained would probably want to violate it; whereas the restraints of decency and good taste and fair play and the desire to see children get a fair chance in life, would operate sufficiently well. I think there are very few persons who would want to bring into the world children they clearly should not have. What they must have, and do insist on having, is a normal sex life. Parenthood is not a necessary part of that. And if the parent urge be strong, there are always children to be obtained by adoption.

In this connection let me say that I have found by long experience that most people want children. There is a com-

mon impression among people who are alarmed by the birth
control idea that if everybody understood the technique of
contraception, nobody would have children, and the race
would die out. These people don't know human nature. It
simply does not work out that way. And obviously, persons
who don't want children are the very ones who ought not to
have them. I should think the absurdity of forcing the human
race to propagate by law would be so evident that even the
solemn moralists would see that it is nonsense. If the human
race has to be kept going by means of obscenity laws it had
better die.

I have a courteous letter from a minister in a southern city
who tells me that he sees two objections to my views on the
companionate. His first objection is that many people would
marry with the intention and thought of quitting if the relationship does not suit them, *and without making any real,
unselfish effort to work out their problem,* since there would
be no pressure from without to compel them to do this. His
second objection is that couples would *"contract marriage
for pleasure, and with no recognition of the divine purpose of
bearing children."* He adds, "It is one thing to believe in a
home with a limited number of children, and quite another
to believe so much in self-indulgence and ease that children
are not wanted at all. I have never been able to see very
worthy motives in marriage that coldly determines that there
shall be no children."

I was very grateful for that letter. It was written in a fair
and kindly spirit, which is by no means always the case with
the letters I receive from orthodox Christian sources; and
at the same time it states clearly two points which I have
perhaps not yet met specifically enough.

Let me take the last objection first. From my long experience with all kinds of people I can positively assure this
critic that the assumption that most persons would not have
children if they didn't have to is an error. There are a few
of whom this is true, but only a few. And obviously it is better

that such persons should find their happiness and their use-fulness without reproach in some field other than parenthood.

I find a tendency, regrettably frequent among the clergy, to assume not merely that people shirk parenthood if they can, but also that they must be induced to have children, either by legally imposed ignorance or by religious persuasion on grounds of "duty." People who have children ought to want them. If they don't want them they are not likely to make a success of parenthood. But an overwhelming majority of people certainly do want children and love children; and this desire on their part is not a "recognition of the divine purpose of bearing children," either. It is natural. They love children and want them about. That is far better and more generous than "duty." This assumption that people never *want* to do what is *right,* and that right acting is accom-plished from a stern sense of "duty," and is made possible only by divine Grace, has some very unfortunate effects on our national habits of thought. The doctrine of total de-pravity has done enough harm in the world, and it is time to throw it overboard.

Now for the first objection, that people would enter the companionate with the intention of quitting if they didn't like it.—Well, why shouldn't they? Why assume that that means that they have no intention or expectation of liking it, and that they will put forth no effort to make a go of the mar-riage? Of course if such an objection applies at all it applies to any marriage.

But anybody who knows anything about human nature and human relationships and human ties knows that most normal people don't behave that way. A tie grows up in the physical and spiritual associations of marriage that quickly acquires a tremendous power to hold the husband and wife together. It binds them with hoops of steel—it is an emo-tional bond, and it is a bond of habit. It develops in every marriage that is based on sympathy, love, and similarity of tastes. Sometimes, so great is its power, it even develops in marriages where these fundamentals of congeniality are lacking. I know many uncongenial couples who are held together by this bond. They may fight, but still they have a certain affection for each other.

The important thing here to understand is that a couple entering marriage may *be mistaken* in their belief that they have a basis for lifelong union, and that *in the companionate such persons would not have to bet so heavily on that belief*. Thus they could take the chance more readily. And why shouldn't they? If they marry frankly facing the fact that they *may* be mistaken, why shouldn't they be that honest? Is being honest with themselves and with each other so dangerous? Must we eternally refuse to face the facts and possibilities of life? There is *obviously* the danger of making a mistaken choice in *any* marriage. Why should people not frankly admit this and provide against the danger by arranging a way to retrace their steps if need be? What is immoral or irresponsible about that? No more so than the immorality and irresponsibility found in present marriage, surely!

Persons who think honestly about these matters are far more likely to make a success of marriage than those who are not honest, who take refuge in orthodox hypocrisy, who have unwanted children from "duty," or from ignorance, or accident, and who stand ready to ruin each other's lives because, as this correspondent puts it, "Jesus insisted on the permanency of marriage."

What if he did?—Are we thereby forbidden to hold our own opinions on these matters? I object to an infallible Book as much as I do to an infallible Pope. As a matter of fact I don't believe Jesus ever taught anything of the sort about marriage. His followers often stupidly misunderstood him, as the record confesses. They were always reading their own traditional views into his teachings, to his great annoyance. Why may they not have done it in this case?

What I vividly feel about Jesus is this: *He consistently*

struck at every ancient law which he found did not accord with human need. He offended the orthodox religionists of his day, and he would offend them today if he were here to comment on present-day conditions.

He used common sense about the Sabbath, and they didn't like that; and he ridiculed their fault-finding by pointing out that they had never seen anything wrong in the fact that David and his followers ate shew bread from the altar when they were hungry; and that if a man's ox fell into a pit on the Sabbath Day he would not refrain from pulling the animal out on that day—not, it is implied, unless he were a manifest idiot, so gone in theological formalism that he lacked sanity. It is my belief that Jesus would unhesitatingly attack our present system of marriage if he were here. He would see—what every minister in the land is announcing with alarm from the pulpit—that too much of its fruit is evil. Jesus had no reverence for tradition and authority, save as these proved their practical value to society. We should do well to follow his great example in this, rather than to be aping and quoting him like parrots, as if we couldn't think and act for ourselves.

This constant reference to *authority* by religionists is the thing that more than any other weakens and discredits the church today, and puts it out of tune with reality, and deprives it of much of its power to do good.

Jesus expressly rejected this reference back to authority, and insisted on the compulsions of present reality. "Ye have heard how it was said by them of old time . . . but I say unto you . . ." Could one ask for a sharper contrast than is afforded in that "but"? He came to fulfill the law, he said. True—he came to show that growth is the law; and to fulfill it as such; and to lay upon the human race the exhortation to *grow.*

Like every preëminent teacher, Jesus was concerned, not that his pupils should memorize his words or make magic formulas of them, but rather that they should *learn to think.*

The plain implication of his teaching is that it is right for people to think honestly and independently for themselves. If the Christian Church would fearlessly apply that principle of independent and honest thought it would be a very different church; and it would have a message for the world the like of which it has not uttered in the two thousand years of its existence. A clergy like that would be a clergy really following the example of the Master. Jesus would be the first to condemn any slavish acceptance of the *letter* of the views he uttered. He would disapprove all attempts to make his utterances apply like a code of fixed rules to conditions he did not have to deal with or to talk about, since they did not then exist. "The letter killeth," he said, "but the spirit giveth life." It is the spirit of his teaching, not the letter of it, that gives life.

One critic has raised a question by letter as to the "mutual consent" idea in the divorce of childless couples. "Suppose," he asks, "one member of the marriage wanted to quit while the other did not? If divorce were granted in the companionate under such conditions, it would not really be by 'mutual consent,' would it?"

I admit that the words "mutual consent" are not quite broad enough to fit precisely. But I find no satisfactory substitute. Obviously, when it happened that one party wanted to continue the marriage while the other wanted its dissolution (that being the one assumption on which divorce is granted in our courts at present, by the way) the case would have to be decided by a judge on its individual merits.—I have seen many such cases. Each is different. Each is a problem in itself. Sometimes a psychiatrist can straighten the couple out and bring them to a basis of understanding. Often I can do it myself. Usually the party who wants the divorce would be glad to change his or her mind if the conditions of the marriage could be made bearable. But sometimes it is impossible to alter the fact that one wants the divorce and that the other does not.

Broadly speaking, it seems hardly conceivable that it could often be wise to maintain a marriage, especially a childless marriage, when it had ceased to be *marriage by mutual consent*. Lacking mutual consent in marriage, then the one alternative in logic and in fact would seem to be divorce by mutual consent. So why not call it that?

These tragedies happen. Unrequited love is common. A wife clings to a husband who no longer loves her; or a husband to a wife who is indifferent to him. No laws can change this; nor can such situations as a rule be made better by forcing the unwilling partner to remain in the union. This might happen *sometimes;* but very seldom unless the unwilling one consents voluntarily to try again, or to sacrifice his or her own preference for what, in the circumstances, seems an adequate reason.

Usually divorce is indicated when a marriage has ceased to be "by mutual consent." It is hard to see how the unloved partner in such a union could reasonably or wisely or rightly withhold "consent" to such divorce, however painful it might be to yield it, except when the rights of children were involved, or else some other vital consideration. And even when there are children, divorce is often the wiser course.

I have a very moving letter from a woman in a large western city whose husband has ceased to love her, and is, with her consent, living with another woman whom he does love. This couple have separated. They remain good friends, and the man contributes to the support of their child.

"Should I be ill," she says, "he would come to my aid immediately; and he does what he can for us financially.—I see them together; and, dear Judge, it is as if a knife were plunged into my very soul, the ache is so tremendous. But what is the use—what can I or should I do? Shall I give him a divorce (he says he doesn't want it) or shall I go on as I have been, hoping against hope that something will happen which will reunite us; or shall I seek happiness and love, the latter being essential to my nature, elsewhere?

"Oh, I know there is fault—chiefly in that I kept at him during our life together, to try and save, and be less extravagant—which he has interpreted as nagging and as mental cruelty."

Now there is a child in this marriage—a child who is being wronged and injured by this situation. Whether this couple could, for the sake of their child, make some compromise in marriage for the sake of providing that child with a home, is a question that depends on many complex things. There is no rule. I have in mind some women who have maintained a home under such conditions by allowing their husbands complete liberty in such outside attachments as the one mentioned here. I have known men who have done likewise in order to find a basis on which they could continue to live with their wives and give their children a home. I have known others, who having formed such outside attachments, gave them up, and who did it for the sake of their children, without grumbling because they thought that was the way to play the game. Sometimes the tensions that result from these compromises prove unendurable to the persons involved. Sometimes the compromise is successful. It depends on the personal equation.

This woman needed expert counsel in the beginning of her marriage. So do all persons who marry. It would be so much easier to prevent these domestic crashes than it is to repair the wreck after the crash comes. This woman began marriage ignorant of certain elementary facts about masculine psychology. Probably he was as ignorant of hers. Why not provide educational facilities to warn men and women against such pitfalls? If the wife had known what she knows now, she could probably have avoided this tragedy. If her husband clearly understood her present point of view, perhaps the situation could be mended even now. Who can say? When I mediate between such persons I can often make them see their common mistakes, and renew the foundations on which their love began. Suppose there were a House of Human

Welfare to which this couple could have gone for counsel—
or to which they could go now. It should be provided.

The point I want to make here is that no system can be
devised that will insure absolutely against such situations.
But the amount of that kind of thing could be reduced to a
mere fraction of what it is at present if we managed marriage
differently.

In connection with divorce by mutual consent, the question of alimony and property is a grave one. This man, for
instance, is not supporting his wife. He would be willing to
support her, but his salary does not permit him to pay the
maintenance cost of two households. His wife, in order to
give him his liberty, undertakes to support herself. He contributes to the support of their child.—Formerly it would
have been difficult for the wife to assume the rôle of economic independence which has made the present relation
possible. Women have of late years become more and more
capable of self-support.

A woman of thirty-five came to me the other day and
asked me to require her husband to contribute to the support
of their two children. They are a divorced couple. She is
making $200 a month; and she explained with pride that she
would not accept a cent from him for herself. "But I do
think," she added, "that he should contribute his share to the
support of the children. There is no reason why that should
fall wholly on me."—Now if this marriage had been a companionate, it would have been easily possible for the couple
to go their ways without the complication of alimony or anything like it.

I encounter more and more of this spirit of independence
among women. It is a very hopeful thing. Some accept alimony for a little while, to tide them over after divorce till
they can dig in and make a living for themselves. They expect to work. But there are others, of course, who accept the
old idea that it is the duty of the husband to support his wife,
whether or no; that no married woman can fairly be expected

to support herself; that support for life was clearly indicated and implied in the bond; and that they are at liberty to settle down in idleness, and live on alimony for the rest of their lives, or for as long as the man can be forced to provide money. Indeed, there is a gold-digger type of woman who marries with the express intention of acquiring an alimony income for life by way of the divorce court. It is easily done— under our present marriage code—especially if the man happens to be rich and able to afford the burden without special inconvenience to himself.

In many of these cases there is an evident injustice. And yet it is impossible to lay down a general rule about it. Each case has to stand on its merits. For instance, some women cannot make a living. Often a woman has been accustomed all her life to a standard of living such that if she had to depend on what she could earn, the change of standards forced upon her would amount to descent into bitter poverty and want. To refuse alimony in such a case might be sheer cruelty. A woman used to a ten thousand or twenty thousand dollar income, but incapable, by reason of her lack of training and capacity, of making more than the wages of a ribbon counter clerk, would be destroyed by such a change of standards.

It all comes down to the human approach. Such problems should be submitted to judges with the power, and the specialized training, to make wise human adjustments which would be fair rather than merely legal. They would seldom be perfect. We have to do the best we can. But at present we make almost no attempt at such adjustments. Justice is not at present dispensed on that plan. It is dispensed rather on a plan that is largely indifferent to equity, and to human happiness. Its chief characteristic is that it arrives at decisions and disposes of human tangles, with a minimum of inconvenience to society. It is a machine processed thing, a flivver,—not a hand-made creation in human artistry, as it should be. Artistry takes time, trouble, and money to achieve;

we haven't time for it. There is nothing so cheap on earth as human lives and human happiness; and nothing so costly as art. So why bother?

There are some terrible abuses in the alimony system as we have it. In my own court, recently, I tried a case before a jury twice. A young man of thirty was sued for non-support by his wife, a woman of twenty-five. They had no children. The husband, at large expense to the county, was brought back from a distant state, under a charge of non-support and desertion. The first jury disagreed because of the fact that the man and woman were both equally able to earn a living. Some of the jury could not see why the woman should not support herself.

Then the county was put to the expense of a second trial, in which the jury convicted the man on the technical arguments of the district attorney, which one of the jurors told me later they could not escape, though they thought them unjust.

I was then compelled to order the man to pay fifty dollars a month for the support of the young woman; and he is still doing it, as the law requires.

This is happening under a statute which does not distinguish between the companionate and the family; and which provides simply that he must support his wife—and children. The fact that there are no children makes no difference, nor does the fact that they are not living together, nor that she could wholly support herself. She is fastened on him like a leech.

A Denver lawyer told me the other day that he lately represented a man of forty in a divorce case against the man's wife, aged twenty-eight. It was shown at the hearing, on application of the wife's lawyer for attorney fees and alimony, that the wife was employed by a large corporation at a salary of $150 a month. The husband was making $200 a month. The court ordered the husband to pay the wife's lawyer $200 attorney fees, and to pay his wife *$75 a month* *alimony*. Thus the husband's income was reduced to $125 a month; and the wife's income was raised, without a cent of cost to her, to a clear $225 a month. The husband had to pay her lawyer and his own lawyer, the court costs—all in addition to $75 a month alimony. Figure out for yourself how long it took that man to get out of debt, and what chance he had of finding happiness again, either in or out of marriage.— There isn't a day that I don't come in contact with these pompous stupidities of the law.

These are some of the conditions that could be remedied if we had, for the companionate at least, a different way of dealing with questions of property and alimony.

In family marriage the conditions would in some ways be different, and the arrangements could justly be made different, because family marriage would involve obligations deliberately entered into. It would have been entered into with the clear understanding that when a man and woman have brought children into the world, the happiness and welfare of those children come before any question of the personal happiness of their parents; and that only under the urge of clear necessity could they expect divorce while their children were of an age to need their care. There would be reason and clear justice in expecting such persons to put their children first; and ordinarily they would see the reasonableness of it and would play the game that way.

It is a curious and interesting fact about divorce as we have it that the courts have habitually put the happiness of the parents first, and have made the welfare and happiness of the children a secondary matter. Couples with children can, under the present system, get a divorce as easily as if they had no children. And when the divorce is granted, the children simply have to make the best of the situation, and get along as they can. Material provision is made for them, but no spiritual provision. They have a right to both their parents; yet they are deprived of that, and of a two-parent home. The real victims of the divorce are thus the children, who are subject to spiritual deprivations which may warp and cripple them for life.

How can we expect anything else with marriage and divorce as we have them? It is inevitable. For we permit couples to rush into family marriage to gratify a sex urge which can find no other legitimate outlet. They often mistake that urge for the basic congeniality which should be the basis of marriage. Romantic love without such basic congeniality is like a plant without roots. Lacking nourishment, or soil to grow in, it dies; whereas properly nourished, it might have lasted and flourished in a lifelong union.

Too late the victims of such hasty marriages discover their mistake. Then it often happens that some relief, through divorce, is essential; *and to hold such people together is often worse for the children they ought not to have had, than divorce.* At best it is an evil choice; for though the divorce mill may be the lesser of two evils, and though it may release the parents, and create a sort of peace where there has been strife, yet it often grinds the lives and the future of the children to pulp. And yet, we must have it; and we shall continue to need a great deal of it till there is some safeguard against the conception of children by people who don't really love each other well enough to stick.

The contention I am making for these changes in our marriage code is in reality nothing but a continuation, another step forward, in the fight I have been making through the last twenty-eight years for the welfare and betterment of the lot of women and children. It is a fight for the rights of women and children.

Years ago a great struggle was waged between progressive forces in this country, and the reactionary forces led by certain of the clergy, for divorce. Liberalism slowly won. Women then found it possible to obtain release from brutal husbands and protection and support for their children. It was not perfect, but it was better than what we had had.

Today it continues as a struggle to obtain for women an

equality of rights, in marriage—including the right to have
wanted children, with the help of birth control, and the right
to control their destiny as individuals who are no longer in
slavery.

It continues as a struggle to give to every child the right
to be wanted when it is conceived, the right to be well-born,
of healthy parents who love each other, and the right to a
home so well founded beforehand that divorce is not likely
to touch it.

More than that, it is a struggle, through the rational application of birth control and the rational ordering of marriage to meet the *problem of overpopulation* which now
menaces the world and threatens it with fresh wars. For war
has, in the past, been in the last analysis a clumsy and
brutal method of keeping within bounds the population of
nations that had no methods of birth control save dangerous
abortion and unnatural infanticide.

The work of settling the Western hemisphere has, for a
hundred years, made population control less necessary than
formerly. But now the saturation point is being reached, and
already the problem, even in this vast country, is becoming
acute. The difficulty is not to populate the earth, but to avoid
an overpopulation that will outstrip the food supply and lead
to wars as the only method of decimation. The howl about
"Race Suicide" is specious nonsense. The breeding of children for quality rather than quantity is the next needful
step. And this, I believe, may best be achieved by birth
control used in conjunction with such a revision of our marriage code as is here suggested. Other factors enter in, of
course, but a right ordering of marriage is basic.

When this is accomplished, one of the most important
fights in history for the rights of women and children will
have been won. There will be more to do; but that achievement will at any rate be posted to our credit.

The ideal of marriage suggested in this book seems to me
to be considerably more exacting than that evidently pre-

ferred by some of my conservative critics—who hold that marriage as we have it is all right, *and that the trouble lies with the men and women who enter it*. This is a characteristically theological view of the matter. What I maintain is that people are rather likely to be pretty decent in their conduct if our institutions and our system of education would give them a chance.

In the ideal marriage we need to seek the union of two *free* personalities, which, without the imposition of any outside force, will by *slow degrees* knit together and grow spiritually into each other.

This is not to be done in a day; and it is not accomplished by an ecclesiastical fiat which, in a five-minute ceremony, performs the magic feat, the sacramental miracle of making two strangers into "one flesh." Time alone can work that miracle.

Nor can this process of growth together be forced. If there be no freedom and spontaneity in it, it fails. The life goes from it. The consciousness of coercive authority often inhibits and blasts it. The only stimulus that can make it grow is the stimulus that comes from within. With such stimulus, men and women will voluntarily make an *effort* to grow into each other's lives; they will surmount obstacles and difficulties and misunderstandings; they will together create between them a love that is real and lasting.—But introduce social coercion, and mutual ownership of each other, and the tyranny of jealousy! Instantly the element of moral responsibility and creative energy vanishes from the marriage.

Held together now by coercive traditions, the couple abandon the efforts at understanding which would have held them together. They become no longer responsible, but irresponsible, in their mutual dealings—because society has given them over each other a tyrannical power of ownership which breeds irresponsibility as the sun breeds maggots.

The very thing which many of my critics accuse me of trying to introduce into marriage was introduced into it long ago by their authoritarian doctrines. *They,* and their predecessors in reactionary thought, have put anarchy and hate and bondage into marriage; and now, quite rightly, they are alarmed when they see the fruit which *their* method and system is bringing forth. Some of us, tired of this ecclesiastical despotism, are minded to find other ways of dealing with this human problem.

In the *freedom* of the companionate, people would have a safe opportunity to grow into each other's lives; and they would accomplish that object only if the elements of such growth were really present in their union. If such elements were lacking, they would discover the mistake, part, and go their ways.

But if such growth *did* take place, then it would be a genuine thing, a real union. Having created that union of their lives out of the physical and spiritual intimacy of their association together in the companionate, they would then usually be able to carry this union effectively over into the graver obligations, the greater strain and stress, the more exacting duties, and the *yet closer bond* of the family—the procreative marriage.

Thus the family marriage would be a step forward—a short step, easily taken, and well prepared for. It would not be a blind plunge into the unknown. And the new joys and responsibilities, the new trials and difficulties, would all serve to bring the man and woman into the kind of union which is real marriage, and real monogamy—growing constantly, and hence capable of lasting their life through, for the reason that it would be *alive,* and neither dead nor static.—They would be ready for it; they would have slowly acquired the strength for it; they would not be trying to leap twenty feet before they had learned to leap ten.

The family would thus crown their lives. It would have grown as grows the oak, slowly. The early companionate would be a mere sapling beside it. And thus there would be created a home which would be a safe nest for children, and a sure refuge for the makers of it.

No marriage, I think, can reach its full possibilities without children, either natural or adopted. To those who have made a success of marriage, with happy children growing up around them, I need not say that here is indeed an overflowing cup.

I do not mean that family marriage is necessarily the most beneficial for all persons. There are those who are not individually adapted to it, and who can find a higher personal development, either without marriage, or with the companionate. Such persons may need to be able to put forth their undivided energies in directions with which the family is not compatible.

But for most of us it still holds true that the family is the ideal to reach for. Approach it gradually, grow into it by the safe route of the companionate, and no other way of life offers such inspiring possibilities. Here is the road by which most of the race can attain greater spiritual heights than by any other. This we comprehend and feel, as by an inner vision. And that is why we cling to marriage and will never let it go.

LOVE, MARRIAGE, AND DIVORCE IN RUSSIA [1]

By V. F. Calverton

It is in the problems of love, marriage, and divorce that the advance in morality in Soviet Russia has been most direct and decisive. Love and the sex life have been freed of the superstitions and silences which had clouded, confused and bound them; marriage has been liberated from the religious and ceremonial rites in which it had once been bound; divorce has been converted into an intelligent device, disenslaved from duplicity and deceit and accessible to all. As a result, morality has been emancipated from the stereotyped stupidities of an enforced convention and an inelastic code.

Love and the sex life are looked upon in Soviet Russia as the private privilege of the individual, and not the concern of the state. This attitude, which English moralists, such as Havelock Ellis, Bertrand Russell and Edward Carpenter, in the vanguard of their contemporaries, have urged in theory, the Russians have put into practice. This achievement is phenomenal. It marks the introduction of an intelligence into morals that is noteworthy and significant. The sex life of individuals is not to be subject to supervision or punishment. It is only when children are involved that the relation becomes a social matter, and necessitates the intervention of the state. This intervention, it should be added, is always in behalf of the woman, and every law concerning it is designed for her protection. The history of moral standards in the West, particularly during the last three hundred years, has been one of close restrictions and confinements. Love and the sex life, once bartered for a dowry or sold for a shilling, had

[1] From *Bankruptcy of Marriage*. New York: The Macaulay Company, 1928.

been regulated by law and rigid social custom. The individual had to fit his impulse into this organized and unnatural order of behavior. In Soviet Russia suffering occasioned by the conflict between economics and impulse has been dissolved.

The education of the individual in sex begins at an early age. Sex instruction is part of the general curriculum in every educational institution of consequence. This instruction is characterized by a candor that endeavors to destroy the foolish confusions and absurdities which ordinarily grow up about the topic in the minds of Western youth. This instruction is not instruction obfuscated by analogy and impaired by properly punctuated omissions. When we recall the statements in reference to the wisdom of such instruction for youth in America, an excellent idea of contrast between prudishness and candor, between convention and reason, between superstition and science, is provided. The American scientist who disapproved of a thorough study in the anatomical differences between the sexes is a splendid example of the surrender of intelligence to custom. Such an attitude is not only absurd, but it is nothing more than a foolish memory of an unenlightened past—in Soviet Russia. It is for this reason that children grow up in that country with an understanding of sex that is uncharacterized by pruriency and evasion. Such instruction after all must be the basis for any sensible study of the problem of sex. Such instruction must begin in youth if it is to be effective in combating the myth and mystery in which sex has been hitherto enveiled. Without it love and the sex life can never be felicitous and exquisite.

Despite our conventions, customs, and codes, men have been mastered by sex, and not the masters of it. The disruption of the old code in the Western world represents only an increasingly concentrated revolt against a set of moral regulations. Preceding this contemporary revolt were the untold individual revolts which were scorned by society, castigated by law, but which had nevertheless not ceased. The double standard of morality evinced likewise the incompatibility of moral regulations with masculine impulse—the male revolted, however, because he could afford to revolt; the female did not revolt because she could not afford it. Now that she can afford it, too, she has revolted also. Sex reaction under the double code became distorted and its expression ruined by monotony or often aberration. The costs of suppression, and the deceptions occasioned by its violation, have left their imprints, deep and often ineradicable in the nervous structure of modern man. Our neurotic and psychotic age is closely connected with this suppression. No sane sex ethic could arise from such a moral outlook. It was only by destroying the concealments that had been perpetuated about sex in the minds of youth, removing the suppressions that had been urged and enforced by bourgeois society, that Soviet Russia has been able to erect a new ethical edifice. Ignorance had to be supplanted by knowledge, suppression had to be removed, and spontaneity of impulse had to replace conformities of conduct.

The new laws regarding marriage and divorce in Soviet Russia have been constructed in such a manner as to provide for the expression of this new attitude. Marriage and divorce are freer in Soviet Russia than in any other part of the Western world. Notwithstanding this advance, even these laws do not yet attain this ideal. As M. I. Kalinin said:

"The new law is not entirely new. It only makes a big step forward." [2] Or as stated in the early edition of the code:

Only time and experience will show how many of the provisions of this code belong to the transitional category, features which are destined to vanish with the more perfect establishment of the socialist order. In certain clauses, however, there is clearly to be discerned a conscious recognition of conditions and habits of life surviving from the old order. Such survivals are inevitable at this time when neither the

[2] Quoted from *Marriage and Family*, A. Prigradov-Kudrin. (Soviet Publication).

economic nor psychological transformation is complete. There are provisions respecting property and income which will inevitably be subject to obsolescence or amendment. The law of guardianship, essentially revolutionary as it is, is yet no more than a first tentative approach to the realization of collective responsibility for the care of the young. The laws of marriage and divorce still bear traces of the passing order, frank and sensible acknowledgment of the existence of certain economic and psychological conditions only to be overcome when the complete change is accomplished.

If all the traces of the old order have not been eradicated from the new marriage laws in the Soviet Union, the mythical, magical, and religious aspects have certainly been discarded. Marriage now is only a civil procedure. While couples may still be married by a religious ceremony, their action is not legal until it has undergone civil sanction. The religious rite, which is discouraged, is unessential; the civil alone is vital. Under the Tzar the opposite situation was conspicuous. If a man and woman lived together for thirty years, and had ten children, the couple could not appear as man and wife unless a church marriage was effected, nor could the children appear as progeny of the father. According to the old Russian law this man was not their father, and in the bureau of births these children were entered as born illegitimately, of an unknown father. The woman had no rights to the property of the man nor did his children; if he died intestate his property went to his relatives. In fact, according to penal statute, every woman who lived with a man, in an unmarried state, could be categorized as a "prostitute." [3] This condition of woman in Tzaristic Russia was akin to that in the England of the pure-passioned Victorians. Today in Soviet Russia such a condition harks back to the archaic. A man and woman are recorded as father and mother, whether their marriage is registered or not. The woman, therefore, suffers

[3] *Ibid.*

no isolation or scorn. Her child has the same rights and is looked upon in the same way whether she is married or unmarried. If she lives with a man without marriage, she is viewed in the same way as if she lives with a man to whom she is married. The registration of a marriage, therefore, has a statistical rather than a moral value.

The attitude toward marriage, which refuses to insert any distinction between registered or unregistered marriage, is indicative of how free marital relations are in Soviet Russia. The equalization of registered and unregistered marriage, for a time was a matter of anxious dispute. Many were opposed to equalizing the two types of marriage. At first only registered marriages were looked upon with favor and those who were registered as married had advantages over those who were unregistered. Soltz and Riazanov were sturdily opposed to this equalization of marriages. The controversy was exciting and hard-fought. Moirova, one of the woman delegates active in this dispute, classified the contentions of Soltz and Riazanov as tainted with remains of bourgeois morality. Her words are a challenge-call:

"What are we? Bourgeois moralists, that we occupy ourselves with such a distinction?"

City groups were much more in favor of equalization than rural groups, although at many of the village-meetings the vote was for abolition of all distinction. The question thus was debated in every part of Russia and it was the masses who finally decided in favor of the equalization of both types of marriage.[4]

Apropos of this dispute over registered and unregistered marriages, one of the statements made in the Ukraine, in protest against the advantage given to registered marriage, is astonishingly clear and concise in voicing the attitude in contemporary Russia:

[4] *Ibid.*

Marriage is a private act of the citizen which does not concern the state . . . a voluntary relationship made by two citizens.[5]

It should be mentioned also that before the masses voted in favor of equalization of registered and unregistered marriages, many statistics were adduced to stress the wisdom of such equalization. D. I. Kurski showed that in 1923 unregistered marriages far exceeded those registered; the actual ratio was 70,000 to 100,000 unregistered. Furthermore, in a study of 300 alimony cases in Moscow state court it was found that 14 of the children resulted from casual relations, 41 from long cohabitation, 68 from short-time cohabitation extending up to one year. It was further estimated by Kurski that at least 15 per cent of couples living together did not register their marriage.

According to the new law, now, both registered and unregistered marriages have the same right and privilege.[6] The husband in an unregistered marriage has the same rights and duties as in a registered; the same is true of the wife. Before this equalization these rights and duties did not exist. Then the right of one person to be supported by the other in case of illness or inability to work did not obtain. Nor was there the right of inheritance at death. The dissolution of these distinctions was a move of not a little importance.

As in the discussion in reference to registered and unregistered marriages, the consideration of the entire marital code which now prevails in Soviet Russia was discussed by the entire population before a decision was consummated. The new marital code is not a device of one group or of one sex to foist a morality upon another. The workers and peas-

[5] *Novy Mir,* February, 1927.
[6] An unregistered marriage is a marriage in which the relations respond to the conditions in the code: Proofs of a marital cohabitation before third parties in the form of personal correspondence and other documents; the jointship of their property in this cohabitation, joint upbringing of children, etc.

ants discussed this marital code for a whole year before it was accepted. S. M. Glikin, describing the procedure, states:

The All-Russian Central Ispolkom decided not to sanction the new law until it could be discussed by the workers. During a whole year the new laws were discussed in factories, shops, village-meetings, and military organizations. . . . The laboring masses of the Republic discussed it with great attention. . . . In its final form, thus, it represents the conclusions of millions of workers in cities and villages.[7]

The statement of another Soviet writer, Kudrin, is also pertinent:

. . . the new code of marriage and family is not only a law forged out by the hands of many millions of laboring people, but it also reflects the spirit of the revolutionary state.

Here is a morality, then, that actually expresses the voluntary desire and choice of a people. Over 6,000 debates on the subject were held in villages alone, and thousands more in towns and cities. It manifests the spirit of an epoch.

Marriage in the Soviet Union cannot bind the woman as it does in other countries. Woman's freedom is not a passive thing, but an active, dynamic reality. In the protest of Moirova flashes the assertiveness and independence of the new Russian woman: "After I read the statement in the code to the effect that the change of location of one of the spouses does not necessitate that the other follow him, I confess I could not understand why, ten years after the Revolution, this must be stated in a special article. Is it not understood that we live at such a time where we can choose as we please the place we desire? Are there still among us people who think that a wife must follow her husband? This is too much, comrades." Very often women sever themselves entirely from their old existence, demand a divorce, and forge their way

[7] *The New Law Concerning Marriage, Divorce, Family, and Guardianship.*

into a freer life.[8] This revolt attests the growth of feminine resolution and intelligence. The working woman is constantly instructed in the nature of her rights, and in the importance of their expression. Her advance is cultivated as much as that of man. Marriage as a consequence can never become an institution of inequality, as it has been in the past, and still is in other nations.

With the removal of the religious element in marriage, and the establishment of the right of the woman to obtain and determine the destiny of her property after marriage, the developments in divorce follow in natural sequence. Just as it is expected that in the "future Communist society of course there will be no registration of marriage at all," and that "if the code of 1918 made registration necessary, it did so only to fit the conditions of the moment, and as a transitory expedient," [9] in the laws pertaining to divorce, it has been necessary to insert, in particular reference to children, clauses that are still without the extraordinary freedom of the socialist ideal. Nevertheless, the most revolutionary factory of the new Russian *mores* is that of the free divorce. It is the advance made in this field which facilitates an easy future development for this entire ethic. Divorce can be got by mutual consent, or even at the instigation of one party, on the ground of incompatibility. The statement of the code is unambiguous:

The mutual consent of the husband and wife or the desire of either of them to obtain a divorce shall be considered a ground for divorce.

Under the Tzar, divorce had been accessible only to the opulent. Today it is a liberating device, attainable by every worker and peasant in the Soviet Republics. The collusion and camouflage that are necessitated in other countries, when

[8] I. A. Rostovsky, *The New Law Concerning Marriage, Divorce, Family and Guardianship.* (Third Edition, Soviet Pamphlet.)
[9] Prigradov-Kudrin, *Marriage and Family.*

the genuine reason for divorce is incompatibility, are superfluous in the Soviet Union. While in Switzerland divorce
upon the basis of mutual consent is valid, there is not in the
Swiss attitude the far-spanning vision that is embodied in
the Russian. Absolute freedom in divorce is the Russian ideal.
Divorce should always be, unless there are children involved,
the concern of the individuals themselves and no one else.
Artifice and subterfuge are at once hostile and alien to this
concept. They stultify its theory. The freedom of divorce
in Soviet Russia, therefore, has been expanded to a maximum.
As S. M. Glikin avers:

> Soviet divorce is so free that if one of the parties wants a
> divorce, it is enough to announce it in the Ispolkom. The
> other of the spouses is then informed about the divorce hav-
> ing taken place.[10]

In other words, if one party wishes a divorce, it is an injury
rather than a benefit to deny it. Continuance of marital
relationships, then, should depend upon spontaneity and not
compulsion. Marriages which continue even when one of the
parties desires discontinuance and separation, or both—as
is so frequent in the Western world—are but a private mad-
house for individual or individuals. That coercion is an un-
healthful and foolish method to be used in marital relations,
no progressive thinker would dispute. Marital felicity certainly cannot depend upon legal enforcements. In reference
to divorce and coercion, the comment of the Soviet writer
Rostovsky is instructive:

> To give any explanations why one of the spouses wants
> divorce is unnecessary . . . for to remain married, or to dis-
> solve the marriage, depends entirely upon the desire of one of
> the spouses; to endeavor to coerce them is impossible, and,
> therefore, any explanation is unnecessary.[11]

[10] *The New Law Concerning Marriage, Divorce, Family, and
Guardianship.*
[11] *Ibid.*

To expedite the simplicity of this process it is not even necessary that the parties desiring divorce appear originally in person:

A petition for the dissolution of marriage may be presented orally or in writing and an official report shall be drawn thereon.

Shortly thereafter the court will

set the day for the examination of the petitions and give notice thereof to the parties and (where necessary) their attorneys.

While in the recent agitation in reference to the expediency of equalizing registered and unregistered marriages, there was a fervor and fury in the clash of pros and cons, and differences waxed intense and vehement, in the question of divorce there were no pros and cons, in fact, no argument at all. I. I. Iliynski, in reporting the recent conference, declared that "the great majority agreed that the freedom to destroy marriage should be preserved in full."

In the problem of children it is the mother and child that are primarily protected. The presence of children is the only impediment to freedom of divorce. Under these conditions a divorce is not granted until the wife and children have been duly provided for against suffering and deprivation. The husband thus seeking a divorce must apportion his wages according to the decision of the court before the divorce is granted. Under ordinary circumstances, one-third of his wage is requisite for each child. Of course, where there are more children, or where his wife is incapacitated for work, other provisions, determined by the case, are made. It can be appreciated at once from these facts that the woman and child are consequently saved from suffering and distress.

Although divorce has now been made open for all, and its pursuit unaccompanied by difficulty of explanation or expenditure, the rate of divorce in Soviet Russia has not been spectacular. The only time when divorces raced beyond normal predictions was at the very beginning of the new code. When the code was first put into effect, it gave an opportunity to thousands who had been oppressed under the marital regulations of the Tzarist régime to take advantage of the new freedom of divorce. Since then the rate has not experienced such exaggerated ratios. In 1922, for instance, there were ten divorces for each ten thousand inhabitants; in 1923 there were eleven; and in 1924 and 1925 approximately the same rate persisted. Fifty-three per cent of the divorcés, it should be remarked, had been married for one year, and thirteen per cent for periods of longer duration. When we recall from our previous studies in divorce ratios that the average in the United States is 15.3 divorces for every ten thousand inhabitants, the statistics in Soviet Russia might appear comforting even to the conservative. With freedom of divorce the ratio of divorces is less than with the lack of freedom—such an argument might be projected by a moralist from these statistics. It would be unfair, however, not to observe certain factors in the Russian situation that are bound to hold the divorce rate at a surprisingly low level. The practice of unregistered marriages would obviously not affect the divorce rate by virtue of their discontinuance. There would be no record of these separations to enter upon the divorce calendar. It would only be the presence of children that would ever bring them up for social study or consideration. In addition it is very likely, despite the wide discussion of the topic all over Russia, that many peasants do not realize fully the opportunities for individual freedom from marital bondage that is inherent in the new code. The presence of these factors, however, should offer no cause for perturbation or alarm. Increase in divorce is a source of destruction only where the perpetuation of the old family is desired. Divorce in the West is a cancerous evil because it signifies the disintegration of the monogamous family which is still entertained as a moral ideal in both western Europe and the United States. In Soviet Russia where this ideal is contemned as obsolescent, and the future is conceived in terms of its extinction, divorce is a benefit and not an evil.

As the hurly-burly of the young days and months of the Revolution subsided into a more orderly change, ideas and impulses once topsy-turvied by the excitement and drama of spreading chaos became more soundly oriented and crystallized. In those tumultuous-spirited years of revolution, counter-revolution, intervention and famine, moral revolt went mad with iconoclastic fury. Everything of the old order was flung aside with a contempt bred in bitterness. All traces of old forms and conventions, however vestigial or attenuated, were beaten and buried beneath the derisive epithet of "bourgeois." The word "bourgeois" became synonymous with everything ugly, hideous and indescribably repulsive. Converted into "boorzhooy," it became the embodiment of even more contempt and hatred. In mystic verse that wove the march of "The Twelve" into the footprints of the Revolution, Alexander Blok fused a fantasy, inspired by religious fervor, with sneer and scorn for the "boorzhooy":

> The boorzhooy, like a hungry mongrel,
> A silent question stands and begs,
> The old world like a kinless mongrel
> Stands there, its tail between its legs.

Youths flaunted with riotous audacity the banners of their revolt. Girls who endeavored to retain the old virtues, or insisted upon delicate discriminations, were spurned with ridicule. Students flashed manifestos upon the walls of schools and colleges; chastity was belittled in quip and epigram, and continence was condemned as insane and ridiculous. Freedom became a fetish, and loveliness was lost in excess. The slow restoration of order inserted the first check upon these impetuosities and indiscriminate enthusiasms. Love and the sex life which had become enmeshed in the confusions of these hectic years gradually disentangled themselves and fumbled about for new foundations. While the old could not be abided, the new could not afford to sacrifice everything precious merely for the sake of novelty. Sex had to be approached with sanity if it was to be mastered by men at all. And so, as the Revolution matured and the new order shaped itself into a new diaphragm, these early exaggerations and excesses dwindled, and the basis of the new morality, organized about the new code, was begun.

It is this new morality which we find expressed in the independent position of woman, and the new marriage and divorce laws written into the legal code of Soviet Russia. In these changes are manifested the first strides in the direction of a new ethic.

V

EUGENICS

HEREDITY AND SEX [1]

By Edward M. East

AFRICAN travelers agree that no ostrich ever tried to out-maneuver a danger by sticking his head in the desert sand. This recipe for solving problems was invented by man in order to deal with matters connected with sex. In a world peopled by men and women, the subject naturally holds an important position. Every social question arises from, or is linked with, the differences between the sexes; yet since the domination of St. Paul's theology civilized nations have tried to manage their affairs, posing the while as if the sexual factor were non-existent.

This pretense is passing, and we are well rid of it. We have begun to realize that the subjective dominance of the sex appeal, which shows so clearly in the love interests pervading our literature, drama, and art, is the emotion to be expected of normal people. The mask of apathy is the abnormal, and psychologists have shown that it often cloaks something more inglorious than mere sham.

Sex *is* an interesting subject. One may say this today without forfeiting his claim to respectability. It is interesting because apart from its other bearings it holds a prominent place among the objective studies of the biologist. And properly so. Sexual reproduction is the keystone of the whole evolutionary structure. This world would have had a monotonous history without it, not because it leads man to become a "chaos of thought and passion all confused," but because there would have been no such noble animal to disturb the music of the spheres. Our humble planet would have rolled

[1] From *Heredity and Human Affairs*, New York: Charles Scribner's Sons, 1927.

on to its final doom of cold and death with the inglorious record of having produced nothing even as momentous and exciting as a jelly-fish or a grasshopper. Variety was the price of life for man, and no one of Nature's numerous experiments in propagation permitted the production of such varied forms as did the creation of a new individual by the union of two cells.

The reasons why such conclusions have been generally accepted are numerous. Perhaps the simplest argument is the following. We know that sexual methods of reproduction were not abandoned because they were too slow. In one week a vigorous fungus like the corn-smut can produce a number of potential new plants in the form of spores, greater than the total human population during the Christian era. The fusion of two cells is a distinct loss of time. We know too that spores, buds, bulbs, offshoots, and other similar methods of multiplication are very good means of keeping species flourishing, for numerous sorts which reproduce in this manner are with us today. But species which did not adopt sexual reproduction remained lowly and unspecialized, and species which abandoned it abandoned the road of progress at the same time. Why? Simply because evolution moves by steps, by mutations, and these changes are inherited independently of one another. When half-a-dozen mutations occur in a given stock of the asexual type, therefore, that stock has only six chances to escape annihilation at the ruthless hand of Natural Selection. There are six opportunities of fitting into the general scheme of things with the alternative of being removed from the scheme entirely. On the other hand, six variations in a sexually reproducing organism where there is an opportunity for crossing gives two to the sixth power possibilities for survival, or 64 all told, through hereditary recombination. It makes a great difference.

Formerly it was thought that species propagating only by asexual methods gradually died out through loss of some mysterious sort of vital energy. Why people drew such conclusions in face of the fact that some of the most ancient types show no traces of sex is an enigma which must be left to the psychologist, but they did. They believed that sexual reproduction meant rejuvenation, a kind of fountain of youth. The idea appears to have arisen because Paramœcium, a one-celled organism which is shaped like a bedroom-slipper, dies under ordinary laboratory conditions after a hundred or so generations of reproduction by division. Given the opportunity, however, these tiny slipper-animals fuse together. The twain become one flesh in physical reality, and afterwards return to asexual multiplication with great activity and vigor. Woodruff,[2] of Yale, and Jennings,[3] of Johns Hopkins, have given us the true explanation of this strange behavior. These animalculæ are poisoned by the by-products of their own life processes. If waste products are removed and new food given periodically, Paramœcium cultures can be kept in a perfect state of health for thousands of generations without conjugation, but conjugation serves as a kind of antidote to bad living conditions. By studying the behavior of the descendants after conjugation, moreover, Jennings found that only certain ones show renewed vigor. It is believed, therefore, that conjugation is not of itself a rejuvenator, but that only those individuals having desirable combinations of hereditary characters profit by the transaction.

Essentially, sexual reproduction is a method of propagation dependent on the behavior of the chromosomes. Again we must focus attention on those protoplasmic freight-trains within each living cell which link generation to generation, and whose operations with the materials they contain build up the body characters of every organism. When a type is sufficiently simple and unspecialized to go on its way living and reproducing its image by mere chromosome divisions, we say that its propagation is asexual; when a type propa-

[2] L. L. Woodruff, "The Life Cycle of Paramœcium When Subjected to a Varied Environment." *Amer. Nat.* 42, 1908.

[3] H. S. Jennings, *Behaviour of the Lower Organisms*. New York: The Macmillan Company, 1906.

gates by a fusion of chromosome sets from two cells, we believe that it has taken on the significant features of sexual reproduction.

Nature is not niggardly in her experiments. She will try almost anything, not only once but many times. She believes in giving new ideas a chance. By all the evidence sex has arisen again and again in both the animal and vegetable kingdoms, and the various guises under which the scheme is carried on are almost innumerable. These various expedients, however, are but cloaks for one process, a shifting of chromosome materials in the preparation of the germ-cells and their further recombination at fertilization.

What appears to be an origin of sex occurs today in the tiny green alga (*Ulothrix*) one finds as a scum in stagnant water. In this species large fat spores are formed when times are prosperous which need only proper housing conditions to germinate and produce their kind. Under the pressure of adversity, on the other hand, it produces starved-looking, lonely little spores which must cast their lot together so intimately as to become one body before they can start life anew. And among primitive animals a very similar round of affairs takes place.

After the origin of sex the evolutionary trend in both kingdoms was in astonishing agreement. First the germ-cells were like ordinary cells, showing their difference only in the attraction they had for one another; yet even so, there is no harm in calling one the male and the other the female. Afterwards, germ-cells distinct in form appeared. Still later, types arose in which specialized organs produced the germ-cells. The final step in each kingdom, the mammals and the seed plants, was the protection of the young.

Let us now forget the sex problems of the plants and turn our attention to the higher animals. We may excuse this partiality by two reasons. In the first place, the sex problems of the vegetable world are superficially even more complicated than those of the animal world. In the second place, we are not interested so much in plant biology as in animal biology. Man recognizes his mammalian relationship even when he will not admit it openly, and he likes to write and talk and speculate about matters that are at least related to his own private affairs.

In most of the higher animals there are males and females. There are hermaphroditic organisms, it is true, where the two kinds of germ-cells are borne in the same individual. There are even animals which are first females, because they bear eggs, and afterwards males, because they bear sperms. But this unusual type of sexuality is nearly always confined to forms that are parasitic or otherwise degenerate. The tapeworm is a good example. The old Hebrew observation, "male and female created he them," still holds as a fair approximation of the facts; and this brings up the question of what determines the proceeding. We know *why* there are males and females. We want to know the *how* of the matter.

The subject has been very popular. A generation or more ago Drélincourt counted some 500 dead theories of sex-determination, and his theory along with a trail of successors long since has gone to swell the number. It would be unnecessary to mention these speculations here were it not that their ghosts are so hard to lay. One meets them time and again in modern publications whose authors ought to know better. There may be germs of truth in some of them, but any spark of life they have is usually so choked with falsehood and ignorance that the theories are doomed from the beginning.

The advantage of most of these hypotheses, from the standpoint of the originators, was the difficulty of putting them to a critical test. Thus they were useful longer than would otherwise have been the case. The idea that the two sexes were controlled individually by the right and left members of the paired reproductive glands was practically useless. Being verifiable, it was killed by the first facts obtained. Let a man with an inferiority complex get started with a compensatory notion of male superiority, on the other hand, and his theory was hard to refute. Queerly enough, though, in the majority of such theories the most highly developed sex, the mentally superior sex, or the physically vigorous sex, which were males of course, was nearly always supposed to produce the opposite sex in proportion to its assumed superiority. No doubt the originators were blessed with large families of girls. Conversely, Girou, who identified the sex of the offspring with that of the most vigorous parent, must have wished to congratulate himself over a preponderant lot of boys.

We now know that sex in the higher animals is largely a matter of heredity, and is usually determined irrevocably by the kinds of eggs and sperm which meet at the time of fertilization. Unfortunately, the word *usually* must be used to qualify the statement, as will be seen later.

The first piece of real evidence on the subject came from a study of human twins.[4] Two kinds exist. There are fraternal twins who look no more alike than other members of the same family. About half of the time they consist of two boys or two girls, the other half of the time there is a boy and a girl. Then there are identical twins, whose features and mannerisms are remarkably alike, and these are always of the same sex. Fraternal twins result from the fertilization of two ova by two sperms, as is shown by the separate sets of membranes enclosing the embryos. Identical twins, since they are both enclosed in one set of membranes, must have their origin in the separate development of two segments produced by a single fertilized ovum. Where development is not wholly separate, such bizarre creatures as the Siamese twins are formed. It is difficult to imagine how such results could have come about unless sex were determined at fertilization.

[4] Two excellent books on twins are *The Biology of Twins* (1917) and *The Physiology of Twinning,* by H. H. Newman (1923). Chicago University Press.

If it were otherwise, identical twins should consist of a boy and a girl just as frequently as fraternal twins.

In the early part of the present century, when the study of heredity by controlled matings became the popular mode of research in biology, another bit of support to this idea appeared. When an individual, hybrid for a single pair of character-determiners, is crossed back with the recessive parent, the resulting progeny are half of the dominant and half of the recessive type. Thus DR × RR gives DR × RR. By analogy one could not avoid suspecting that one of the sexes is similarly a hybrid producing two kinds of germ-cells, and the other a pure type producing germ-cells all of one kind, since the sex ratio in so many animals is very close to equality. Several slightly different hypotheses were published interpreting sex in this way, but the first direct proof was put forward by Dr. C. E. McClung,[5] of the University of Pennsylvania, in 1902. A few years earlier a German investigator had noticed an unpaired chromosome in half of the sperm-cells of certain insects he was studying. He reported the matter, but thought little of it. McClung now found the same feature in the reproductive cells of various insects, and suggested that this odd chromosome element was the sex-determiner.

Other American cytologists then began to investigate numerous species of animals, and corroborated McClung's observations in wholesale fashion. In most insects, in many worms, and in all mammals studied, including man himself, the male was the sex-determiner. Half of the sperm-cells contained this sex chromosome, which became known as the X Chromosome, and half were without it. The egg-cells all contained it. When a sperm carrying an X chromosome fertilized an egg, a female was produced who had two X chromosomes in each of her body-cells. When a sperm having no X chromosome entered into fertilization, an individual

[5] C. E. McClung, "The Accessory Chromosome Sex-Determinant?' *Biol. Bull.*, 3, 1902.

was formed with only a single X of maternal origin in the body-cells, and this individual was a male.

In some instances the X chromosome was found to be an unpaired element which, at the maturation of the germ-cells, passed to one of the daughter cells undivided. Its behavior therefore could be studied easily. In other species the X had a mate, a Y chromosome; but even then the behavior of these particular elements during the formation of the germ-cells was different from that of the other chromosomes. As if conscious of the importance of the rôle they played, they often hung back during cell division, joining their sister chromosomes at a slightly later stage. The entrance and exit of star performers belonged to them, and they took it.

Here then are several great groups of organisms where the male controls the sex by virtue of producing two kinds of sperm. The female is a passive actor, for all eggs are alike. But Nature showed no favoritism. She gave the female an opportunity to show her efficiency at this performance in moths, butterflies, and birds. There the sperms are all alike and the eggs are of two kinds. The determination of sex thus comes about in essentially the same old way.

If sex control is a chromosome function [3] similar in character to the chromosome control of other inherited traits, body qualities ought to be found that are transmitted by the particular chromosome which determines maleness and femaleness. Such a situation has been discovered, not once but a hundred times. In man, for instance, there are two recessive characters, a bloody abnormality called hemophilia and color-blindness, where the affliction is more common in males than in females, and where the hereditary transmission is peculiar. They are not transmitted from father to son, nor do they appear in the son's descendants, yet the daughters

---

[3] See *Heredity and Sex*, by T. H. Morgan, New York: Columbia University Press, 1913. It contains a fuller description of these matters as well as a nearly complete bibliography.

of an affected man, though normal themselves, transmit the abnormality to half their sons.

This exceptional type of inheritance is understandable if the determiners of the traits are assumed to be located in the X chromosomes, since the distribution of the latter parallels their own distribution. When a color-blind man has children by a normal woman, the sons are normal because their X chromosome comes from their mother. The daughters are also normal because the normal X chromosome inherited from the mother dominates the defective X chromosome inherited from the father, but these daughters will have defective sons whenever those sons get their X heritage from a defective egg, because sons are dependent entirely on the mother for their X heritage.

A similar type of crisscross, sex-linked heredity naturally ought to be found, and is found, in birds, where the female is the controller of sex. The best known case is a dominant character, barred feathers, such as are found in the Plymouth Rock. When a Barred-Rock cock is mated with a hen of a black breed, the offspring of both sexes are barred; but these in turn produce progeny in which half of the hens are black, though all the cocks are barred. The reverse cross, a black cock mated with a Barred-Rock hen, gives barred cocks and black hens, and these when mated together produce barred individuals and black individuals of both sexes in equal numbers. Anyone ought to be able to work out the way the inheritance goes after the explanations given above. Crisscross inheritance is an easier puzzle than one of crisscross words.

In all the higher animals which have thus far been investigated, sex appears to be determined at fertilization by the particular chromosome inheritance received. Yet it is well to be cautious. There are still a great many unsolved problems connected with the subject. Sex, in fact, is a precarious proposition; just when one thinks it is mastered, he finds that he is mistaken, as St. Anthony discovered long ago.

In man the sex ratio varies from 104 to 108 males for

every 100 females. We would like to know why, but as yet we have not the slightest inkling of the truth. Under the chromosome theory there ought to be an equal number of male-producing and of female-producing sperms, and if there is no differential viability of fertilizing power between them, the sex ratio ought to be equality. But one must face the facts, and the truth is that there is an excess of males born alive among the people of every race. And if premature births only are considered, this excess is sometimes as high as 50 per cent.

Possibly equal numbers of each sex are produced at fertilization, and a considerable proportion of the females eliminated at early stages of gestation because they find this particular portion of the life cycle difficult to pass. Such an assumption would account for the disproportionate number of males at later ages, and also, from the early elimination of feeble females, for the fact that the so-called weaker sex is really the stronger sex and has a lower death rate from birth to old age. The theory is submitted here because it is worth investigating, and it is thought that some of our readers may possess the necessary data to confirm or to refute it.

Slight differences in the sex ratio which can be accounted for by selective elimination of the weaker sex do not disturb the view of sex-determination through the chromosomes very seriously, but what is one to say of the experiments of Richard Hertwig [7] and Miss Helen King? [8] Hertwig obtained as high as 100 per cent of male frogs when he delayed the fertilization of frogs' eggs until they were overripe and had taken up large quantities of water. Conversely, Miss King obtained 80 per cent of females, with a mortality of only 6 per cent, by lowering the water content of the eggs of toads.

[7] R. Hertwig, "Uber den derzeitigen Stand des Sexualitäts problems nebst einigen Untersuchungen." *Biol. Centr.* 32, 1912.

[8] H. D. King. "Studies on Sex-Determination in Amphibians." V. *Jour. Exp. Zool.,* 12, 1912.

Miss King [9] also obtained some very strange results in an experiment with a strain of white rats in which the sex ratio is normally 105 males to 100 females. By selection, a male-producing strain was originated in which the sex ratio was 122 males to 100 females. Selection in the reverse direction, on the other hand, resulted in a strain of female-producers in which the sex ratio was only 82 males to 100 females.

Not less confusing are the experiments of Riddle with pigeons and of Goldschmidt [10] with the gypsy moth. In pigeons more or less complete sex reversal apparently can be forced by changing the environmental conditions after fertilization has taken place and development begun. Goldschmidt has even found strong-male and weak-male, and strong-female and weak-female races of the gypsy moth, in which the various possible matings give different results in both the primary and the secondary sexual characters of the progeny.

Still more of an enigma is the remarkable case of sex reversal reported by Crew [11] in Scotland. It is an authentic case of "functional" sex change occurring in poultry. The word functional should be emphasized because numerous instances of superficial changes in the sex organs have been found among human beings, but in no case has an individual become both a father and a mother. The facts are as follows: A hen which had laid eggs and hatched chicks from them later took on the appearance and behavior of a cock. Mated with a hen, the erstwhile mother became the father of two chicks, one a male, the other a female. A post-mortem examination showed that the ovary had been destroyed by a tumor and male organs had developed.

[9] H. D. King, "The Sex-Ratio in Hybrid Rats," *Biol. Bull.*, 21, 1911.

[10] The points of view of Riddle and of Goldschmidt are given in *The Mechanism and Physiology of Sex Determination* by R. Goldschmidt, translated by W. J. Dakin. London: Methuen, 1923.

[11] F. A. E. Crew. "Complete Sex-Transformation in the Domestic Fowl." *Jour. Heredity*, 14:361, 362, 1923.

These data are somewhat contradictory, it is true. But one must expect contradictions. Life is complex. What we must hold fast is that the two sexual states, maleness and femaleness, are not mutually exclusive. They are quantitative characters like many others with which the geneticist has to deal. The germ-cells in numerous species have become male-determiners and female-determiners respectively in the sense that they have inherited qualities which in ordinary circumstances hold the balance of power in the control of sex. Generally speaking, they cast the deciding vote; but there may be a recount.

Perhaps an illustration will make our meaning plainer. One may think of men or of women as possessing attributes both of maleness and of femaleness. The controlling power which makes one actually a man and the other actually a woman is inherited constitution. The possessor of one X chromosome is a man, the possessor of two X chromosomes is a woman. And this chromosome distribution has so far shifted the balance of conditions that no environmental changes can reverse it. In some of the lower animals the balance of the sex complex is not shifted thus far by the particular inheritance received. Under extraordinary circumstances, conditions may be such that the sex is really changed.

In these lower forms where the influence of external conditions is relatively great, there is still a considerable possibility that man may be able to control sex at will. The possibility is slight, but the hope is there. That man will ever be able to control the sex of his own offspring is improbable. The possibility remains, like that of making gold, but the chances weigh heavily against it. And to tell the truth, the first is about as undesirable as the second. The one would result in a terrible economic muddle, the other would bring about a social chaos.

There is, as we have seen, a plethora of evidence that the principal determinant of the characters of all animals and

plants which reproduce sexually is the chromatin. Because
chromatin is distributed in a particular manner at reproduction, inheritance is what it is. In other words, the ordinary
mechanism of heredity is furnished by sex. And now, paradoxically enough, sexuality is found to furnish the means
by which the two sexes inherit their differences. The evidence
which has been cited is only a fragmentary sample. Direct
experimental proof has been made on dozens and dozens
of species. Is there, then, good reason for doubting Thomases
to be skeptical of the philosophy of genetics and to equivocate
concerning its application to human affairs?

Do these genetic ideas of sex throw any light on the ever-
popular question as to the relative capacity of man and
woman? It seems to me that they do. The heritage of the
female is precisely that of the male in 46 of the 48 packets
of genes which each possesses. The distinction between them
is that the female possesses two X chromosomes, while the
male possesses one X and one Y. It is possible that the extra
X does something more than make its possessor a female,
but this is not genetically probable, for usually one member
of a pair of chromosomes functions as well as, and similar to,
both members of the pair. It is likewise possible that the Y
chromosome possesses other functions than that of giving
maleness to its possessor, but no such additional duties have
been demonstrated except in the case of certain fishes.

Man and woman are different. Yes. Havelock Ellis [12] has
demonstrated that the differences in the sex glands and the
hormones they release produce radical alterations of the whole
structure. Woman is different from man from the crown of
her head to the soles of her feet, but presumably all of these
distinguishing marks are merely sex. There is no crucial evidence that either is more capable than the other in logical
thinking or capacity of making intelligent adjustments in
life. It would be odd if there were a psychological differentia-

[12] Havelock Ellis, *Man and Woman.* New York: Charles Scribner's
Sons, 5th ed., 1914.

tion other than one useful in the matter of reproduction and care of the young, for Nature is not usually careless and purposeless.

What then are we to make of the historical fact that men have done more creative work than women? How are we to interpret the undeniable truth that men have furnished the great constructive geniuses? Emotionally, women are great; witness the long roll of celebrated actresses ending with Bernhardt and Duse. But there are no philosophers among women. And in science and the arts there are few names to conjure with. The work of Madame Curie is not to be compared with that of Rutherford, though their special interests have been the same. Women inventors are rare, and are distinctly below the highest grade. Madame Le Brun and Rosa Bonheur make a sorry showing beside Rembrandt and Velasquez. Even the great designers of women's clothes have been men, as has often been noted with great glee by militant males.

I cannot persuade myself that these specific data are decisive. It may be that women labor under a physiological handicap which makes it more difficult for them to do sustained constructive work of the highest type. Their part in weaving the thread of life is overheavy. But it is doubtful whether woman's specialization as potential mother or that considerable part of her life devoted to actual motherhood means any more than a comparative lack of opportunity for other pursuits. The tyranny of old folkways has kept her out of competition with men. If we could make a true comparison of the eminence attained by men and women in proportion to their opportunities, the story might be quite different. Think of the millions of men entering the crafts, the tens of thousands entering the arts, the thousands entering the sciences. How many of them attain prominence? Naturally, very few. Similarly estimated, particularly if relative opportunity for training is given due weight, it is possible that women would show a record of past greatness in as high proportions as have men.

In the future, men had best look to their laurels. Customs are changing. Opportunities are increasing. More and more women are entering the world arena. And Terman's studies [13] appear to show that they are just as capable as their brothers.

[13] L. M. Terman *et al.*, *Studies of Genius, I. Mental and Physical Traits of a Thousand Gifted Children.* Calif.: Stanford University Press, 1925.

EUGENICS [1]

By Franz Boas

THE possibility of raising the standards of human physique and mentality by judicious means has been preached for years by the apostles of eugenics, and has taken hold of the public mind to such an extent that eugenic measures have found a place on the statute books of a number of states, and that the public conscience disapproves of marriages that are thought bound to produce unhealthy offspring.

The thought that it may be possible by these means to eliminate suffering and to strive for higher ideals is a beautiful one, and makes a strong appeal to those who have at heart the advance of humanity.

Our experiences in stock and plant breeding have shown that it is feasible, by appropriate selection, to change a breed in almost any direction that we may choose: in size, form, color. Even physiological functions may be modified. Fertility may be increased, speed of movement improved, the sensitiveness of sense organs modified, and mental traits may be turned in special directions. It is, therefore, more than probable that similar results might be obtained in man by careful mating of appropriately selected individuals—provided that man allowed himself to be selected in the same manner as we select animals. We have also the right to assume that, by preventing the propagation of mentally or physically inferior strains, the gross average standing of a population may be raised.

Although these methods sound attractive, there are serious limitations to their applicability. Eugenic selection can affect

[1] From *Anthropology and Modern Life*. New York: W. W. Norton & Company, 1928.

only hereditary features. If an individual possesses a desirable quality the development of which is wholly due to environmental causes, and that will not be repeated in the descendants, its selection will have no influence upon the following generations. It is, therefore, of fundamental importance to know what is hereditary and what not. Features, and color of eyes, hair and skin, are more or less rigidly hereditary; in other words, in these respects children resemble organically their parents, no matter in what environment they may have been brought up. In other cases, however, the determining influence of heredity is not clear. We know that stature depends upon hereditary causes, but that it is also greatly influenced by environmental conditions prevailing during the period of growth. Rapidity of development is no less influenced by these two causes, and in general the more subject an anatomical or physiological trait to the influence of environment the less definitely can we speak of a controlling influence of heredity, and the less are we justified in claiming that nature, not nurture, is the deciding element.

It would seem, therefore, that the first duty of the eugenist should be to determine empirically and without bias what features are hereditary and what not.

Unfortunately this has not been the method pursued; but the battle cry of the eugenists, "Nature not nurture," has been raised to the rank of a dogma, and the environmental conditions that make and unmake man, physically and mentally, have been relegated to the background.

It is easy to see that in many cases environmental causes may convey the erroneous impression of hereditary phenomena. Poor people develop slowly and remain short of stature as compared to wealthy people. We find, therefore, in a poor area apparently a low hereditary stature, that, however, would change if the economic life of the people were changed. We find proportions of the body determined by occupations, and apparently transmitted from father to son, provided both father and son follow the same occupation. The more far-reaching the environmental influences are that act upon successive generations the more readily will a false impression of heredity be given.

Here we reach a parting of the ways of the biological eugenist and the student of human society. Most modern biologists are so entirely dominated by the notion that function depends upon form that they seek for an anatomical basis for all differences of function. The stress laid upon the relation between anatomical form or constitution and pathological conditions of the most varied character are an expression of this tendency. Whenever the anatomical and pathological conditions are actually physiologically interdependent such relations are found. In other cases, as, for instance, in the relation of anatomical form and mental disturbances, the relation may be quite remote. This is still more the case when a relation between social phenomena and bodily form is sought. Many biologists are inclined to assume that higher civilization is due to a higher type; that better social health depends solely upon a better hereditary stock; that national characteristics are determined by the bodily forms represented in the nation.

The anthropologist is convinced that many different anatomical forms can be adapted to the same social functions; and he ascribes greater weight to these and believes that in many cases differences of form may be due to adaptations to different functions. He believes that different types of man may reach the same civilization, that better health may be produced by better bringing up of any of the existing types of man.

The anatomical differences to which the biologist reduces social phenomena are hereditary; the environmental causes which the anthropologist sees reflected in human form are individually acquired, and not transmitted by heredity.

In view of what has been said before it will suffice to point out a very few examples.

Sameness of language is acquired under the same linguistic

environment by members of the most diverse human types; the same kinds of foods are selected from among the products of nature by people belonging to the same cultural area; similarity of movements is required in industrial pursuits; the habits of sedentary or nomadic life do not depend upon race but upon occupation. All of these are distributed without any reference to physical type, and give ample evidence of the lack of relation between social habits and racial position.

The serious demand must be made that eugenists cease to look at the forms, functions, and activities of man from the dogmatic point of view according to which each feature is assumed to be hereditary, but that they begin to examine them from a more critical point of view, requiring that in each and every case the hereditary character of a trait must be established before it can be assumed to exist.

The question at issue is well illustrated by the extended statistics of cacogenics, of the histories of defective families. Setting aside for a moment cases of hereditary pathological conditions, we find that alcoholism and criminality are particularly ascribed to hereditary causes. When we study the family histories in question, we can see often that if the individuals had been protected by favorable home surroundings and by possession of adequate means of support against the abuse of alcohol or other drugs as well as against criminality, many of them would have been no more likely to fall victims to their alleged hereditary tendencies than many a weakling who is brought up under favorable circumstances. If they had resisted the temptations of their environment they would have been entitled to be classed as moral heroes. The scales applied to the criminal family and to the well-to-do are clearly quite distinct; and, so far as heredity is concerned, not much more follows from the collected data of social deficiencies than would follow from the fact that in an agricultural community the occupation of farmers descends from father to son.

Whether or not constitutional debility based on hereditary

causes may also be proved in these cases is a question by itself that deserves attention. It remains to be proved in how far it exists, and furthermore it cannot be assumed without proof that the elimination of the descendants of delinquents would free us of all those who possess equal constitutional debility. Of these matters more anon.

It is an observed fact that the most diverse types of man may adapt themselves to the same forms of life and, unless the contrary can be proved, we must assume that all complex activities are socially determined, not hereditary; that a change in social conditions will change the whole character of social activities without influencing in the least the hereditary characteristics of the group of individuals concerned. Therefore, when the attempt is made to prove that defects or points of excellence are hereditary, it is essential that all possibility of a purely environmentally or socially determined repetition of ancestral traits be excluded.

If this rigidity of proof is insisted on it will appear that many of the data on which the theory of eugenics is based are unsatisfactory, and that much greater care must be exerted than finds favor with the enthusiastic adherents of eugenic theories.

All this does not contradict the hereditary transmission of individual physical and mental characteristics, or the possibility of segregating, by proper selection from among the large series of varying individual forms that occur among all types of people, strains that have admirable qualities, and of suppressing others that are not so favored.

It is claimed that the practical application has become a necessity because among all civilized nations there is a decided tendency to general degeneration. I do not believe that this assertion has been adequately proved. In modern society the conditions of life have become markedly varied as compared with those of former periods. While some groups live under most favorable conditions that require active use of body and mind, others live in abject poverty, and their activities have more than ever before been degraded to those of machines. At the same time, human activities are much more varied than formerly. It is, therefore, quite intelligible that the functional activities of each nation must show an increased degree of differentiation, a higher degree of variability. The general average of the mental and physical types of the people may remain the same, still there will be a larger number now than formerly who fall below a certain given low standard, while there will also be more who exceed a given high standard. The number of defectives can be counted by statistics of poor relief, delinquency and insanity, but there is no way of determining the increase of those individuals who are raised above the norm of a higher standard. Therefore they escape our notice. It may very well be that the number of defectives increases, without, however, influencing the value of a population as a whole, because it is merely an expression of an increased degree of variability.

Furthermore, arbitrarily selected, absolute standards do not retain their significance. Even if no change in the absolute standard should be made, the degree of physical and mental energy required under modern conditions to keep one's self above a certain minimum of achievement is higher than formerly. This is due to the greater complexity of our life and to the increasing number of competing individuals. When the general level of achievement is raised, greater capacity is required to attain a high degree of prominence than was needed in earlier periods of our history. A mentally defective person may be able to hold his own in a simple farming community and unable to do so in city life. The claim that we have to contend against national degeneracy must, therefore, be better substantiated than it is now.

This problem is further complicated by the advances of public hygiene, which have lowered infant mortality, and have changed the composition of the population, in so far as many who would have succumbed to deleterious conditions in early years enter into the adult population and have an influence upon the general distribution of vitality.

There is still another important aspect of eugenics that should make us pause before we accept this new ambitious theory as a panacea for human ills. The radical eugenist treats the problem of procreation from a purely rationalistic point of view, and assumes that the ideal of human development lies in the complete rationalization of human life. As a matter of fact, the conclusions to be drawn from the study of the customs and habits of mankind show that such an ideal is unattainable, and more particularly that the emotions clustering about procreation belong to those that are most deeply seated, and that are ineradicable.

Here again the anthropologist and the biologist are at odds. The natural sciences do not recognize in their scheme a valuation of the phenomena of nature, nor do they count emotions as moving forces; they endeavor to reduce all happenings to the actions of physical causes. Reason alone reigns in their domain. Therefore the scientist likes to look at mental life from the same rational standpoint, and sees as the goal of human development an era of reason, as opposed to the former periods of unhealthy fantastic emotion.

The anthropologist, on the other hand, cannot acknowledge such a complete domination of emotion by reason. He rather sees the steady advance of the rational knowledge of mankind, which is a source of satisfaction to him no less than to the biologist; but he sees also that mankind does not put this knowledge to purely reasonable use, but that its actions are swayed by emotions no less now than in former times, although in many respects, unless the passions are excited, the increase of knowledge limits the extreme forms of unreasonable emotional activities. Religion and political life, and our everyday habits, present endless proofs of the fact that our actions are the results of emotional preferences, that conform in a general way to our rational knowledge, but which are not determined by reason; that we rather try to justify our choice of action by reason than have our actions dictated by reason.

It is, therefore, exceedingly unlikely that a rational control of one of the strongest passions of man could ever succeed. If even in matters of minor importance evasion of the law is of common occurrence, this would be infinitely more common in questions that touch our inner life so deeply. The repugnance against eugenic legislation is based on this feeling.

It cannot be doubted that the enforcement of eugenic legislation would have a far-reaching effect upon social life, and that it would tend to raise the standard of certain selected hereditary strains. It is, however, an open question what would happen to the selected strains owing to the changed social ideal; and it is inexcusable to refuse to consider those fundamental changes that would certainly be connected with eugenic practice, and to confine ourselves to the biological effect that may be wrought, for in the great mass of a healthy population the biological mechanism alone does not control social activities. They are rather subject to social stimuli.

Although we are ignorant of the results of a rigid application of eugenics, a few of its results may be foretold with great certainty.

The eugenist who tries to do more than to eliminate the unfit will first of all be called upon to answer the question what strains are the best to cultivate. If it is a question of breeding chickens or Indian corn, we know what we want. We desire many eggs of heavy weight, or a large yield of good corn. But what do we want in man? Is it physical excellence, mental ability, creative power, or artistic genius? We must select certain ideals that we want to raise. Considering then the fundamental differences in ideals of distinct types of civilization, have we a right to give to our modern ideals the stamp of finality, and suppress what does not fit into our life? There is little doubt that we, at the

present time, give much less weight to beauty than to logic.
Shall we then try to raise a generation of logical thinkers,
suppress those whose emotional life is vigorous, and try to
bring it about that reason shall reign supreme, and that
human activities shall be performed with clocklike precision?
The precise cultural forms that would develop cannot be
foretold, because they are culturally, not biologically, determined; but there is little doubt that within certain limits
the intensity of emotional life,—regardless of its form,—and
the vigor of logical thought,—regardless of its content,—
could be increased or decreased by organic selection. Such a
deliberate choice of qualities which would modify the character of nations implies an overestimation of the standards
that we have reached, which to my mind appears intolerable.
Personally the logical thinker may be most congenial to me,
nevertheless I respect the sacred ideal of the dreamer who
lives in a world of musical tones, and whose creative power
is to me a marvel that surpasses understanding.

Without a selection of standards, eugenic practice is impossible; but if we read the history of mankind aright, we
ought to hesitate before we try to set our standards for all
time to come, for they are only one phase in the development
of mankind.

This consideration applies only to our right to apply creative eugenic principles, not to the question whether practical
results by eugenic selection can be attained. I have pointed
out before how much in this respect is still hypothetical, or
at least of doubtful value, because the social factors out-
weigh the biological ones.

At the present time the idea of creating the best human
types by selective mating is hardly a practical one. It dwells
only as a desirable ideal in the minds of some enthusiasts.

The immediate application of eugenics is rather concerned
in eliminating strains that are a burden to the nation or to
themselves, and in raising the standard of humanity by the
suppression of the progeny of the defective classes. I am

doubtful whether eugenics alone will have material results in this direction, for, in view of the fundamental influence of environmental causes, that I set forth before, it is perfectly safe to say that no amount of eugenic selection will overcome those social conditions that have raised a poverty- and disease-stricken proletariat,—which will be reborn from even the best stock, so long as the social conditions persist that remorselessly push human beings into helpless and hopeless misery. The effect would probably be to push new groups of individuals into the deadly environment where they would take the place of the eliminated defectives. Whether they would breed new generations of defectives may be an open question. The continued presence of defectives would be a certainty. Eugenics alone cannot solve the problem. It requires much more an amelioration of the social conditions of the poor which would also raise many of the apparently defective to higher levels.

The present state of our knowledge of heredity permits us to say that certain pathological conditions are hereditary and that apparently healthy parents who belong to defective strains are very likely to have among their descendants defective individuals. We may even predict for a number of such cases how many among the descendants will be normal and how many defective. The eugenist must decide whether he wants to suppress all the normal individuals in these families in order to avoid the development of the defectives, or whether he is willing to carry the defectives along, perhaps as a burden to society, to their relatives and in many cases even to themselves, for the sake of the healthy children of such families. This question cannot be decided from a scientific point of view. The answer depends upon ethical and social standards. Many defective families have produced individuals who have given us the greatest treasures our civilization possesses. Eugenists might have prevented Beethoven's father from having children. Would they willingly take the responsibility of having mankind deprived of the genius of Beethoven? Another aspect of the problem is of much more vital importance to mankind. The object of eugenics is to raise a better race and to do away with increasing suffering by eliminating those who are by heredity destined to suffer and to cause suffering. The humanitarian idea of the conquest of suffering, and the ideal of raising human efficiency to heights never before reached, make eugenics particularly attractive.

I believe that the human mind and body are so constituted that the attainment of these ends would lead to the destruction of society. The wish for the elimination of unnecessary suffering is divided by a narrow margin from the wish for the elimination of all suffering.

While, humanely speaking, this may be a beautiful ideal, it is unattainable. The performance of the labors of mankind and the conflicts of duties will always be accompanied by suffering that must be borne, and that men must be willing to bear. Many of the works of sublime beauty are the precious fruit of mental agony: and we should be poor, indeed, if the willingness of man to suffer should disappear. However, if we cultivate this ideal, then that which was discomfort yesterday will be suffering today, and the elimination of discomforts will lead to an effeminacy that must be disastrous to the race.

This effect is further emphasized by the increasing demands for self-perfection. The more complex our civilization and the more extended our technical skill and our knowledge, the more energy is demanded for reaching the highest efficiency, and the less is it admissible that the working capacity of the individual should be diminished by suffering. We are clearly drifting towards that danger-line where the individual will no longer bear discomfort or pain for the sake of the continuance of the race, and where our emotional life is so strongly repressed by the desire for self-perfection,—or by self-indulgence,—that the coming generation is sacrificed to the selfishness of the living. The phenomenon that characterized the end of antiquity, when no children were born to take the place of the passing generations, is being repeated in our times and in ever widening circles; and the more vigorously the eugenic ideals of the elimination of suffering and of self-development are held up the sooner shall we drift towards the destruction of the race.

Eugenics should, therefore, not be allowed to deceive us into the belief that we should try to raise a race of supermen, nor that it should be our aim to eliminate all suffering and pain. The attempt to suppress those defective classes whose deficiencies can be proved by rigid methods to be due to hereditary causes, and to prevent unions that will unavoidably lead to the birth of disease-stricken progeny, is the proper field of eugenics. How much can be and should be attempted in this field depends upon the results of careful studies of the laws of heredity. Eugenics is not a panacea that will cure human ills; it is rather a dangerous sword that may turn its edge against those who rely on its strength.

RACE CONSCIOUSNESS AND EUGENICS [1]

By André Siegfried

Up to the beginning of the twentieth century, America believed in the theory of environment which was fashionable at that time, but when the Melting Pot began to overflow with immigrants she adopted the views of Mendel and de Gobineau. Their theories were popularized by brilliant writers who converted a large following to the thesis that, in the long run, heredity is the most important factor, and that the hierarchy of races with the Nordics in the lead is an established scientific fact. Eugenics, which in reality is a mixture of biology and politics, looked to this doctrine for a scientific basis on which to develop the future American race. This was quite in keeping with the nationalistic reaction that has taken place since the war. If you visit the United States you must not forget your Bible, but you must also take a treatise on eugenics. Armed with these two talismans, you will never get beyond your depth.

Lothrop Stoddard [2] and Madison Grant [3] have spread these ideas throughout America in their widely read books. They have firmly implanted the theory that civilization, like a delicate flower, survives only as the result of continuous human energy; for its creative force depends on superior germ plasm. Fundamentally, therefore, it varies with the race. In our day we are no longer menaced by invasions of hordes of barbarians, but peaceable penetration by inferior

[1] From *America Comes of Age*. Harcourt, Brace and Company, 1927.
[2] *The Rising Tide of Color* and *The Revolt Against Civilization*, by Lothrop Stoddard. New York: Charles Scribner's Sons.
[3] *The Passing of the Great Race*, by Madison Grant. New York: Charles Scribner's Sons.

human elements is an insidious danger that is equally formidable. The backward peoples of the world are the most prolific, just as they are often the most vigorous physically. They are attracted to civilized centers by high wages and better living conditions, but their advent spells disaster, for they dislocate the established order of things and sterilize the original superior races. The mingling of the races is equally fatal, as it undermines the ethnic foundations of civilization and introduces a mongrel strain which leads to decadence. Today everyone knows that acquired characteristics cannot be handed down to posterity, and as the influence of environment is strictly limited, the individual cannot pass on more than he has actually received from his ancestors. The supreme importance of heredity is the great biological discovery of modern times.

According to this theory, what can we expect from the influx of immigrants into the United States? Since 1890 they have been mostly of inferior races that do not amalagamate, and though they may have individual qualifications they also have definite limitations. History shows that the inferior races multiply on account of their vast inferiority, whereas the superior do not tend to perpetuate themselves. The aristocracy of America is thus in jeopardy, for we might almost say that the race is giving way to another that is being surreptitiously substituted for it. If we write Anglo-Saxon in place of "superior," and Slav, Latin, or Mediterranean instead of "inferior," without mentioning Negroes or Asiatics, we have the political aspect of this scientific theory, in fact the doctrine of the Ku Klux Klan. Once we admit that superiority can be transmitted only through blood, we arrive at the same conclusion as the eugenists, that the character of the race must be preserved by legal measures. The Spartans were striving for the same ends when they evolved the theory that the race could be improved only by eliminating the mediocre and multiplying the best elements. It is interesting to note that the idea of caste which has been rejected by Europe appears attractive to certain Americans.

The attitude toward natality is bound to be entirely different in France and the United States. For political and military reasons our great ground of anxiety is a decrease in the total population, but this does not apply in America, where, according to the Malthusian doctrines inherited from England, an excess of population is regarded as an evil. Public opinion there is alarmed by the fact that in the South and certain parts of the West, the Anglo-Saxon stock is not reproducing itself, whereas the birth rate among the immigrants is high. In Massachusetts, for example, the foreign-born woman is twice as prolific as the American-born. After a thorough investigation, Professors Ross and Baber discovered that in the middle class of the central states, which is purely American, the families of the present generation have decreased 38½ per cent in size as compared with the previous one; 13 per cent of the marriages are childless, and 18 per cent have only one child. On the other hand, among the Czecho-Slovak immigrants only 2.4 per cent of the homes are childless, 2.5 per cent among the Russians, 2.6 per cent among the Poles, 3.9 per cent among the Germans, and 4.9 per cent among the Italians.

In certain classes of Americans, reproduction seems almost to have ceased. Intellectuals and university graduates marry late and have practically no descendants. Sixty per cent of the women with university degrees do not marry at all; of those who do, 36 per cent have no children, or in other words, three-fifths of the most cultured women do not leave descendants. These figures have been published and quoted all over the country. Professors Ross and Baber come to the melancholy conclusion that the old Anglo-Saxon element is diminishing, not merely absolutely, but also relatively, and that in a century it is probable that it will only constitute a negligible factor in the American population. In view of these incontestable facts, the eugenists prophesy dire results. On the basis of the present ratio, 1,000 Harvard graduates, according to Dr. Davenport, will have only fifty descendants at the end of two centuries, whereas 1,000 Rumanians in Boston will have 100,000.

These sensational deductions, so dear to the New World, do not take into account the changes that are operating among the immigrants themselves. When their standard of living is raised by assimilation, they also adopt the customs of the country as regards natality. The second generation still has more children than the original inhabitants, but the fecundity of the third and fourth differs very slightly from the general level of the country. All these pessimistic calculations, though they are obvious exaggerations, favor the foreigner as against the American, the Catholic as against the Protestant. The present attitude of the 100 per cent American, in the towns at any rate, is fatal for his race. When he has few children or none at all, he excuses himself by saying that he cannot afford more, that there would be so many difficulties about housing and servants, and he really has to buy a car; or else his wife's professional career makes a family inadvisable. Also, in many cases, marriage comes too late in life, and the sex relation therefore is only secondary. The problem is not so much depopulation as maintaining the racial equilibrium, and the danger of the present race's being replaced by another. The two chief influences reacting on American thought are the neo-Malthusian or birth control movement on the one hand, and the Catholic Church which preaches unrestricted fecundity on the other. Morals, hygiene, and social welfare are the arguments invoked by both sides, but underneath it all lie political considerations; for it is this question that will decide the center of gravity of the nation in the future.

As in England, the birth control propaganda has been conducted in the spirit of a crusade, supported chiefly by the intellectuals, often from among the best people, and by a few fanatics. It is difficult to understand why they should be so vehement, for after all the average Protestant was converted long ago to voluntary birth control. Quite apart from theory, experience has taught them that nothing is more deplorable than a heavy birth rate coinciding with a heavy death rate, and that large families are apt to be a charge on the community. Anyway, the world has quite enough of the lowest classes already, certainly if a decent standard of living is to be maintained. The Malthusians accordingly concentrate their efforts on the "poor whites" of the Alleghanies and the South, and more especially on the aliens of the first and second generation, who through either their own ignorance or the influence of their priests leave nature to determine the size of their families. Good or bad, the real meaning of the propaganda is that the inferiors have many children, the superiors few, to reëstablish the balance by trying to increase the fecundity of the superiors would be both undesirable and hopeless, although it is possible to slow up the reproductive speed of the inferiors. These are the ideas that are taught at the special clinics of the Birth Control League. Their activities correspond perfectly to the outlook of the responsible classes who have taken it on themselves to care for the poor. If some humorist were to propose a Conference on the International Limitation of Births, the Americans would take up the idea in a twinkling!

The eugenic movement, which was originated in England by Francis Galton, has become quite important in the United States during the past twenty years. After making due allowance for the exaggeration of the enthusiasts, we must admit that it expresses the American line of thought exactly, and therefore we should not be astonished if a new code of racial ethics and reproduction laws should be evolved from it. The eugenist lays stress on the importance of heredity in the development of the individual. He maintains that nothing can replace inborn qualities, and that it is futile to try to develop any particular traits if the character lacks the initial germ. Hence, if we wish to improve the race, we must determine which individuals should be allowed to reproduce. There is thus to be a rational selection based on biology and not on individual sentiment, for the matter is of too great consequence to be left to the caprices of ir-responsible people. The program is to consist of medical, legal, and social measures designed to bring about an increase in the number of children from the superior grades of society, a decrease in the number from the inferior grades, and an absolute cessation from those below a certain mental and physical level.

The effect of such a movement is enormous. It means creating a new eugenic conscience and involves a code of morals based on reproduction, which is practically non-existent at present. The eugenists go even further and pro-pose to legislate to reduce degeneracy and so deliberately construct a new race. The Americans love the classical Greek ideals, and in their sanctimonious way they are always ready to accept a theory if they think it is scientific. In fairness we must add that like their British cousins, thoughtful Ameri-cans possess a strong racial sense. For example, look at the way they keep the Negroes and Asiatics in their place, and even the Portuguese and Mediterraneans, if they suspect them of a touch of the tar-brush. For over a generation the idea has been growing among them that a superior race is under a moral obligation to maintain its ascendancy and produce offspring that are healthy and free from doubtful strains. This is not exactly a religious ideal, but the Protestant churches encourage it; for they consider themselves rather the élite, and extol anything that is considered pure. Neither is it entirely a matter of nationalism, for an American looks on reproduction from much the same angle as a breeder of dogs.

The European individualist resents having his most inti-mate relations organized for the good of the community, but the reformers of the New World hope to make short work of "passion," for they have made such magnificent progress that they are beginning to believe they can accomplish everything. Efficiency has such prestige on the American side of the Atlantic that all objections are set aside, and even the most extreme measures are approved in its name. Eugenics, in fact, is part of what in the United States is called "service."

A whole system of new legislation is being developed on the subject. Many of the measures no doubt are not eugenic, but simply social hygiene, such as for example the law in Wisconsin that makes pre-nuptial examination obligatory. Other laws are eugenic in their effect, although they were originally adopted for very different reasons. When the law of 1911 in Nevada orders a murderer to be sterilized as a punishment it is simply a matter of repression, but it is pure and simple eugenics when similar laws are applied either to favor the reproduction of the better elements or to prevent it among the feeble-minded. Sterilizing to improve the race is like restricting immigration to exclude certain races. Both are distinctly eugenic.

Eugenic sterilization aims to destroy the reproductive capacity of the individual by means of certain surgical operations which are carried out in accordance with the law, and which are used principally in cases of degeneracy such as lunatics and criminals. "Vasectomy" and "salpingectomy," as these operations are termed, are not the same as castration; for the patient can still have sexual intercourse, although he cannot produce children. Since 1907, twenty-three states have passed laws of this nature, and they were still being applied in 1926 in nineteen [4] of them.

A certain amount of confusion as to the exact objective is apparent in the declarations of various legislatures. In Nevada the intention was only to punish criminals guilty of raping girls of less than six years of age. Such vengeance against

[4] California, Connecticut, Delaware, Idaho, Iowa, Kansas, Maine, Michigan, Minnesota, Montana, Nebraska, New Hampshire, North Dakota, Oregon, South Dakota, Utah, Virginia, Washington, Wisconsin. In four other states, Indiana, Nevada, New Jersey, and New York, the laws have either been declared unconstitutional or repealed.

sex is undoubtedly puritanical, but when people came forward voluntarily to be sterilized it was decided that it was not always a punishment; and the courts ruled the law unconstitutional. On the other hand, the operation was considered legal when the aim was the improvement of the race rather than punishment. The legislation actually in force at the present time comes under this category, as it is applied to idiots, incurable degenerates of all kinds who are not necessarily shut up in asylums, second offenders in cases of certain crimes, and the irresponsible and vicious who, if given their liberty, would probably procreate undesirables.

The ambition of the eugenists reaches still further. When the diagnosis of depravity has been finally perfected, they hope by legal sterilization to eliminate not only idiots and degenerates, but also drunkards, tubercular persons, syphilitics, epileptics, and even the blind, the deaf, hunchbacks, and in a general way all potential parents of inadequate offspring. As in the case of vaccination, the individual will be forced to submit for the welfare of the community. But is such a program legal? Does it not violate the rights of the individual as laid down in the Constitution? In the states where such legislation has been confirmed as constitutional by the courts, it has been decided that the decision of a criminal court or of a committee of doctors from an asylum or a hospital is sufficient guarantee that the operation is advisable. In Indiana, Nevada, New Jersey, and New York, however, these laws have been declared unconstitutional, because they do not grant to every citizen the legal recourse laid down in the Fourteenth Amendment to the Federal Constitution. The controversy goes back to fundamentals, for if a state were to assume the right to compel the individual arbitrarily, it would mean the beginning of a new epoch in human civilization.

We are far from this, however, for legal sterilization is still very restricted. Up to July 1, 1925, there had been altogether 6,244 operations, of which 4,636 were in California,

355 in Kansas, 313 in Oregon, and 262 in Nebraska. We must not overlook the fact that in future the rights of the individual will be protected less by the text of the law than by the interpretation of judges who are apt to be sensitive to the pressure of public opinion. If we inquire into what the public thinks of such extreme ideas, we discover that there has never been any popular demand for them. In order to vote a eugenic law, it is generally sufficient for it to be taken up by a few individuals, such as the director of the Board of Health, a prominent surgeon, and some university professors. The text is drawn by this handful of experts and is then quietly passed by the local legislature, always provided, of course, no organized opposition is stirred up. Hostility to such laws has generally come from the Catholic clergy, who maintain that the community has no right to prevent the birth of a human being. Doctors also have protested occasionally, and governors have even opposed their veto; but generally the public has not been aroused. The specialists tell them that the measure is for the welfare of the community, and they remind the taxpayers what it costs the budget to care for the scum of humanity. In any case, as the Americans are imbued with the spirit of progress, they are quite willing to vote a new law even if they never apply it.

In spite of these reservations, the eugenic movement is typical of present-day America, for it indicates a keen, though not necessarily intelligent, preoccupation with the future of the race. Against such considerations the rights of the individual are powerless, for by a sort of mysticism America considers the needs of the community supreme. Ever since Plato's *Republic*, this collective spirit has lain dormant, or at best has been maintained by a few dreamers. In the hands of a people who are conscious of their superiority and are ready to sterilize remorselessly Negroes and Asiatics, or in fact any inferior races, eugenics may eventually relegate the "sacred rights of man" to the limbo of half-forgotten achievements.

VI

THE PROBLEM OF BIRTH CONTROL

ARE TEN TOO MANY? [1]

By Marjorie Wells

I suppose I am old-fashioned. I am quite sure many of my friends and neighbors think so, while some of them do not stop at so kindly and sympathetic a judgment. I am aware sometimes of their pity, condescension and amusement, and even of contempt and a veiled antagonism.

The reason is that I have a large family, stretching already as far as the eye can reach and with the end not yet in sight. In an age when two or three children are considered the civilized and respectable achievement, I have ten to date and am still unchastened and unrepentant. I am even mildly ostentatious about it, and find a reprehensible satisfaction in projecting my oversized family like a bombshell into polite society, where it is variously greeted with congratulation, consternation, interrogation or condemnation. The friendlier reactions concede that this is indeed an old-fashioned family, supposedly endowed with indefinite but admirable old-fashioned virtues and advantages. But I am aware of other attitudes beneath the polite surprise or careful congratulations of casual conversation. There are those who clearly count me as no better than a deluded female, unkindly outlawed from the pleasures and privileges of modern life by an unfortunate biological habit. There are some who would weep for me and with me, if I gave them but half a chance. There are others who probably think me a scab and blackleg, traitor and backslider, in these days of feminine emancipation.

I have no intention of apologizing for my family. I have never done so nor tried to keep it a secret, which would in

[1] From the *North American Review*, March, 1929.

fact be difficult. I am, indeed, candidly and brazenly proud of it. A large family is liable to have that effect upon its perpetrator and proprietor. All ordinary parents are publicly proud of two children or even three. Most parents become a little reticent about five or six. But when the score mounts up to nine or ten, parental pride gets a second wind. There is something monumental about such a family, and it is asking too much of human nature to expect its parents to keep it entirely to themselves.

But I sometimes feel like speaking out against the undertones of unpleasantness which often answer my parental pride. Especially I resent the insinuation that I am somehow related to the old lady who lived in a shoe, who had so many children because she didn't know what to do. In this age of grace and gossip, ignorance must keep company with stupidity in order to preserve itself entire. There is a clinical candor about our reading, our conversation, and even the advertising in the most respectable of our family magazines, which makes it difficult to retain the innocence of ignorance unless one is firmly determined upon it. Ordinary curiosity has been enough to introduce me to Dr. Marie Stopes and all her works, and the name of Margaret Sanger is not as unfamiliar to me as might be supposed. I am, in fact, reasonably sure that I know as much about keeping the stork from the door as do most of my friendly and unfriendly critics, and that I know vastly more about practical biology than most of these young modernists who regard me with such a pitying and patronizing eye.

So in the natural course of events I come upon Mrs. Sanger's latest book, *Motherhood in Bondage,* and am thereby much tried and exercised. It is a tragic and terrible book. It is made up principally of letters— hundreds of them—from women and some few men overburdened with the bitternesses of too much parenthood. It is a grim collection of hard luck stories, every one of them outlining a human tragedy. It is a compilation of case records in marital misery, full of pain and poverty and protest against the blind inhumanity of natural law. Its purpose is clear, even though it is published in a country where there are still some things which must not be talked about. The letters are chosen and grouped to prove that families should be made to measure and not left to luck or the lack of it. It is overpowering in its picture of human misery and entirely sincere in its conviction that something should be done about it, but its specific plea is for public approval and dissemination of a practical doctrine of birth control.

I am really not much interested in this particular question. It seems likely that the curse of Anthony Comstock might well be lifted in this age of reason, but it also seems likely that a certain amount of damage might result from too much eating of the tree of knowledge. It strikes me as a delicate problem, as delicate as some of those which every parent knows who tries to bring youngsters safely through adolescence. As I have suggested above, the vast majority of parents have access to all the knowledge there is on this subject, and the fact that it is sometimes a little difficult to get at is probably a moral safeguard rather than a national calamity. Knowledge is an excellent thing, but it won't cure all our personal or social diseases. It never has. And it is often, much too often, turned to evil account.

But my complaint against Mrs. Sanger's book is that it lacks a certain letter. I have never felt the urge to write to Mrs. Sanger, but I think now that I should have done so. I should have written in the following fashion and thereby contributed my share to the great American tragedy.

DEAR MRS. SANGER:

I am only thirty-eight years old and have been married less than fifteen years, but we already have ten children and I am beginning to feel that there is no reason why I should not have ten more. When we married, my husband was earning just ten dollars a week as a school-teacher, and at the end of ten years he was getting less than three thousand a year and we had seven children. We have never had any income except what we could earn, so I have always done practically all my own work, including the cleaning, cooking, washing and everything. For years we hardly ever went to a theater or concert or took a vacation. Four years ago my husband lost his job and had to start in an entirely new line, but the children kept right on coming. Now we have ten of them and the oldest not yet fourteen, while the youngest is about six months. During the time before the last one was born my husband was taken ill and had to go away to a hospital for a serious operation, and my mother was also taken ill and died. I had to let my own work go in order to help nurse her. Through all this trouble I wondered many times what would be the effect of it all on the new arrival.

When I was married I knew very little about marriage and all its responsibilities, and had to learn as best I could by experience. Just now I have a cold in the head and the boys have kicked a football through the living-room window and the dishes aren't washed and the coal man has sent a bill with "Please Remit" on it, and what's going to become of us I don't know.

Perhaps Mrs. Sanger would have published this confession; perhaps she wouldn't. The point is that while its facts are all true, its implications are all false. I don't feel sorry for myself, and I never did. There's nothing the matter with my family, and there's nothing the matter with me that I can blame on the family. There's nothing the matter with the latest arrival, who is a healthy, happy, good-looking little rascal and the pride and joy of the whole household. Other people may feel sorry for us because we have practically the largest and noisiest family east of the Mississippi, but we don't feel sorry for ourselves. We have a tremendously good time with our family, and we don't much care who knows it.

The trouble with all this loose talk and careful propaganda about birth control is that it implies, more or less subtly, that the large family is in itself a dangerous, undesirable and even reprehensible performance. It is inferred and even stated that overproduction involves a tempting of Providence, an invitation to poverty, and a gamble with maternal health and childhood happiness. It ignores all chances that the large family may have positive and intrinsic advantages of its own, and its own rewards and compensations for all the toil and trouble attached to it. It implies—without actually saying so—that the small family is the right family and the large family the wrong family, and that therefore people like myself are in some sense a public nuisance or a public menace.

So although I have been steadfastly uninterested in birth control propaganda as such, I find myself compelled to have some ideas on the subject. I have, in fact, been publicly debating the problem in a definitely practical fashion through fifteen years and by means of ten children. Every new bud on the family tree has been not only a hostage given to fortune but a challenge and even an affront to all these people who seem to know what is good for me and good for my children and good for the human society in which we all find ourselves. Mrs. Sanger might conceivably approve of my family, but only as an exception to prove her rule, for we are fundamentally on opposite sides of the argument. I am doubtful of my abilities as a debater, and therefore when the subject came my way I have kept quiet. But there is nothing quiet about a family of ten. It is an assertive, obvious and concrete argument in itself.

But apart from particular cases and present company, I feel that the vital consideration in the birth control discussion is the matter of proper proportion. Nobody denies that there are many mothers who have more children than they know what to do with. Everybody must agree that the world holds too much misery which is a by-product of unrestricted child-bearing, particularly now that Mrs. Sanger has filled a book with it. But it should be remembered that other books of human misery might be filled readily enough with the dreadful things wrought by tight shoes, aspirin tablets, radio sopranos, home cooking and cocktail shakers, without actually proving anything except that it is all too bad.

Mrs. Sanger has collected abnormalities and horrors in such quantity that the whole of humanity seems tarred with the same brush. In effect she preaches that uncalculating parenthood is a sort of universal disease, which can only be relieved by the universal practice of her pet doctrine. She is deeply distressed by all the troubles she has seen, so that her theories have become badly scrambled with her emotions and she attempts to be both sympathetic and scientific at the same time. Therefore she at last makes the usual mistake of women who attempt the guidance of public opinion, and tries to transfer to public responsibility what is essentially and inevitably a private and local problem.

I have said that this seems to be a matter of proportion, and it is certainly so in a private sense. Every married woman must draw up her own balance sheet of debits and credits in this business of motherhood. Every married man must do the same. Children are both a liability and an asset, and in order to reckon the net values of the family—natural, moral and spiritual—the parents must have an honest showdown with their own consciences and convictions. What they do about it is their own business, and should have nothing to do with the current fashions in families or the legal status of this doctrine or that. When the sub-surface agitation in favor of birth control begins to assume shape as a popular notion that three or four or five children are enough, it takes away from the most conscientious parents something of the freedom to which they are entitled.

It is a matter of proportion. Each and all of us have our own scale of values by which we measure the worth of the pleasures, privileges, duties, comforts and satisfactions of life. Our attitude toward children, real and potential, will reflect pretty closely what we think and feel about these various elements. It really has nothing to do with the rights and wrongs of birth control. Birth control, rightly or wrongly, is no more than another device which we use or decline in deference to our sense of what is important. We ought, in honesty to ourselves, to resent the suggestion that it is anything more, that it is an article of faith for the scientific age. We ought, in a word, to feel free and be free to take it or leave it alone.

So though I do not believe in birth control, neither do I disbelieve in it. To announce that I believe in it means that I believe in it for somebody else, which seems to me to be none of my business. It happens that I don't believe in it for myself, under present circumstances and conditions, but that also is an entirely personal conviction and one which has no relation or importance to any other woman's problem. But I do believe that the contraceptionists are unwittingly making things uncomfortable for the large family, by giving scientific encouragement to the human liking for scandals. People do love to think the worst of their neighbors, and there is no such likely target as the parents of a large family. There ought, I think, to be a closed season for such parents, during which it would be a breach of the peace for mere theorists to add bedevilment to their burdens. Bachelors, maiden ladies and scientific reformers should in particular be warned to stay off the matrimonial grass where they have no proper business.

It is a long time since anyone made out a case for the large family. The argument has all been on the other side. I find at least four general arguments in favor of the small family. (1) Its cultural advantages. (2) Its possibilities for health and intelligence. (3) Economic necessities. (4) Racial hazards and obligations. To keep my conscience clear I must make some sort of a settlement with each of them.

The eugenists tell us that the small family is the really civilized achievement, in the face of all experience that one child or two may be totally unpleasant products and that the small family is perilously near to extinction with the first epidemic of whooping cough. They argue that the small family gets its full rations of educational and other advantages and turns out a higher type of citizen thereby. The answer is that it doesn't. Other things being equal, the large family gives better social training than the small one, and offers more stimulus to imagination, enterprise and intelligence during the most critically formative years. My own children knock the corners from each other, sharpen their wits on each other, and practice the social virtues on each other. They must necessarily learn to work together and play together. They must take small responsibilities early, and their affections and ambitions have small chance to get self-centered. It is possible that they may go short some day on the high-priced privileges of education and travel, but it won't matter much. They are learning already how to find their way about and make themselves a place in the world, and they are learning it at home.

In regard to the second point I take refuge in the record. My children are perfectly healthy and reasonably intelligent, and the later ones seem to have a slight edge on the earlier experiments. The suggestion that they might have been more so had there been fewer of them does not much interest me. Children, it seems, are healthy and intelligent principally according to the health and intelligence of their immediate ancestors and the parental progression in mutual development and usefulness, and if there is any rhyme or reason to the matter the later child has the best chance. Concerning my own health I am equally free from anxiety. I weighed a scant hundred pounds on my wedding day, but since I have increased by nearly four per cent per annum the family regards me as a good investment.

The third argument concerns the economic probabilities. To this my answer is that we have never yet been justified by our income in extending our family. We have extended the family, and then done what might be done to bring the income up to scratch. We were as financially embarrassed by one child as we are by ten, and we shall probably continue that way. Nothing in our married experience leads us to suppose that a small family guarantees financial independence or a large family forbids it; the two things simply don't have any cause-and-effect connection. We have no certainty as to what the morrow may bring forth, any more than do our more cautious neighbors, but we are sure of this, that the constant challenge and spur of increasing responsibilities and necessities have been fundamentally good for us. If we ever amount to anything—socially, financially, and particularly as to character and worth—my husband and I are agreed that we shall blame it on the children.

I am not entirely clear about the racial obligations involved in the doctrine of the small family. Very few people seem to be clear on the matter, with the exception of Havelock Ellis and a few others whose opinion, I suspect, is a fairly academic one. But I understand that a certain Mr. Malthus, aided and abetted by higher mathematics, has demonstrated that the human race, unless checked in its mad career by Act of Congress, is due either to be squeezed to death or starved to death. This is important if true, though it is probably not my business. But it may not be true. History is full of the dead bones of prophecies that have come to a sad end and the future is full of unknown quantities to upset all human calculations. Further, I am impressed by the obvious standstill and even retrogression of population increase within my own range of experience. Despite all my own contributions to the cause, the generation to which my children belong is falling short of its predecessors. There are families of my near acquaintance that are literally dying out; and nobody knows why. Civilization, I suppose, is taking its own toll by many secret ways, without much direct help from statisticians and scientists.

One other thing I have discovered by dabbling a little in vital statistics. The apparently alarming population increases of the past generation or so don't mean all that they seem to. Many children were born, for our country attracted chiefly the young and hardy; few old people died, for the dying generation belonged to a previous period of much smaller population. But now the numerical advantage shifts up the line, aided as it has been by the lengthening of the expectation of life during the past generation, and a lot of people must die soon as the consequence of having been born in the busiest times of the last century. Looking around a small circle of acquaintance, particularly in our cities, I can't see that the coming generation will do more than compensate for the ordinary wear and tear of time on the ones that are passing. My friends and acquaintances aren't having any too many babies to take the place of all the uncles and aunts and grandparents and such whose time is nearly over. So much for statistics, which don't mean much anyway.

To get back to my own family, which—as usual—is in danger of neglect whenever I mess around with speculations, the four popular arguments in favor of the job-lot of children simply don't apply, so far as I am concerned. And I am aware of substantial arguments on the other side. I leave out of the discussion certain spiritual considerations which are entirely personal, and I prefer to ignore all unconvincing statistics about everything. I rest the case for the large family on the simple fact that children are desirable because they are pleasant and stimulating things to have around the house. They vastly increase the happiness of life. Happiness is made up of responsibility, ambition and achievement, of mutual appreciations that are a bond and blessing for two people who understand each other, and of numerous intelligent appreciations. A family of ten children will supply these in quantity and variety.

Children are, of course, sometimes a nuisance and always an embarrassment. They keep you out of bridge clubs, poker games, golf tournaments, uplift movements and the movies, and even out of the divorce court. They insist that you shall make a reasonable attempt to live happily with your own husband or wife, which is not a very dramatic, exciting or fashionable accomplishment. They demand that you shall devote most of your time to plain and unvarnished hard labor, but if this is undesirable or abnormal then the world was very badly designed on the first morning of creation. And they keep it up without much interruption until they pack up and leave you, which is an eventuality to be regarded as philosophically as possible.

I concede that my philosophy, such as it is, ignores such charming contingencies as inherited lunacy, disease, and abject poverty; also pathological abnormality, confirmed criminality, and inherent immorality. These things do not belong in my personal problem; they belong rather in Mrs. Sanger's book. But I claim that the code of normal people is not to be determined by the behavior and condition of the unfortunates.

For myself I am deeply thankful for all those enriching accidents which permit me the pride and delight of an old-fashioned family. I admit that I am fortunate—fortunate in having good health, a home in the country, kindly and forbearing friends, and a calm and perhaps cowlike disposition. For some of these advantages I thank the children themselves, and my family doctor is inclined to agree with me. And since I am fortunately free of some of the bogies that are frightening family folk out of their proper rights and responsibilities, I can enjoy my family as the veritable "heritage and reward" of the Biblical phrase. For I have found that a real family of children pays an adequate daily dividend of satisfaction and delight, and if you don't believe it you may ask at least one woman who owns one.

WOMEN AND BIRTH CONTROL [1]

By Margaret Sanger

I was one of eleven children. My mother died in her forties. My father enjoyed life until his eighties. Seven of my brothers and sisters are still living. If I am not an "old-fashioned" woman, at least I was an old-fashioned child. I have never thought it necessary to call public attention to these circumstances of my life. Not that I am ashamed of them, but, on the other hand, neither am I brazenly proud of them. I do not believe that these facts are sufficient as a foundation upon which to erect a code of morals for all men and women of the future to follow. I do not say: "My mother gave birth to eleven living children, seven of whom are still alive and more or less healthy. Ergo, all women should give birth to eleven or a dozen children." There are, it seems to me, a few other things to consider.

I have been impelled to cast aside my habitual reticence because I have just finished reading a highly personal essay in the March number of the *North American Review,* written by a lady known as Majorie Wells. Mrs. Wells confesses herself the mother of ten children. Her family stretches "already as far as the eye can reach and with the end not yet in sight." This biological fact seems to endow Mrs. Wells with the glib authority to hand down decisions concerning complex problems which have puzzled humanity since civilization first began. I rejoice with Marjorie Wells in the peace and happiness she has found in her "monumental" family. But I confess that I am not convinced that feminine wisdom increases in direct proportion with the number of one's offspring.

[1] From the *North American Review,* May, 1929.

Implicit in Marjorie Wells' confession I discover a certain condescension toward the mothers of smaller families. She knows all there is to know about keeping the stork from the door. She admits her vastly superior knowledge of practical biology. She has read my book *Motherhood in Bondage,* which is a compilation of case records in marital misery, of protests from slave mothers against the blind inhumanity of natural law. From the citadel of her self-satisfaction, Marjorie Wells asserts that my theories have become badly scrambled with my emotions and that I attempt to be "both scientific and sympathetic at the same time"—as though that were quite impossible! I have made, according to Mrs. Wells, "the usual mistake of women who attempt the guidance of public opinion, and try to transfer to public responsibility what is essentially and inevitably a private and local problem."

Intellectually speaking, she "high-hats" me. A mere woman who has borne only three children instead of ten, who can therefore never hope to reach that peak of serene Olympian indifference to the cries and moans of my less fortunate sisters which Marjorie Wells has attained, I cannot hope to equal in dialectic skill a lady who has enjoyed the educational advantages of ten pregnancies. I have not yet attained that point of self-confidence which enables me to cast aside as irrelevant and unimportant the conclusions of scientists who have devoted their lives to the study of genetics, nor can I close my eyes to the statistics of government workers who have made deep researches into the conditions productive of the alarming maternity death rate in these United States. Having been only one of eleven hungry little brothers and sisters, I was not able to profit by the early educational advantages which Marjorie Wells evidently enjoyed. Her philosophic poise enables her to look upon the birth of a child as "a purely private and local problem." I have always assumed, and I do not believe that I am egregious in this assumption, that the birth of a child is an event of the utmost importance not only to the family into which it is born, but to the community, to the nation, to the whole future of the human race. I agree with President Hoover:

The ideal to which we should strive is that there shall be no child in America: That has not been born under proper conditions; that does not live in hygienic surroundings; that ever suffers from undernourishment; that does not have prompt and efficient medical attention and inspection; that does not receive primary instruction in the elements of hygiene and good health; that has not the complete birthright of a sound mind and a sound body; that has not the encouragement to express in fullest measure the spirit within which is the final endowment of every human being.

I suppose those of us who subscribe to these ideas are in the eyes of Marjorie Wells hopeless sentimentalists.

My opponent sharply crystallizes a definite point of view not only concerning the theory and the practice of birth control, but toward all the social problems which confront us today. Hers is the attitude of "splendid isolation," of enlightened self-interest, of laissez-faire. She tells us in effect that she is the mother of ten healthy children, that she and her husband enjoy from them a daily dividend of satisfaction and delight, and that therefore she "should worry" about the behavior and condition of the less fortunate. "Am I my sister's keeper?" asks in effect Marjorie Wells.

It is late in the day to point out that all human experience teaches that an attitude of "splendid isolation" can no longer be logically maintained by any individual in the face of the problems which confront American civilization. If only from the motive of self-protection the well-born and the well-bred can no longer shirk responsibility concerning "the behavior and the condition of the unfortunates."

Time after time, it has been demonstrated in all the countries of Western civilization, that as we descend the social scale the birth rate increases. Dependent, delinquent and defective classes all tend to become more prolific than the average normal and self-dependent stratum of society. With this high birth rate is correlated a high infant mortality rate. This law is true in all countries. More children are born; more babies die. So likewise, the maternal mortality rate jumps correspondingly. Out of the surviving infants are recruited the morons, the feeble-minded, the dependents, who make organized charities a necessity, and who later fill prisons, penitentiaries and state homes. To compute the cost in dollars and cents of these industriously prolific classes to society is beyond human power. Every one of us pays for their support and maintenance. Funds which legitimately should go to pure scientific research, to aid the fine fruition of American civilization, are thus diverted to the support of those who—in all charity and compassion—should never have been born at all.

We cannot ignore, as Marjorie Wells confesses she does, "such charming contingencies as inherited lunacy, disease and abject poverty." They press in upon us on all sides. These things, she says, do not belong in her personal problem. I beg to remind her that they do. For, despite her valiant efforts to bring up her own brood, Mrs. Wells will, in time, find out, if she has not already found out, that the children of the defective and the diseased will crowd into the schoolroom with her own children, and that standards of intelligence must perforce be lowered to meet their limited capacities. The community in which she lives will call upon her to aid the alleviation of the poverty and distress of the all too prolific. Her property and income will be taxed to maintain state institutions for the support of the dependent and the delinquent. She will resent bitterly this enforced expenditure of funds that should go for the higher education and the cultural development of her talented children. That is, if her resources are as limited as she admits them to be. And finally she will discover that her own good luck in life is not the general rule, but a fortunate exception, upon which it would be the utmost folly to attempt to generalize concerning this exceedingly human race.

"But," she may now retort, "you are speaking dogmatically, making a special plea for public approval of the dissemination of birth control." Marjorie Wells is convinced that the cases recorded in my book *Motherhood in Bondage* are abnormalities and horrors, gathered together merely to foist the practice of contraception upon unwilling parents.

Let us turn, then, to less prejudiced and partisan sources. Let us consider the findings of impartial investigators who have no interest in what our critics call propaganda. Let us find out, if we can, the truth concerning the conditions under which children are brought into our American world. For this evidence we need not go far afield. In a recent report published in the *Survey*, Hazel Corbin, R.N., general director of the Maternity Center Association of New York, states that year after year, more than twenty thousand women die from causes due to childbirth—one mother for every one hundred and fifty babies born! The Newton bill had as its aim government responsibility for the health of American citizens including the special needs of the mothers of the country. This bill died when the last Congress expired. The Sheppard-Towner Act expires June 30, 1929; and unless Congress provides a further federal subsidy, the government aid for mothers and children which its funds have furthered during the last six years will be brought to a close.

When correlated with the refusal of state legislatures to consider bills which would make birth control education permissive, these facts assume new significance. Our government pronounces itself unwilling to assume responsibility in alleviating the hazardous trade of maternity. At the same time the state and federal authorities refuse to countenance legislation which would allow American mothers to help themselves—which would permit them to choose the time and the conditions best suited for the fulfillment of the maternal function. "The birth of a baby is such a common, everyday occurrence," writes Hazel Corbin, "that people do not realize that during pregnancy the margin between health and disease becomes dangerously narrow, and only by skilled medical supervision can the maintenance of health be assured. Every mother in the country needs skilled medical supervision, nursing care and instruction during pregnancy, at delivery, and for the six weeks that follow. Many families do not know of this need. Not all families can provide this care. It is not available at any price in many parts of this rich country. There are no doctors, nurses and midwives properly trained to give adequate care to all mothers."

Yet two million women in America are compelled, by law, to descend annually into the valley of the shadow of death, to bear two million children in a country that has enacted drastic immigration restriction laws to prevent overpopulation. No: we are not underpopulated—there is no need for a "full speed ahead" policy of procreation. Since the revelations of *Motherhood in Bondage* are condemned as exceptional, let us listen further to the testimony of Hazel Corbin: "There are, caring for our mothers, midwives so ignorant and superstitious as to suppose hemorrhage can be controlled by placing an ax upside down under the patient's bed. *Of about fifty thousand practicing midwives only a small portion are well-trained and the majority are untrained—yet in most instances they are licensed or registered by their states.*"

Let us turn to the testimony of Julia Lathrop, ex-chief of the Children's Bureau, under whose supervision government agents made extensive investigations into the conditions surrounding infant mortality in eight typical cities of our country. Infant mortality rates concern all children who die during the first five years of life. On the whole, according to Miss Lathrop in the *Woman's Journal*, the evidence is overwhelming that poverty, ignorance, or both, lack of medical and nursing care, unwholesome living conditions, overworked mothers, remoteness from doctors and nurses in rural areas, and other types of inability to give babies needed care are in marked degree coincident with high infant mortality rates. A vast number of babies and of mothers die needlessly every year in this country. This fact is well known to statisticians, doctors and to some social workers, but details as to social and economic conditions under which the parents live are seldom disclosed or frankly discussed.

Today the situation remains fundamentally unnoticed. Women clamor for deliverance from compulsory motherhood. Yet dull-witted legislators, both state and federal, refuse to sanction the dissemination of harmless contraceptives to those unable or unwilling, due to the conditions discovered by government agents, to undergo a pregnancy that may be fatal to mother or child. Yet measures aiming to improve by governmental agencies dysgenic conditions surrounding maternity and infancy are condemned and defeated as "paternalistic." The situation calls for a Shaw or a Swift.

Perhaps this dilemma has been created not so much by the laws and the legislators themselves as by the smug and bland indifference of women themselves—of those fortunate, well-bred, well-educated women who refuse to concern themselves with the sordid tragedies of those they consider their social inferiors.

Whether birth control is right or wrong, moral or immoral, a need or a nuisance, one thing is certain. Mothers of ten or of one can no longer, by the mere exercise of a function common to all living creatures, consider themselves exempt from social responsibility. As Miss Lathrop has expressed it: "One thing is in my opinion certain—only mothers can save this coöperative work for maternity and infancy. If prosperous, intelligent mothers do not urge the protection of the lives of all mothers and all babies, why should we expect Congress to come unasked to their aid?"

Though Julia Lathrop is here making a plea only for government protection of maternity and infancy, the same truth is applicable to the doctrine of birth control. The most stubborn opposition to birth control has come, not from the moralists nor the theologians, the most distinguished of whom recognize its legitimate necessity, but from those women who, like Marjory Wells, "know as much about keeping the stork from the door as my most friendly and unfriendly critics," yet nevertheless assume that such knowledge, simple, harmless and hygienic as it is, must be kept for the privileged few and from the very women most in need of it. Such an attitude seems to grow out of a frantic feminine desire to retain a certain superiority, social or otherwise, over one's less fortunate neighbors.

Even for that very limited and very special type of woman who is gifted by nature and natural inclination—and also by wealth—to undertake a specialized career in maternity and to become the mother of ten or a dozen children, there is need for the practice of birth control. For if she be intelligent and farseeing, such a woman will recognize the necessity of "spacing" her children, of recuperating her full physical strength and psychic well-being after the birth of one child before undertaking the conception of another. Mothers of large families have written me expressing their gratitude for the benefits of birth control. It has enabled them to give each of their children a good start in life. It has prevented crowding, and has moreover permitted them to enjoy marital communion which would otherwise have been impossible. But let us recognize today—with the ever-increasing cost of living and the high cost of childbirth—that the large family must more and more be considered the privilege of the moneyed class. A large family, if the income is small, is a crime against the children born into it. I was one of eleven, and I believe that I am slightly more entitled to speak on this subject than Marjory Wells, who is, after all, only the mother of ten! I may be prejudiced, but I feel that the testimony of a child born into a large family is of more

interest and importance than that of the mere progenitor of
a large family. It all depends on the point of view!

American civilization has long passed the pioneer stage of
its development. We no longer have a vast continent to
populate. We no longer need mere numbers. But we are only
beginning to realize that there are other values in life than
those of mere quantity. We have not yet outgrown the
adolescent habit of worshiping the biggest this, the largest
that, the most of the other thing. So, I think, no one need
take any excessive pride in the production of a large family,
even though the rotogravure sections of our Sunday news-
papers will undoubtedly, for the delight and amusement
of their millions of readers, continue to publish photographs
of large families which imitate visually a long flight of steps.

The attitude of those who have been rewarded by life, and
cannot see the punishment inflicted upon others, reminds
me always of Dr. Pangloss in Voltaire's *Candide*. "It has
been proved," said Dr. Pangloss, "that things cannot be
otherwise than they are; for, everything being made for a
certain end, the end for which everything is made is necessarily the best end." And though the world went to wreck
and ruin about him, he still maintained that "it does not
become me to retract my words. Leibnitz cannot possibly be
wrong—the preëstablished harmony is the finest thing in
the world. All events are inextricably linked together in this
best of all possible worlds."

Rather, I think, in this matter of mothers and children—
whether we be the mother of ten, or the sister of ten—we
must heed the counsel of Candide himself and cultivate our
garden.

WHY THE CHURCH SHOULD CHAMPION
BIRTH CONTROL [1]

By Charles F. Potter

At St. Mark's in the Bouerie, Charles Rann Kennedy and Edith Wynn Mathison presented that tremendous drama of the crucifixion entitled, *The Terrible Meek*. Those of you who have seen it will recall that the curtain rises in darkness. There are heard the voices of a woman and of a cockney captain of the guard discussing the fact that the woman's son has recently been hanged. It is only as hints are occasionally dropped in the conversation, and as the light gradually increases that you find that the woman is Mary and that her son who has been hanged or crucified is Jesus, and the remarks that she makes and the rather unusual point of view which the author makes or has give you a fresh view of that great drama of all history.

The whole dénouement of the play centers around a certain awakening in the soul of Mary, who finally comes to make this supreme statement, recognizing that all her anguish, all the suffering of herself and of her son, were for a definite purpose, and she says, "All this suffering and the death of my peasant boy were in order to make the world better for women and children."

Now, I maintain that if the Christian church can center its attention upon that great drama of Calvary and recognize with Mary that the suffering there and the suffering in her mother heart were in order to make the world better for

[1] Lecture delivered by Dr. Potter, Founder and Leader of the First Humanist Society of New York. Published in *Religious and Ethical Aspects of Birth Control* (edited by Margaret Sanger), The American Birth Control League, 1926.

women and little children, no informed person will dare to say that the church should not champion birth control.

For the Christian church has taken upon itself this peculiar task, to make the world better for women and little children. In whatever other task it has attempted, it may or may not have succeeded. It at least has tried at times to make the world better for women and little children. Paul gave things a wrong turn at first, and we have hardly yet recovered from his attitude toward women, but we are gradually coming, in Christianity and in other religions as well, to recognize the proper place of woman, which is a place equal to the place of man, and we are gradually coming to see that we must pay more attention to the comfort and the happiness and especially to the education of the little children. It is, as Dr. Reiland has so well said, coming to be recognized that the biological is extremely important in all human activity, and, thanks to such pioneers as the one whom we have with us today, we are coming to see that the church should champion birth control because birth control does make the world better for little children.

Poetically and æsthetically the church exalts motherhood. The time has come for the church to coöperate actively in practical measures to make that poetical, dreamy Mother's Day superstition a reality, a definite, active thing in the lives of men.

Every day I pass the Convent of the Holy Child, and there I see, enshrined in marble, high above the city traffic, the Mother and the Child, beautiful, poetic, mystic, Christian in a sense. But so often I think what a terribly tragedy, that the church should put motherhood and the child so far above everything else that they fail sometimes even to lift their eyes and see. There they are—exalted, put upon a pedestal and forgotten, whereas the motherhood and the childhood are the great opportunity of the race to retrieve some of its past wrongs.

The church—the very one which enshrines the Mother

WHY CHURCH SHOULD CHAMPION BIRTH CONTROL 269

and Child upon the outside of its convents—insists that to take practical measures to insure the happiness of the mother and child is what? Obscene and immoral. Is there a more contradictory thing in history than that? The time has come for every church, every synagogue, every temple, every group of people pretending to be religious and moral, to maintain that the practical measure of birth control affords our best opportunity of assuring to the child the proper welcome in the home and to the mother that leisure which is absolutely imperative if she is to develop the spiritual side of her nature.

Whatever may be our particular theological relation to Jesus of Nazareth, I doubt if there is one person here this afternoon who would deny that his most important statement, or at least one of his most important statements which have come down to us, is this: "I am come that they might have life and that they might have it more abundantly."

I am devoting my own particular leisure to the advocacy of birth control measures because I believe that in a practical sense there is no other reform which so fundamentally assures to the *genus homo* life, and life more abundantly.

The trouble is that that passage has been misinterpreted to mean physical life, and we have had churches, we still have churches, which insist that the thing to do is not to interfere with nature but to allow nature to produce life more abundantly. Now, that reproduction of physical life until it becomes such an incubus and burden that it weights down and blots out all spiritual nature, is not the meaning, of course, of this phrase—not physical life, for when that comes too fast the spiritual is swamped, and the spiritual is what Jesus emphasized. I am confident that spiritual life will come not in an increase in the birth rate, and not in the having of families of fifteen and eighteen children, but rather in the producing of children properly spaced who will have adequate time for their own development given to them by the mother.

In this way, by the modern church dealing with conditions as they are to help this world become better, we shall find ourselves nearer the happy land of heart's desire than we have hitherto been.

I believe that the church should champion birth control for several very definite practical reasons. In the first place, birth control protects the mother against the exhaustion of body and spirit which results from too frequent child-bearing. I believe the church should champion birth control because birth control will assure to the child a welcome and a fair start in life, and certainly everybody deserves that; it will assure to the child a mother's care and a home environment conducive to health and morals.

I believe that the church should champion birth control because birth control will mean less child labor and better educational opportunities for the young by making it possible for parents to have only such children as they can care for properly.

I believe that the church should champion birth control because it will cut down our tragically high infant mortality, because it will make early marriage economically possible for thousands of our young men and women and thereby diminish immorality, illegitimacy, prostitution and its accompaniment, venereal diseases. And to speak frankly and plainly to an intelligent audience, may I say this, I believe that the church should champion birth control because only by the spread of contraceptive information through Birth Control Leagues can we check the growing practice of abortion among married women whose husbands do not earn enough to support a large family.

I believe the church should champion birth control because birth control will increase the number of marriages, lessen divorce and desertion, enrich and strengthen the marriage bond by making possible normal and complete companionship between husband and wife without the haunting fear of too many children.

I believe that the church should support these measures because birth control will mean, in short, happier homes, healthier children, better men and women, a stronger nation and a nobler race.

And if I may add a postscript to this rather hasty summary of a few of the reasons why the church should champion birth control for its own sake—if the church should champion birth control, the general public would say, "Why, the church does care for men and women and real things, and we thought it didn't."

It is my custom to travel incognito in various parts of New York City, to dress not exactly as a clergyman ordinarily dresses, to mix in Third Avenue restaurants with people who earn their daily bread by the sweat of their brow. I steer the conversation toward the church, and if I told you the things which those men and women—ninety per cent of them—say about the church, you would leave this room in disgust, but those things are true for them. Why not make a practical demonstration of the fact that the church does care for the living conditions of men and women, and why not have the church champion birth control? Birth control is coming. If it comes with the help of the church, the church will be strengthened, but if it comes without the help of the church, then the church will topple from its present rather precarious position.

BIRTH CONTROL OR WAR? [1]

by Henry Kittredge Norton

BIRTH CONTROL or war? Those who have a liking for either will readily countenance the elimination of the other, but the choice between the two, if it is a necessary one, has a horrific aspect for many. Its moral aspects cause confusion and its practical aspects are difficult.

The crux of the question is found in the demand of certain countries for additional territories because their homelands are crowded. Italy is the most forthright of such countries at the moment, although Germany's insistence upon the restoration of her colonies is of the same stamp, and Japan, while less vociferous than a decade ago, does not forget her narrow confinement in a string of mountainous islands. Intellectuals throughout the Orient, in fact, express resentment against the white man's preëmption of the unoccupied lands of the globe and his exclusion of the colored man therefrom.

There is no accepted standard of size for a nation, either as to the number of its people or the extent of its territory. The meat of the matter is in the proportion these bear one to the other. The United States with its 120,000,000 people is not overcrowded, while Japan with half as many people feels congested in a territory less than one-tenth as large. And 7,000,000 Australians fairly rattle around in a land as large as the United States.

In this disproportion the Japanese find ground for complaint, just as do the Italians when they consider their efforts to maintain 40,000,000 people on an area hardly more than half that possessed by the same number of Frenchmen. The underlying thought in both cases is that the world's arable

[1] From the *Outlook and Independent*, March 26, 1930.

land should be distributed more uniformly. The ideal would be a distribution such that each man, whatever his nationality, would have soil of approximately the same productive value back of him.

As an ideal, such a distribution would have its merits. Let us suppose some super-dictator should so distribute it and that all should forthwith arrive at millennial happiness. Then let nature take its course and the next generation grow to maturity. Some of these ideal one-family farms would still be maintaining one family in prosperous circumstances and others would be groaning under the weight of six, eight or ten families. The first group would be white—probably French—and the others colored—Japanese, Chinese or Hindu. Another generation would repeat . . . but we are leaving our millennium far behind!

What should the super-dictator do? Redistribute the lands equally among the men of each generation? Such a course would mean periodically taking land from the one-family peoples to supply the ever-increasing hordes of the ten-family peoples. General prosperity would give way first to general privation, then to destitution, then to squalor and degradation and then to the final struggle for mere existence. That way madness lies. The things of the spirit—art, literature, philosophy, religion, civilization itself—would all go down in a brutishly relentless fight for a bare existence on the lowest animal plane. Too much of the world's history is already written in such characters.

Yet the present plea of overcrowded nations for more land as an outlet for their surplus population leads logically in just this direction. They are in effect demanding additional farms for their multitudinous offspring. The only way to obtain such farms is to take them away from the less prolific peoples. Quite naturally these peoples refuse to give them up unless they are compelled to do so by superior force.

Japanese statisticians have declared that there is room in the world for 2,500,000,000 people living on the Japanese standard while the world can support only 1,000,000,000 on the American standard. Therefore, they triumphantly conclude, Americans should move up a bit and make room for these extra hundreds of millions. But should we? Pursue this reasoning in the other direction. The world might support 3,500,000,000 people on the Chinese or Indian standard. Are the Japanese ready to move up a bit closer to make room for these extra hundreds of millions merely because the Chinese and Indians can breed faster and live lower than they can?

The complaint of overcrowding will come only from a people which is dissatisfied with its standard of living. The solution proposed by the Japanese statisticians, however, would not raise the Japanese standard. It would only bring down all the more favored peoples to that standard. And then, if the same course were faithfully pursued, all would continue to sink together to the plane of the very lowest.

On this basis, the one criterion of race survival becomes the sheer animal capacity to procreate. No other quality would count because mere numbers would carry the day.

It is fair to assume that neither the Japanese nor any other people of higher standards of living would care to adopt the Chinese or Indian standard. Our own immigration situation would indicate that all of them would readily adopt the American standard if they could. But they cannot do it on the theory that more land is the means to that end.

There was a time when Japan and Italy, even China and India, were no more densely populated than the United States is today. In other words, they were then in exactly the position which they claim justice would give them today. And what did they do about it? They proceeded to breed at a rate which filled up their territory to overflowing and laid upon their sons an almost insupportable burden of competition for the barest essentials of existence.

These sons demand a larger share of the world's acres. To give it to them is utterly futile so long as they carry on the procreative tradition of their fathers. Give them a province, give them a hemisphere, and in a moment of history they will fill it as full as the land they have today. They will have gained nothing, but the more continent peoples will have lost. Civilization will have lost. Humanity will have lost. And peace will be further from our grasp than ever.

Yet war or the power to make war will still be necessary for many generations if we are to hold the gains which civilization has made. Mass-procreation is as expansive in its nature as mass-production. It will constantly raise the human pressure and its output will clamor ever more stridently for a share of the advantages of those who refuse to diffuse their energies in prodigal reproduction. That pressure must be held back by force or civilization must surrender. That surrender may be either wholesale or retail. Whenever the world tolerates the seizure of the territory of one country by another and recognizes its legal validity, that is wholesale surrender. Retail surrender is involved in some aspects of the immigration process.

An undeveloped country welcomes immigrants. The more people there are, the more work, production and development there are. But sooner or later a point is reached when a further influx of people does not raise the average well-being. Instead it lowers it. This point is somewhat difficult to locate with exactitude because it varies with the degree of technical development, the social organization and the psychological attitude of the people. A Chinese might feel there was plenty of room where an Englishman would feel fearfully annoyed.

But the point of population balance exists. Undoubtedly Italy, Japan, China and India have gone far past it. Australia and the Argentine have not yet reached it. The United States is probably very close to it. And thus there are emigrant countries, immigrant countries and countries which have no desire to be either.

Critics of the exclusion laws of the United States, Canada, Australia contend that there is within the borders of these countries an enormous amount of arable land which is un-used. This land it is asserted would maintain, in what for them would be affluence, millions of immigrants from the overcrowded countries. The conclusion is that the lands should be made available for the immigrants. But remember the ten-family farms. Those unused lands, beyond the margin of profit for Americans, Canadians, Australians, are the very bulwark which sustains their higher standards of living. Admit the highly procreative peoples to them and those high standards begin to sink. This is retail surrender to mass-procreation.

There is but one way to a satisfactory solution for those who desire the peace and progress of all mankind. That is for each nation to adjust its population to such numbers as its present territory will support on whatever standard of living it desires. It should not be permitted to seize the territory of others to make room for its increasing numbers. Nor has it any right to send its surplus people into other countries and overcrowd them to the detriment of their peoples. It can regulate the pressure of population in its own land as it sees fit, but every other nation is entitled to the same opportunity. Population must be adjusted to territory and not territory to population.

The colored peoples make prompt rejoinder. It is all very well, they say, for the white race, now that it has secured much of the Americas, most of Africa, and all of Australia, for its own expansion, to cry quits and suggest that everybody keep what he has. The colored spokesmen can see no justice in that. They insist that the races are equal and that the yellow and the brown are entitled to as much land per capita as the white. Reduced to its fundamentals, this is simply a claim that because the yellow and the brown races have produced more children, therefore they are entitled to more of the earth's surface. If there be any injustice in the proposal to maintain the *status quo*, it will be less than the injustice caused by unending efforts to change it by military power.

But how much of injustice is there in maintaining the *status quo?* India and China had an advanced civilization 3,000 years ago. Japan makes hers 2,500 years old. In comparison, the civilization of Europe and America is hardly out of its swaddling clothes. During all those centuries before it had found itself, the Americas, Africa and Australia were sparsely peopled by savages. Did the yellow and brown races make any effort to reclaim them for civilization? If the white race had never existed, how long would it have been before India, China or Japan would have peopled these lands? Without the achievements of the white race, the yellow and brown would be just where they are today so far as room for expansion is concerned.

Whichever way the scales of justice may tip, it is perfectly obvious to any person who prefers fact to fantasy that the peoples who possess lands on this shrinking globe of ours are not going to hand them over to others, no matter how great the need of those others may be made to appear. It is equally obvious that the crowded peoples will never miss an opportunity to get more land whenever it offers. This is such stuff as wars are made of. If wars do not come, it will be because the less crowded peoples remain so well prepared that the outcome is a foregone conclusion. Thus it is clear that we shall have war or menace of war until such time as the mass-procreation peoples consent to restrain their reproductive proclivities.

It was the fashion for a time to smile condescendingly at the predictions of Malthus. It was held that the Industrial Revolution had utterly invalidated his conclusions so far as England was concerned. And this appeared to be the case. For England's population doubled and trebled beyond the limits he had set for it. England was able to accomplish this, however, because there were other parts of the world untouched by the Industrial Revolution. The great undeveloped areas of the New World and the backward masses of Asia absorbed her industrial products and enabled her to sustain this increased population on a standard of living higher than that of Malthus' day. But those halcyon days have passed. The rest of the world is not only increasingly able to supply its own industrial demands but is increasingly jealous of its right to do so.

Even the Industrial Revolution did not help the population problem in the overcrowded Asian lands, nor did it help it much in Italy. Now that the world is beginning to feel its unity, it becomes evident that the conclusions of Malthus, while temporarily upset as to England, may have a new validity when applied to the world as a whole. To invalidate them in this larger field, there must be a world-wide economic advance comparable in intensity to the Industrial Revolution in England but universal in its operation.

This is unlikely enough, but to have any permanent effect upon the standard of living in the mass-procreation countries. it must be accompanied by a resolve on the part of their peoples to become more temperate in some of their habits. Otherwise they will in all too short a time find themselves again exactly where they are now.

So, strive to escape it as we will, the inevitable alternative seems still to face us. If the prolific peoples insist upon the unlimited indulgence of their procreative abilities, it will be impossible to restrain their land-hunger except by the presence of overwhelming force. War and the menace of war will thus remain with us until its alternative is accepted.

In some highly influential quarters birth control is condemned as an immoral practice. All the powers of ecclesiastical authority are marshaled against the dissemination of information regarding it. Practice, of course, consistently ignores precept in this regard, and quite without reference to the moral aspects of the question. Whatever these moral aspects may be, whatever may be the arguments deduced in their support, it seems clear that those who denounce birth control thereby—whether intentionally or not is immaterial —increase the possibilities of war.

It would appear to the layman that the inevitability of such a choice involves moral considerations of quite as high an order as may be found in the question of birth control itself. The choice may be between two evils but the choice is there. There are only the two alternatives and humanity must choose—birth control or war?

VII

THE ADOLESCENT

THE SEX URGE, ITS ONSET AND MANAGEMENT [1]

By Joseph Collins

"TELL me a story," is the child's continuous appeal to a parent. "Write me the truth about sex," is the publisher's frequent appeal to me. The inventive and resourceful parent yields; the prudent and foreseeing physician hesitates. There is a reason.

The truth about sex is a large order. No one knows the whole truth, and if he did he would not be allowed to tell it. Church, convention and commerce do not want it and will not have it. Were I to tell as much of the truth as I know about sex, society would frown at me, the postal authorities would forbid its printed circulation, some self-constituted censor would hale me before a tribunal, and were I dependent upon patients for a livelihood, want would soon stare me in the face.

On the other hand, the physician has unparalleled opportunity for observing the course and fate of love and its effect upon those who experience and display it. It is his help that is usually sought when the ship Matrimony goes upon the rocks. I write from my own observation and experience. One who has practiced medicine for a third of a century, who evolved from family physician to neurologist, who has spent seventy-five thousand days in more or less successful attempts to succor footsore travelers on the roadway of life, should have made some observations of love's displays and love's disasters, and should have reached some conclusions about the rôle that maldirection and manhandling of the reproductive energy plays in the causation of

[1] From *The Doctor Looks at Love and Life*. New York: Doubleday, Doran & Company, 1926.

disease and distress. He should be willing to submit them to his fellows. They should be willing to receive them.

I am not a theologian so I do not know how man was made, but I believe that the God who has been revealed to me through my intelligence made him. There has been much discussion in recent years, as man has become more arrogant, national and predatory, as to whether it was done in just the way described in the first book of Moses. It really does not matter. We know that He made the caveman before He made the manikin and that He made unicellular organisms that reproduced their kind without fertilization or impregnation before He made the intricate morphological mechanism called man.

Mankind has two fundamental urges: to stay alive, and to reproduce its kind. It is not germane to this discussion to express an opinion as to which is the stronger. There is no uniformity about them. The one is stronger in one individual, the other in another, and their strength varies in the same individual at different times. The nutritional or self-welfare urge has always been given free rein and encouragement, but the other has been so curbed and weighted that it seems, on casual consideration, to be by far the more dominant. Nothing could be further from the truth. The purpose of mankind like that of all creation is reproduction; the nutritional urge is accessory and contributory to it. A third urge, not fundamental, but one that has possessed man during the entire period of recorded history, is the self-expression urge. It is responsible for all of our sins and most of our salvation, for our accomplishments and our derelictions. Another subsidiary but conspicuous urge, the herd urge, makes the earth a paradise for the many, a hell for the few.

It does not transcend my understanding that mankind originally received instruction from its Creator as to the management of its urge. God told the ancestors of the human race His reasons for creating them, their duties and obligations. He left it to those who took upon themselves the responsibility of carrying on His work to tell those whom they created their duties and obligations. They have failed to do so and it is likely they will continue to fail: from that failure, most of the inadequacies and infirmities flow. When God's masterpieces became sentient He blessed them and assured them of the plenitude of the earth and admonished them to subdue it. His injunction was that they be fruitful and multiply; that they direct, coördinate and display the energy with which He had endowed them. They made a mess of it and their descendants have done worse. The instruments that they have used to accomplish the jumble are religion, convention, expediency. Religion maintains that procreation save under the seal of matrimony is a sin; convention makes pariahs of those who essay it; and prudent, forward-seeing human beings uphold the family as the only safe rock upon which to perpetuate society, the ark of the covenant.

Procreative capacity comes to living creatures after a definite period of existence; to mankind it comes after about fourteen years of life. To some it comes like a hurricane; to others like a warm wind in spring. It steals upon some like a thief in the night; it affronts others like an armed highwayman in full day. To some it does not come at all; to others it comes but does not stay. To the male it seems to come far more blusteringly than to the female. This may be an entailment of her long bondage, an artefact of her artificial life. Its onset and early display, in women especially, vary with the nation and the race. It is widely held that Latin races are more easily upset by it than Anglo-Saxon. It is my experience that the reverse is true. It may be because for a number of years my contact in the Neurological Institute was with a race of great emotivity that I believe it comes with greater awareness to Jew than to Christian. It is unsafe to generalize; there is little uniformity in its onset or early manifestations. Many women have told me that they never experienced sexual feelings previous to marriage. In the majority of women it is subordinate to love.

Religion, conviction and expediency say it matters not how it comes, or how much comes; it is to be handled, managed, administered in the same way. They say so but nature says no, and the result is that the world is divided into three classes: antinomians who are in the vast majority; conformers; and cripples whose immobilities have resulted from fear engendered by threats of punishment by God, state and society should they transgress, and whose exhaustion is the result of battling with their most godlike possession.

Religion has not been very successful in keeping man continent. Its most widely conceived and perfectly administered organization, the Roman Catholic Church, counsels and urges its adherents to marry soon after puberty, and the Talmud when its followers acquire sixteen years of age. But the state with forward look to its exchequer is averse to matrimony until the contractors have means of support or can gain them; and society is definitely in favor of postponing marriages until the breadwinner of the team has got a good start on the roadway of life, and his helpmate has had some experience in peeping beneath men's masks to learn if they are kind, loyal and otherwise marriageable. Also man himself has become what he calls prudent—what was once called more timid—as he spins the evolutionary wheel. He hesitates to take on responsibilities that will burden him in the success race and handicap him in the pleasure race.

As the result of all this, despite the Roman Catholic Church and orthodox Jewry, the average age when matrimony is contracted steadily mounts. The sap of life courses through the human tree for ten years before it can legitimately be transmuted into blossom or leaf and before it can do its share toward bathing the world in beauty.

The astonishing thing, then, is not that it often oozes through the cortex, but that it does not rush into limb and twig whenever it feels its bursting ascent. The wonder is that it can halt its ascent before reaching the arena of display, and that it can do so repeatedly.

The struggle to keep it back, the ruses adopted to stem it, the subterfuges employed to divert it from its legitimate channel, the labor expended in digging canals to carry the outflow, the unwillingness to admit its coursing—these are the materials from which the devil fabricates psychoneuroses, from which he cuts the pattern of the semi-insane and whittles the square pegs to be thrust into round holes.

Were I obliged to answer categorically the question: Is continence prejudicial to health? I should have to answer in the affirmative, but I should want to qualify my answer. I should want to say that this is one of the many things about which one cannot be dogmatic. To some it is injurious, to others it is not. Protracted continence, unless some other wish or determination can be substituted for the procreative desire, is not contributory to health or sanity. The determination to save one's soul is not the only substitute. There are conditions under which continence may contribute to efficiency and happiness. Those conditions are that the individual should be proud of his creative possession and desires rather than ashamed of them; that the reward for keeping his jewels in their cases should be not the promise of happiness in the dead but in the quick—the knowledge that he can offer them whole to one who is worthy of them. This makes it worth while to be continent. Things that are worth while are never injurious.

It may be said that this is a variety of sublimation, and it is true. Love vaporizes the powerful urge and respect re-solidifies it. Self-sacrifice is the touchstone of nobility, self-control the patent.

The same problem of control confronts everyone, though its clamor for solution varies with the individual, his temperament, age, race, and gait. If he is gaited to idealism and not to materialism, continence should make powerful appeal to him.

Then comes the question: How long is continence compatible with well-being? To which my answer is: the shorter the better. Man and woman individually would be healthier, happier and more efficient were they to gratify their genesic instinct soon after nature intended they should, but collectively they would doubtless be far worse off than now.

Nature has provided mankind with sex safety valves. They are adequate if too much strain is not put upon them. It is wholly beyond belief that nature intended that they should last very long; probably until the sex dynamo develops its full capacity.

Sex hunger clamors for appeasement in the majority of human beings soon after puberty, about the time when Minerva takes them in charge. Fortunately this clamor usually comes on so insidiously and develops so gradually that many are not even aware of its existence, but the world is full of things that increase the speed and is getting fuller every day. This same world says that it shall not be appeased. The result is that some eat of the forbidden fruit; others seek and readily find a substitute; a few go hungry.

With the antinomians I am not here concerned save to pity them. They spill their vial of life's perfume before they have developed olfactory bulbs to appreciate it. When these grow—after Minerva has discharged her duties—the priceless essence has been exhausted.

Those who abstain after they have reached the age of discretion have no problem, and if occasionally something looking like one thrusts up its head the church solves it for them.

With those who find and use the substitute I have had much to do. Many of them are of the salt of the earth, modest, sensitive, temperamental, talented, often overburdened with emotional awareness and penetration. They are entitled to our counsel and to our guidance.

Practically all men and a considerable proportion of women strive for and obtain some form of appeasement. Fortunately, in the majority the indulgence is moderate and

the period of addiction comparatively brief. Sex enlightenment has already accomplished a great deal in this field.

Vicarious sex appeasement, often spoken of as "the sin
of youth," is offensive to God and man. I base this statement
on the tenth verse of the thirty-eighth chapter of Genesis
and a life's experience with those who have indulged in it.

It is, however, injurious to self-respect only. Indulgers feel
themselves walking among their fellows with a need to
conceal a shameful feature of their life; they dread the
scorn that revelation would bring and they regard themselves as whited sepulchers filled with unholy desires.

The terrorizing admonitions of well-meaning but ill-advised
and misinformed parents and teachers, and the ghastly literature that worms its way into the hands of schoolboys and
young men, which alleges, by word and picture, that physical
decay and mental agony flow from such practices, are far
more injurious to mind and body than the indulgence itself.
Onanism of any variety does not make an invalid or misfit
of its practitioner. The shame that it engenders, the fear
that parents and physicians thrust upon him, tend to do so
At one time it was charged with capacity to derange the mind.
This accusation has been withdrawn. Its protracted indulgence, and continuation of the practice after maturity comes,
often testify a mind prone to lose its balance. Its recom-
mendation as a therapeutic measure by psychoanalysts testi-
fies their turpitude and their insensitiveness.

Parent, teacher and victim may ask: "Then does it do no
harm save to one's self-respect?" To the phlegmatic, none;
to the hypersensitive, to those who overreact to pleasure or
pain, kindness or cruelty, sights or sounds, it may do great
harm. It makes them more timid, more bashful, more anti-
social and it has a tendency to accentuate the amplitude of
their emotional waves, alternately to exalt and to depress
them, and to increase the frequency of occurrence of such
states. In other words, it prepares the soil for nervous, mental
and emotional instability; it causes nervous and mental ex-

haustion; it thrusts preoccupation and self-censure on the victim, and it is the worst training for matrimony.

How the disgusting habit is formed depends upon the individual, his sex endowment and emotivity. In some it is the result of local irritation; in others, chance or accident initiates it, but usually it is a companion or a conversation. Rarely is it the continuation of a habit dating from early childhood. In some cases it is a bolt from the blue—no warning, no suggestion, no teaching. The magazine is ready and a chance shock determines the explosion. In some intuitive way or through warning, the youthful practitioner realizes that it is wrong and immediately he is seized with remorse. This remorse continues for a time and then gradually spiritual appeasement comes. But after a while the tension increases again and there is the same search for relief; then repetitions, until the unfortunate young person feels that he is between the devil and the deep sea. Thus frequently the foundation of anxiety states, apprehension and self-solicitude is laid. If it is his good fortune to have a parent or a teacher with whom he is on terms of intimacy, he may be spared protracted suffering; on the other hand, he is often such a good boy that nothing of the sort is suspected and he has to carry his burden alone. Tact, kindliness, sympathy and understanding are the measures to use to prevent and to cure the habit. Threats, harshness and punishment are measures that are frequently used, and with small success. The masturbation which most young children practice usually ceases before sex consciousness develops.

As the problem presents itself to me, the physician, it is a simple one: the function of human beings is to procreate. The male element must germinate the female element and to accomplish it a specific embrace is essential.

It is to the welfare of human beings, individually and collectively, that procreation be carried on by people who are married.

It is a lie to teach that procreation or any step of it is a sin—a cowardly, malicious lie.

It is contemptible conduct, wholly beyond justification, to endeavor to impose continence upon those as yet bereft of understanding with threats of punishment after death. Does one value the respect of the community? Is the welfare of the world one's concern? One may secure the first and contribute to the second by refraining from sexual intercourse save in the marriage state. But marriage must not be too long delayed. If it is, the individual takes the chance of becoming a sexual cripple—that is, of developing some sexual anomaly which will impede his usefulness and stultify his happiness. Amiel is a good example.

Marriage is theoretically a sacrament, but practically it is a matter of economics. The question therefore arises: is the man or woman, powerless to solve the economic problem, justified in renouncing the pleasure and profit of carrying love to its full blooming? That is a question that everyone should be permitted to answer for himself, after he has reached the age of reason and found out that to trust to sense and conscience makes for greater happiness and usefulness than to trust to instinct and emotion. Priest, moralist, pedagogue, physician, economist, statesman, are all entitled to an expression of opinion, to exhortation even, but to nothing more. The voice I raise is to say that none of them has the right to threaten or intimidate the individual, to freight him with the potentialities of disease, disorder and disequilibrium before he has sense or strength to handle them.

Sex orientation is a problem for parents, not for priests. Priests who are parents do not seem to be more successful in dealing with it than those who are not. It should be no more difficult to teach children about sex than it is to teach them about God. It is a subject on which we do not lack specific information founded upon experience.

There is no doubt that repression of sex desires modifies

character, dwarfs and biases emotions and predisposes to nervous and mental disorder. For that reason, such desires should be recognized, discussed and dispersed. To accomplish this means supervision of youth's life; its contacts with persons and things, its reading, diversions, exercise; its spiritual awakenment and enlightenment. The time to sublimate sex repressions is before they are repressed; the place, the home; the person to suggest it, the parent.

But where do the majority of children get their sex information? They get it from gutters and latrines, from vicious schoolfellows and from more vicious elders, and later they get it from pernicious pamphlets that mysteriously find their way to them and from books the sale of which is limited "to the medical profession, psychoanalysts, scholars and such adults who may have a definite position in the field of psychological or social research" but which anyone, regardless of sex, age, creed or color, may buy if he has the money; and they get it from fiction. Invariably this is misinformation. Some get instruction from teachers, a few get it from parents. Most of that is misinformation too. Parents tell me that their children are enlightened about sex in school, but when I encounter the children they are ignorant. There is one person from whom a child should get sex enlightenment: a parent. It is as much a parent's duty as providing food for it. What would be thought of a parent who shut off his child's food supply and what would society and the state do to him? The question need not be answered. What do they do to the parent who shuts off the most important source of the child's happiness and efficiency? They applaud him.

When should a parent tell the child about sex? When it begins to ask questions. What should he or she tell the child? The truth. It is not necessary, not even prudent or advisable, to tell the whole truth. Neither the receptive apparatus nor the interpretive mechanism of the child is ready for it. In His wisdom God permits His mysteries to be submitted to us gradually; some of them come only with senescence. But nothing save the truth should be told. The mother who tells her child that the stork or the doctor brings the brother or sister who is such a source of wonderment does it an injury that she can never compensate. She not only lies (which the child will soon discover and always remember)—she inflicts a wound which will leave a sensitive scar. We do not hesitate to tell children, even in their infancy and most dogmatically, things that are beyond proof and that we accept on faith; why should we balk at telling them things we know, which it is vital for their spiritual welfare and physical health that they should know? "They are too young to know about such things," is the customary rejoinder. Then why were they given curiosity, the determining antecedent of all knowledge? Children have little or no curiosity about any feature of what is summarized by the words "religious training." It is thrust upon them like food upon Strasbourg geese. But they have an insatiable appetite for information about nature and its display which centers in themselves and their kind. Hence their investigation of themselves and of those with whom they come in contact.

We answer as best we can every question the child asks save the important one. When he asks that, we say, "Nice people don't talk about such things." Nice people don't, but wise people do.

A child is never too young to be told that the baby comes from within the mother. Its supreme helplessness is so obvious even to a child that it will not marvel that the babe should have been hidden and protected there. If it does, there are countless analogies, such as the chicken and the egg, that will suffice to satisfy the young curiosity. Why should a mother be more ashamed of her womb than of her breast? The inquiring child sees the babe at her breast and realizes that it is thus being nourished. He can easily understand that once it was even more helpless and had to be provided for otherwise and elsewhere. But the mother will not explain and the result is that the child invents and fantasies and thus lays the foundation of a structure that will one day fall upon and crush him. The part that the father plays in the procreation of the child should be explained soon afterwards. The supreme embrace is but an exaggeration of the parental embrace which the child witnesses every day. He will display no more astonishment at its revelation, if properly explained, than he does at such familiar marks of affection, nor will he gabble his information. The only reason we should have compassion for the educated mother who does not know enough about flowers to explain sexual matters to her daughter of seven is that we ourselves are compassed with infirmity. My experience has been that having the knowledge, she cannot be persuaded to enlighten her daughter of seven or seventeen save in exceptional instances.

"Mother is the last person in the world to talk to me about such things," was the stereotyped reply I received from nubile girls and young women brought to me for nervous disorder when my profession required that I investigate their sex life. Later when I charged mothers with their dereliction, the customary reply was: "When I attempted to talk to Julia about such matters, she stamped her foot and said ragingly, 'Mother, if you go on talking about those things I shall leave the room. I don't want to hear about them!'" The trouble was that mother had procrastinated. She was under the delusion that sex curiosity and sex feeling occur simultaneously, whereas one precedes the other by a decade or more.

Fathers give a somewhat better account of their intelligence in dealing with their sons than mothers with their daughters. Nevertheless, it is astonishing to note the chances that many fathers take. I recall a splendid, highly intelligent boy who was not giving a satisfactory account of himself in school. During his first two years there he had never led his classes but he was always a close second to the leaders, and having habituated himself to concentration, he had earned a reputation for learning easily. Study had never been a bore and play had always been a delight for him. Now they were both antipathic, and he had become distractible, morose, solitary and preoccupied. The marks of his examinations indicated that he had not the smallest chance of getting into college. Exhortation and threats having failed to improve matters, the director of the school sent him to me. Inquiry revealed an absorbing sex complex, which quickly yielded to explanation, enlightenment and assurance. His father, a conspicuous figure in the law, an executive and college president, and a pillar of the church, had never told him a word about the management of the tremendous force that seeps or sweeps into boys soon after their thirteenth year.

It is in infancy and childhood that children should be taught about sex, when we instill into them the principles of morality: honesty, truthfulness, their relation to property and to persons, their rights and obligations to themselves, the community and the state. Children have to be taught how to manage all the features of the self-preservative urge, and we begin the instruction before they can lisp; why should they not be taught how to manage the race-preservative urge as well, and before they can lapse?

Lubricous Puritans have striven to make love's fulfillment a Gorgon Medusa, and prurient psychoanalysts have made it an Augean stable, but the world is finding a Perseus in the shape of Rights for Women and a Hercules in the shape of public enlightenment which are making ready to decapitate the one and clean the other.

The church, by which I mean organized religion of any variety, has a large responsibility for the reputed uncleanliness of sex. Just so long as religion holds that debasement of the body not only enhances but determines elevation of the soul and that punishment and humiliation of the former contribute to and insure the salvation of the latter, it will stand as a bulwark against sex enlightenment and sex decency. I express no opinion as to whether the church should be reformed, but I am sure that it will continue to have small determining weight in shaping the conduct of individuals and nations so long as it continues some of its present and past day teachings.

Human beings should be proud, not ashamed, of their sex and their potency, and prouder still that they can dominate its display. During their youth they should be told, by those they love and to whom they look up, the reasons for dominating it: why continence pays. Fright is the most treacherous of all levers. It is sure to break when the cause it is lifting to fortune is farthest from safety. The reasons for continence are no risk of disease to the body or death to the soul; the reason is that virtue is its own reward. The man or woman who brings to the love partner virginal offerings makes a priceless gift. The giver blends with the beauty of the universe, the recipient proclaims its joy. What is it in humans that excites our greatest admiration? Self-control and courage. In no way may they be more brilliantly displayed than in management of the sex urge.

We think about sex a great deal of the time, waking and sleeping; we talk about it very little and both thinking and talking are surreptitious. We may not be ashamed to think about it but we are to talk about it, just the reverse of our ego urge. It is with the greatest difficulty that we refrain from talking of ourselves, but we are warned not to think about ourselves because introspection is bad for us. It would make enormously for our welfare here, and I think beyond, were we to balance our treatment of the two primitive urges. "Would you have people go about talking of their sex potency," I shall be asked, "its inhibitions and display, as they now talk about their attitude toward food, their lust for drink, their determination to be thin and how they achieve it?" Scarcely. But I would have them put their sex possession above every fortune that has been vouchsafed them. I would teach them neither to jeopardize it nor to squander it, but to utilize it to their happiness and welfare, and I would tell them that though sex tries constantly to suggest behavior, it usually succeeds only in influencing, not in determining it, and the smaller its success, the greater one's self-respect. I would tell them that the rumor spread by lyricists, and the message broadcast by novelists, that the joys of the world are circumscribed by sexuality are exaggeration and falsehood; sexuality sweetens life but it is not what makes life worth living. It is a priceless possession to be wreathed in pride, not wrapped in shame, to be lifted from darkness to light, from sin to virtue.

There are some parental sins which should be labeled "unforgivable." One is failure to tell children about sex; another is to tell them in such a way that it engenders fear and anxiety. Horace may be right in saying that though one be richer than the unrifled treasures of the Arabs or rich India, he shall not free his soul from fear, but parents can do a lot to prevent fear from entering their children's souls. We shall never be delivered of the burden that our way of looking upon sex has strapped upon us until we deal with it as we do with any other display of nature: in a simple, matter of fact way.

If the parent has not the requisite tact, patience and intelligence for this task, it should be intrusted to teachers. The enlightened rich would have no hesitation, because it is their custom to trust the bringing-up of their children to servants and teachers; the ignorant poor would protest at first, as they always do against every hygienic enforcement, and end by yielding.

Though this is not a discussion of pedagogy, I must interpolate a word about teachers. My observation is that the teaching profession has more atypically sexed members than any other. This is a great misfortune. To no calling is normal sexuality more becoming. Successful education of children rests on two fundamentals: love and facts. The person who has not both cannot be the ideal teacher. That is one of the reasons why celibacy and pedagogy are enemies.

There should be a teacher of social hygiene attached to every public and private school. He should teach the principles of bodily and spiritual health. The obstacle to the success of such a department would be the teacher. Unless he were the right sort, could separate sheep from goats, venomous serpents from benign, and had the right outlook on life, more harm than good might result to the pupil. The right outlook is the biological one. To have sex taught by a celibate woman, stored with sex repressions, or by a pious man spiritually warped by vicarious sex appeasement in his youth, or by one whose sex endowment is feeble or errant, as is the case in so many private schools and colleges today, is to stage a tragedy. But the solution of the problem should not be beyond pedagogy and administration. A country that can accept the risk attached to the activities of so-called psychoanalysts would not be hazarding its chances of salvation by instituting departments of social hygiene in its schools.

The teacher should instill into the child the elemental facts of biology without which no one can claim to be educated even though he can read, write, figure and poetize. Barriers to knowledge are lack of curiosity and of interest on the part of the pupil. Arouse his curiosity and interest and he will learn anything. There is no surer way to accomplish this than to point out the mysteries of his own organism and to show him how the web of life in nature is woven into the woof of life in man. Every child is always interested in his own body. He can be informed about it and its functions by being taught the life histories of familiar plants and of the lower forms of animal life. When the time comes in the course of instruction for the teacher to put before the pupil the facts of sex and reproduction, the child will be purged of prurient prudery and ready to accept a natural attitude toward sex and its display. He will realize that he is not a fountain of vileness and evil constantly seeking an outlet, but the most supreme expression of nature subtly and masterfully controlled by the supremest endowment of God, his spirit or soul.

I can hear such a teacher explaining to the children on whom puberty is about to descend that time, patience and money had been expended to teach them how to manage their self-preservative urge. I hear him reminding them that they were trained like little animals while their intelligence was undeveloped, but that now, confronted with an urge that is oftentimes clamorous and sometimes imperious, they are endowed with the intelligence to direct, subdue and satisfy it. I hear him putting before these young aëronauts about to essay life's flights the things they should know about sex so that they may have successful adult love life, just as a physician explains to a young man about to start for Ecuador how he may avoid yellow fever and malaria. Naturally, I also see the bad boy or the incorrigible girl who is panting to escape from the class that he or she may inject some obscenity and ribaldry into the subject. Like the poor we shall always have them; they are one of our endurance tests.

But if the matter is presented in a scientific spirit, it will be received by the vast majority of children as teachings of botany or of geography are. Proper parental supplementation will readily keep it out of the realm of pruriency.

It is in some such way that sex hygiene should be taught these same children when they reach the age of puberty. Why should we tell them all about tuberculosis and leave them ignorant of syphilis from which the bulk of organic nervous diseases flow? Physicians know that the majority of diseases "peculiar to women" have their origin in a microscopic organism which husbands harbor without knowing it, the relic of an infection that has perhaps even been forgotten. Yet it is considered immodest for a young woman to know the names of the diseases! Both of these diseases are preventable and curable, but every year they claim their victims by the thousands and all because parents have not the moral courage to enlighten their offspring. The only reason they can offer for not doing so is that it might be construed as a license to "immorality." There is a choice between immorality and general paresis.

THE SEXUAL AND MATERNAL INSTINCTS OF THE ADOLESCENT GIRL [1]

By Phyllis Blanchard

WHILE Jung was of sufficiently philosophical turn of mind to enable him to develop the hypothesis of a great evolutionary force of life and the theory of the unconscious to the fullest extent, he was at the same time too much the scientist to neglect the fact that the vital impulse has a somatic as well as a psychic side. We find, therefore, that he describes the organism as equipped with an infinite variety of physical structures, the functioning of which is the physiological mechanism through which the *élan vital*, or libido, finds an outlet in manifold activities. The first expression is an entirely selfish one, and is the desire for nutrition which is manifested through the motor reflex of sucking in the human infant.

In its broadest and most inclusive interpretation, this hunger-motif becomes one of the two great dominating factors in the existence of mankind; the other is the sexual impulse, which, although the Freudians have demonstrated its activities at an exceedingly early age, attains its full significance only at the critical period of adolescence, which is, in a sense, a rebirth of the individual, since with its advent, there must be made readjustments almost as radical as those attending the transition from the prenatal state to the external world. It follows that if we are to make an intelligent study of the adolescent girl, we must know something of the manner in which this second motive is manifested in her feelings and conduct, a knowledge which can be gained only

[1] From *The Adolescent Girl*. New York: Dodd, Mead & Company, 1920.

by a concrete analysis of her erotic life in all its phases.

The most obvious physiological phenomena which characterize the onset of puberty in the female sex are the establishment of the periodic menstrual flow, and the rapid development of the mammary glands and other secondary sexual characters. Besides these, there is a less apparent but equally important change in the whole body metabolism, for as Blair Bell has shown, it is not merely the reproductive organs and their hormones which control the physical manifestations of sexuality, but all the glands of internal secretion, acting together, which determine the erotic life of the individual. Bell concludes that before adolescence, there is very little difference between the metabolic processes of the male and female organisms; but at that period, the endocrinic glands, interacting harmoniously by means of mutual control through the hormones which are produced by them, form a metabolic synthesis which may well be termed the *sex complex* and thus determine the degree of masculinity or femininity.

There are thus seen to be two types of phenomena which compose the physiological side of adolescence: the specific sexual stimuli from the pressure of internal secretions formed within the reproductive glands proper, and a general change of feeling-tone which is conditioned by the functioning of the other glands of internal secretion. This second factor is not at all of a strictly sexual nature, but as Cannon and Crile have shown, is the common metabolic background characteristic of all powerful emotions, whether of fear, anger or sex.

In the case of the adolescent girl the emotional state is of undoubted sexual origin, and is probably produced in response to hormone secretions from the ovaries, which stimulate the other endocrinic glands to activity. It is the general sensations from this increased endocrinic functioning which produce the affective changes in the mental life of the adolescent girl, since in her case there is no direct source of constant stimulation such as that furnished by the accumulation of spermatic fluid in the male. Moreover, this emotional energy does not require a specifically sexual outlet, for by its very metabolic nature, it is readily capable of passing over into some other emotion, such as anger, fear or religious ecstasy. However lightened may be her task of self-control on this account, the adolescent girl has nevertheless entered upon the definitely sexual phase of her existence, a phase which Dr. Frink has very well characterized in these words:

"Sexual emotion, tension, or preparedness is less dependent on external situation than are other normal emotions. We do not feel continual normal anger or fear unless we are continuously subject to an external menace. But sexual tension, or preparedness, may arise in the absence of any external stimulation, and tends to persist until relieved by some suitable action, of which coitus, in the adult, is normally the most satisfactory one. Thus, in the absence of actions adequate in quality or in frequency to discharge the libido, there may come about a state of organic sexual preparedness which is chronic. (This does not mean that the individual need be continuously aware of sexual desire.) In other words, a lack of adequate sexual outlet (and by this is not meant simply abstinence from intercourse) may result in the accumulation in the blood of abnormal quantities of thyroid bodies, and perhaps of sugar, adrenin, and other substances which constitute also an important part of the state of preparedness for non-sexual exertion, such as attack or flight, and this very likely is accompanied by corresponding changes in the sympathetic-autonomic balance."

Correlated with this increased metabolic activity, there is an augmented sensibility of afferent nerves and end-organs, both visceral and peripheral, and it is upon the basis of this organic instability and readiness for reaction that we can best explain the conduct of the pubescent girl. Through all her seeming inconsistencies, she is seeking an outlet for the great reproductive energy which has thus taken possession of her being, and this motive, taken into consideration with the increased sensitivity of the afferent nervous system and the consequent exaggeration of motor response, furnishes the key for a right interpretation of her demeanor.

The first evidences of the awakening *vita sexualis* in the young girl is an inordinate desire to attract attention from the opposite sex. Who has not observed the various ways in which the high school girl, while not admitting her motive even to herself, endeavors to draw the regard of her male companions? Incessant giggling seems to be a veritable disease with her, and although partly due to her new consciousness of sexual differences, and the tension of meeting social situations for which she as yet feels herself lacking in poise, it has also the ulterior purpose of attracting the glances of those erstwhile everyday comrades who are now surrounded by the glamour and fascination of their masculinity.

In addition to these causes for the epidemic of giggling, G. Stanley Hall notes a more useful function, in that it forms one extreme of the hedonic scale whereon the emotions play up and down, in preparation for the joys and sorrows which must be experienced later, in contact with real life. The opposite extreme of the pain-pleasure scale is apparent in the tendency shown by the adolescent girl to weep at the least occasion, or even with no occasion at all. Sometimes she seeks the solitude of her room or of some outdoor nook to indulge in the luxury of tears, especially if their flow is simply the result of nervous fatigue and tension. More often she uses them to obtain the love and sympathy of which she cannot have too much at this time, and finds them a potent means to gain the affection which she craves to a degree almost abnormal in its intensity.

Even more eloquent of her desire to prove attractive in the eyes of others is the passionate love of dress which possesses the girl in her teens. Watch the girls on their way to school. The kaleidoscopic nature of feminine fashions does not dismay them—they follow the modes with the dexterity and nonchalance of practiced lightning change artists. But whatever the fashion, the same adolescent tendency is exhibited,—happy the girl whose dress is more strikingly of the hour than the daring styles worn by her mates. The vogue for colors is as inconstant as that of lines, and no one can prophesy what shade the future will bring forth, yet we may rest assured that we shall see it in hair ribbons and sport coats the very instant that it is first rumored in the latest magazines. The Mary Pickford curls have gone the way of the pompadour, and styles of bobbing change; but the young girl has little thought for past styles in hairdressing,—her one concern is to see that her newly put-up locks are arranged according to the latest vogue. And so it goes, until we wonder when they ever find time to look at the books they carry under their arms, and whether there is ever any thought in their minds beyond the fascinating subject of dress.

It is to be noted that another motive may lurk beneath this love of adornment than the naïve desire to arrest the roving attention of a male. With the dawn of adolescence comes a new self-consciousness as the awakening sexual and social instincts induce comparison with others and emphasize personal deficiencies hitherto disregarded. Psychologists have recognized that every piece of apparel serves to extend the personality, becoming, as it were, an integral part of the wearer's own ego. Hence the adolescent girl seeks to reenforce her self-respect and conceal her failings under the gaudy attire which she assumes. Thus she accomplishes a double purpose, winning the admiration of the other sex at the same time that she wards off social humiliations, which are agonizing to her new-born consciousness of self.

So deep is the adolescent longing for attention and sympathy, and so keen the sorrow over personal failings and criticism, that the girl is prone to indulge in long fantasies wherein she pictures herself lying cold and still in death while a throng of friends and relatives laud her to the skies as they mourn her untimely demise. Oversensitive to the least rebuke, which she interprets as a symbol of lost affection, she also thinks of death as a fitting revenge upon parents or others in authority who have denied her wishes, or treated her harshly. If any proof were needed to demonstrate the fact that at this time of life the death wish is most foreign to the whole organic make-up, which is never more flushed with the joy of living, the very attitude of the girl in these reveries would furnish it. Never does she conceive of death as the absolute end of all things. Instead she always pictures her feelings as she stands apart and sees the mourners gathered around her body and hears their regret and praise. She only dreams of what would happen *if* she were dead.

When the adolescent girl really does commit suicide, and occasionally she does do it in more than a day-dreaming way, it is because of actual mental disease or emotional conflict which only the psychoanalyst can understand. At the period of adolescence, the necessity of transferring the libido from infantile fixations to goals which have a wider social relationship becomes insistent. With normal individuals, this transference is made with little apparent struggle, but with neurotics, there may be a flight from the too stern realities of adult existence, and a seeking for refuge in insane delusions and neurotic obsessions, or even in an attempt to seek a pleasant oblivion like that of the prenatal state in death. Thus, the very will to live, unable to make proper adjustments, and with its energy turned in upon itself, torments the soul in its futile attempts to find expression until it succeeds in the utter negation of its own purposive impulse.

After the first general reaction toward any member of the male sex, there follows a period in the career of the adolescent girl when she begins to exercise her powers of discrimination to a slight extent, and to evince a preference for some particular individual among her acquaintances. Ordinarily, this choice depends upon certain physical traits which become veritable erotic fetishes upon which the young girl lavishes her devotion, while the personality below them is a minor detail. G. Stanley Hall, Slaughter, Smith, and others, have noticed this fetishistic tendency, and commented upon its common occurrence and dominating influence in the girl's life. It is noteworthy that the various characteristics which are thus idolized are all more or less intimately connected with sex from a genetic viewpoint,—for Scharlieb and Sibley have remarked, as have other writers, that the hair, eyes, complexion, etc., grow brighter or clearer at puberty, while Holmes has emphasized the fact that the voice, laugh, etc., had their origin in the mate calls of our animal forefathers. It is safe to conclude that concealment of the primary organs of reproduction has resulted in the focusing of the attention upon the secondary sexual characters, so that these have become as stimulating to the senses as were the genitalia proper when our ancestors first assumed the upright position that brought them into prominence.

Quite as pronounced as the fixation on erotic fetishes is the ideal love for an older person which is almost invariably a part of every girl's development. This, too, has been remarked by a large number of authors,—Kohl and Slaughter having given it especial attention. The psychoanalysts regard it as a normal stage in the transition of the libido from its fixation on the parent to its final goal outside the family group. To what lengths this infatuation for an elder person can carry an impulsive girl, is beautifully illustrated in the autobiography of a prominent woman writer of the day, published anonymously under the title *Me: A Book of Remembrance*.

After several interesting adventures, the heroine, an 18-year-old Canadian girl, "picks up" a traveling acquaintance who occupies her thoughts thenceforth. By the time he has rendered her timely assistance in her endeavor to gain a livelihood, she is desperately in love with him, and begs him to say that her affection is returned. She bends all her energies to living up to what she believes to be his idea of her.

"I deliberately blinded myself to every flaw in Roger," she states. "His selfishness and tyranny I passed over. It was enough for me that he descended into my life for a few days each month and permitted himself to be worshiped like a God. . . . Lolly called my love for him an infatuation. . . . She said that I was a hero-worshiper, and made impossible ideals of unworthy clay and endowed them with fictitious traits and virtues. She said girls like me never really loved a man at all. We loved an image we ourselves created."

Whether it is a real love or no, under its impulsion Nora is spurred on to do more than one act which she regrets bitterly afterward. Because Roger seems loath to declare his affection, she feels that her sentiments are not returned, and in wounded pride, takes pleasure in becoming engaged to other men,—no less than three simultaneously,—in order that she may prove the attractiveness which he thus treats so slightingly. Only when she makes the heart-breaking discovery that her idol is not only a married man but one of notoriously bad morals as well, does she attempt to control her madness, and instead of accompanying Roger on a trip to his hunting lodge, begins her life anew in devotion to her chosen profession.

Perhaps the best summary of this love of the young girl for a man much older than herself, although it neglects the psychoanalytic interpretation, is to be found in these words of Slaughter's:

"There is in the love of the older person a larger element of respect and the mystery of complete development, joined as a rule with sympathetic and gracious treatment. The situation is often one that gives opportunity for beneficial influence and guidance; the older person must not be flattered too much by adolescent affection; it is a passing phase and involves the projection of an ideal to which the older person may, in reality, only remotely approximate."

The psychoanalytic school would offer the explanation of a father substitute to account for the fixation of the young girl upon an elderly man.

The indefinite feeling of attraction which the adolescent girl at first feels toward the opposite sex, is often replaced, a little later, by a state in which a very conscious element of physical sexual desire predominates. That there is vast individual variation in regard to this is obvious to anyone who has observed the adolescent girl even in a cursory and idly speculative fashion. The reason for this wide variation, as Blair Bell has shown, is to be found in the metabolism of the ductless glands. This endocritic theory, while undoubtedly correct, does not explain the absence of a similarly broad degree of difference in the case of individuals of the male sex. In order to understand this phenomenon more clearly, we must seek the aid of genetic psychology, and it is just there that we find further facts which furnish us with an adequate explanation.

In the beginning of human life as such, man, like all other animals, had a definite mating season, of which traces remain even to this day. In proof of this statement, Havelock Ellis quotes examples of the outbreaks of venery that occur among the primitive tribes of Africa and Australia in the spring and fall, and among the Eskimos at the end of the long winter during which they are devoid of sexual desire. Other evidences are found in the May Day and Harvest festivals of the rural British population and in the holiday celebrations of the European peasantry at these times of the year, which tend to assume orgiastic characters. The Chinese holiday called "Walking on the Green" is the survival of the old springtime mating ceremony. A less obvious trace of the old periodic function of sex is the favoritism accorded to June weddings, which have become traditional, and the universally prevalent outbreak of "spring fever," which owes its origin to the restlessness created by sex tension.

As Corin points out, when the struggle for existence became less acute with man's increasing mastery of his environment, the necessity for a definite breeding season passed away, and the human species lost the pairing season which natural selection has generally preserved throughout the animal kingdom. The bi-pedal position, the loss of hairy covering, the intimate throwing aside of garments and the huddling together in the cave-dwellings, and the use of the hand for purposes of stimulating desire, all tended to focus the attention on the organs of reproduction, and to emphasize sexuality as it had never been emphasized. The vast fund of energy which man had developed in his long battle with the environment and with other men, now turned to the sex function as an easily accessible and pleasant outlet, and he demanded that his mate give up all vestige of her old periodicity of function, in order that he might satisfy his new passion.

It was at this time that woman lost her place as the free and equal comrade of man. Previously, her share in social progress had been as great as his, for as Mason has shown, while he had been developing militarism, she had been initiating and perfecting industrialism. Now, however, man came to see in woman, in place of the co-worker, an object wherewith to gratify his lust. There was produced, by the slow process of natural selection, a race of wives too weak to resist such treatment, together with a second type who came to possess the ability to feel the sexual impulse at all times, with only traces of the old periodicity. Thus there came into being the erotic and maternal types distinguished by Ellis, Forel, and others, with all degrees between these two extremes. It is an undisputed fact that these types exist today, and it is herein that we have an explanation for the varying degrees of sensuality which are characteristic of the adolescent girl as of the adult woman.

The adolescent girl who is most deficient in the sexual side of her life may complete her existence without feeling any noticeable sexual desire; indeed, physicians report that they find a large number of cases in which female patients are utterly unable to experience any·such feeling, and ·hence find their marriage vows extremely irksome. Repression of sex feelings in harmony with the demands of society must also be considered in accounting for these types. In some instances, auto-erotic practices interfere with the development of normal impulses.

Normally, the physical sensations of sex longing do appear in women during some period of their adolescence. They are usually very much intensified just preceding menstruation, and again after the third day or so from the beginning of that function, becoming relatively quiescent midway between two menstrual periods. Some girls say that it becomes so strong at this time as to prove a temptation to masturbation or to illicit intercourse. Often this feeling is first aroused by an accidental touch, for touch is intimately connected with the reproductive function. One girl states that she experienced her first sensual thrill when her bosom touched that of her partner during the dance; another that her first sensation of this kind was received as she clung to her escort in an agony of terror; and many are thus awakened by the kisses and caresses of their lovers. Most often, the waking consciousness succeeds in inhibiting a sensation that it has been taught to regard as sinful, and it is carried over into the dream life, where such vigilant censorship is impossible, due to the relaxation of the higher nerve centers in sleep.

Until the psychoanalytic practice came into being, the dream life of the adolescent girl, like that of everyone else, was in large measure a sealed book, but with the aid of careful analyses made by Freud, Jung and their followers, we can at least formulate some general statements which will hold true in the majority of instances. To Dr. Sigmund

Freud belongs the credit for giving us a key for the interpretation of dreams, a contribution as significant for the proper understanding of the psychic life of the adolescent girl as it has been in the treatment of neurotic cases, in which connection it was evolved. Stated in the briefest possible terms, the Freudian theory holds that the dream is the fanciful fulfillment of a suppressed wish, which the waking consciousness will not admit into its ken, but which escapes from this inhibitive influence or censorship, during sleep, and runs riot in the dream life.

It is hardly surprising that the unconscious sexual desires form a large part of this suppressed impulsive energy, for their normal satisfaction is very often incompatible with established social standards, and the dictates of conscious morality even go so far as to forbid the slightest thought of their existence. So deeply, indeed, is the necessity of denying such wishes impressed upon the mental life that very often the sexual meaning of the dream itself has to be cunningly hidden in order to escape the vigilance of the *censor*, so that there must be distinguished in the dream content a whole series of symbolisms which have received an erotic meaning through the old phallic ceremonials of ancient religions, although their sexual meaning has long since been obliterated from the conscious memory of the race, and persists only in the submerged levels of the unconscious psyche.

The suppression of any crudely sexual desire, even in dreams, is especially typical of women, because they have been taught for centuries that passion was the unique possession of the male organism, while the female merely submitted to this sinful act in order to insure the birth of offspring. Thus it has happened that former students of sex psychology have noted the sexual dreams of the man who is practicing continence, but have been strangely silent as to the experiences of women along this line. The psychoanalysts, however, have broken through this barrier of delicate reserve, and have described symbolic dreams of purely sexual charac-

THE INSTINCTS OF THE ADOLESCENT GIRL

ter which they have brought to light in their treatments of nervous diseases. An especially good example of such a dream in the case of an adolescent girl who came to him for treatment is described by Dr. Frink in his latest book.

Miss Sunderland, the patient in question, dreamed "that she was struggling with a large, long-nosed, gray dog which was trying to bite her, while she endeavored to prevent it by holding its mouth shut with her hand. The dog finally did bite her somewhere in the thigh. She saw a little blood flow from the wound, and then she awakened, terrified. This is evidently a sexual dream. Its symbolism is very typical. Young girls are apt to conceive of sexuality as something animal-like or violent. When, therefore, a girl dreams of some violent attack or assault, one can feel assured that she has in mind something sexual. And when this attack results in the shedding of blood and is followed by swelling of the body, the analogy to defloration and a resulting pregnancy is so striking that there need be little doubt as to what the dream means." In this case, further analysis showed that the dog of the dream represented a young man with whom Miss Sunderland was really in love, though hesitating to admit it, and whom she finally married.

An elaborate set of the sexual symbolisms which most frequently occur in these erotic dreams has been worked out by the psychoanalysts, and is probably more or less universally applicable, although it is far from being the all-inclusive content of the dream psyche which was at first claimed for it, as further analytic work with cases of war shock has shown. Herbert Silberer, too, has emphasized the multiple factors of dream interpretation, and concludes that its symbolisms not only veil a suppressed wish of lowly somatic origin, but also express the idealistic strivings of mankind to sublimate this unconscious energy into forms which shall be higher and more beneficial to the individual and to society, just as the alchemists of old tried to transmute the baser metals into pure gold.

It has been the habit of psychologists to deal with the sexual dream of the girl as entirely symbolical, if at all occurrent, for the assumption is made that she never experiences the definitely sexual dreams of her brother. Exchange of confidences with other girls has justified the conclusion that this is an entirely erroneous impression, for the adolescent girl very often dreams of ardent love-making with some man of her acquaintance, or even with someone who is an entire stranger to her waking thoughts. Often these dreams end with the fantasy of sexual intercourse, and even result in a complete sexual orgasm. Day-dreams, too, may take on a specifically erotic character, particularly in the case of girls who have been involved in more or less ardent love affairs and who are temporarily forced to forego the accustomed caresses of the lover.

There is one other aspect of the sexual instinct in the adolescent girl which has received all too little attention except as it has been seen in manifestations so extreme as to be pathological in nature. Intimately connected with the emotion of sex, as the psychoanalysts have noted in their studies of neurotics, is the sentiment of fear. In woman, the fear element is especially predominant, not only because the results of sexual intercourse are more involved in her case, but because for the inexperienced, at least, a vast body of tradition emphasizes this element,—the fear of defloration pains, the horror of passion which she has often been taught is unwomanly, and in cases of extreme ignorance, dread of the unknown processes of the sexual act itself.

In the face of so many terrors it is to be wondered that almost every girl dreams of marriage, and more especially is it astonishing that so many defy conventional morality to become mothers outside the sanction of wedlock. In order to understand this apparent courage, we must recollect the masochistic tendency which is to some extent a part of the female sexual nature. Through a long biological history, man has been the aggressor to whose advances woman passively yielded her charms; he has been the wooer, she the wooed. And this long accustomed compliance with the desires of the more ardent male, necessary for the continuation of the race, has become the natural heritage of woman, so that the impulse to yield to her mate, lawful or otherwise, is stronger than all the fears of present or future pains which may result. Thus it is that we see in our present social system the wife who is faithful to a brutal husband and the girl who is a social outcast, both equally anomalous until we recognize that the masochistic sacrifice of self is a fundamental concomitant of the sexual life of womankind.

These generalizations concerning the sexual instinct of the adolescent girl are more forcibly illustrated by some of the concrete examples which led to their formulation. Except for the description of Mary MacLane, which is drawn from her books, the exact words of the girls are quoted. Nearly all the girls who have been under close observation are the college and university type, and this makes their cases the more significant when it is remembered that many of them have been brought up under the strictest possible code of repression, so that for a long time their sex life was wholly a matter of instinctive response, unguided by any definite information. It is my impression, gathered during two summers' work with factory girls (not in social welfare, but as co-worker with them, so that the observations were perfectly free and natural), that with girls of this class the awakening of physical sexual desire is earlier and more intense. This is due partly to their different environment in which the sexual side of life receives more emphasis, and partly to the fact that they lack adequate means for sublimating their biological energy into intellectual and artistic effort.

Mary MacLane carries her sensualism over into every other sensory domain, so that the red line of the sky at sunset becomes a symbol of the passion which shakes her body, the feel of her garments and even the prosaic eating of food becomes tinged with erotic pleasure. But far from being contented with these symbolic and substitute erethisms, she longs most intensely for the hour which shall give her the supreme satisfaction of physical love in its intensest form, and all her day-dreams center upon the supreme height of her ambitions. Her dream-partner is visualized as a gray-eyed gentlemanly devil, who may ruin her soul if he will, so long as he gives her the supreme satisfaction which her being craves. Thus all her desires converge to the moment in which she can experience in her own person that acme of pleasure, sexual love. One does not wonder that when she writes her third book, Mary confesses that she has never found her dreams realized, for such elaborate visions, whatever their theme, could scarcely hope to find their counterpart in the world of reality. It is noteworthy that in this last volume, too, she replaced her first dreams of a lover with quite as passionate a fantasy of little dream-children whom she holds in her arms, and warms against her breast.

Case 1.[2] My ideal of life after college is marriage, with opportunity to continue work in designing. My plans and interests have broadened with my increase in knowledge. For instance, before entering high school my highest ambition was to be a public speaker and wear a black spangled gown, for I had once seen a reader so dressed and greatly admired her.

Quality of work is lowered during the first part of menstruation, increased during the last part. Marked mental depression during first two days of menstruation, followed by an opposite mental attitude. Languid for first two or three days, then emotions greatly increased in intensity, desire to dance,

[2] These reports were obtained from friends, and girls who wrote me at the request of mutual friends, in answer to very plain questionnaires. I have given the selected answers verbatim, at the risk of reproducing irrelevant material, because they afford such remarkable insight into the mind of the adolescent girl. The questions concerned day-dreams, erotic dreams, experience at menstruation, ideals for the future, religious beliefs, etc. The last question (on religious beliefs) has no bearing on the subject of this chapter, therefore the answers to it are omitted from the reports.

etc. Yes, I know that a girl who has had no actual sexual experience can have dreams of that nature. In myself, they occur after a dance, or any occasion where there has been unusual sexual stimulus. I have spring fever, too, which is similar to the emotion before and after menstruation. It seems to be due to an accumulation of superfluous energy, and I usually indulge in some strenuous exercise.

Case 2. When I entered high school, I had no plans further than going to college so as to have some good times, living in a dormitory. Then, towards the end of my course, I realized that after college one earned one's own living. I thought it would be delightful to be a librarian, for one who loved books must be happy if always with them. But after applying for entrance at Simmons, I solemnly decided that I'd better not become a librarian, since all I knew of that species were withered old maids. I then thought it would be so satisfying to have taught school, and be able to say of great men, "I used to teach him." After a few years of teaching I wanted something tangible as a result of my work, so I decided to become a trained nurse. Only one friend approved this idea. Finally in selfish desperation, I planned on a delightful time studying German at college. Then I was surprised to find my dreams realized in the science of sociology.

For a while the fascination of psychology lured me away from sociology, but I gave that up as I had given up nursing. Jones' book on psychoanalysis made the work of an alienist the most attractive that could be done, just as Alice Freeman's life and Jane Addams' *Twenty Years at Hull House* made an unselfish life seem attractive.

I am always depressed at the menstrual period. Consider myself a failure, unworthy of success. The third day I have always been very lonely, and strongly attracted by the idea of masturbation. Still, I always feel with unusual strength the sanctity of sex at this time, so that I never experience any rebellion against the occurrence of menstruation.

When I was seven, my father told me that the baby sister

came out of mother, not out of the doctor's bag. . . . Two years ago, Dr. X—— said something about a woman who was trying to appear young. He knew that she was older than she said, because he had known her for years. Besides, she had had a Cæsarean operation when her child was born. Did I know what that was? No? Well, right then I learned that babies were not commonly born through the navel. From Havelock Ellis I learned all else there was to know about sex. It was marvelously interesting. For the first time in my life, I became curious, but Ellis went into so much detail that my curiosity was satisfied before it was aroused, almost. I earnestly hoped I was normal sexually, and despised women who were not. Marriage seemed a much more definite thing, and more interesting, really a career in itself. Men now seemed different from women. They all appealed to me rather strongly for a time, but gradually I was forced to find sublimation, as I found that I did not appeal to them any more than I ever had. My fondness for children ran a parallel course with my desire for masculinity.

In my nineteenth year, I remember being much shocked at my moral depravity because of two dreams. In the first, I was sitting on a beam in the barn with a grammar school boy pal, when I felt very much elated in a peculiar manner because my bare foot touched his, and we swung our feet together a moment without speaking. Not many nights later, I dreamed I went down through a hole in the ground, as did Alice in Wonderland, till I came to a beautiful garden. Here, a radiant man, naked, embraced me with his hands and feet so that we seemed welded together. After reading Havelock Ellis I dreamed several times of having sexual intercourse.

I used to think it was simply preordained that somewhere in this big world there was a man whom I should meet in the far future, who would be the perfect complement of myself. We would love each other when we met, and until death. I never would do any cooking, so he must be willing to eat raw food. My career would not be interrupted. We would have fifteen children, who would take care of each other. Now, I have been seriously looking at every man I meet, but I do not find him. I realize that I may never find him. But it does not mean so much to me as I used to suppose that it would. It means simply a choice between a narrow and a wide circle of interest. For children do not take care of each other. And I don't think I'd like to eat raw food myself. My day-dreams are of success, and of self-sacrifice. I have never dreamed of lovers or of love in them.

Case 3. During menstruation I am weaker physically and overcome with weariness for a day, sometimes, but I do not notice any tendency to be irrational, excitable or morbid. I am simply depressed somewhat by physical languor and sometimes pain. I have attacks of spring fever, but have not noticed any similar difference near the menstrual period. I should say my spring fever was attacks of the blues, due to nervous fatigue, discouragement in my work, and desire for masculine company, to put it mildly. I find relief in physical exercise, or work, or writing, usually *to* someone.

At the age of ten, my mother explained most of the physiological phenomena concerned with reproduction, and showed me the big colored illustrations in my grandfather's medical books. I was assured in beautiful language that it was all very lovely, but it took me some years to have any respect for sexual intercourse or see anything but pain and horror in childbirth. At present, though I love children, I do not like the idea of being tied down. If I could combine my ambitions with married life and motherhood without hurting either, I should be most happy. I cannot tell which call will prove the strongest, but at present it seems that art is.

I cannot recall definitely any erotic dream, though I often have them. They are usually vague, unconventional, but not naughty. Complete sexual experience is not necessary for erotic dreaming. My sexual experience has been all but complete, and I have dreamed only a small part of it, such as kissing, physical contact and pressure, but other girls of my acquaintance have dreamed all this and more.

When I was about thirteen, my day-dreams were romantic adventures with handsome men. With the more picturesque events, such as narrow escapes from being murdered by brigands, etc., I imagined all the ramifications of sexual experience. This last I do today, but with added details taken from real life. Books do not tell us so much of the actual workings of such things. Nowadays, my day-dreams are less romantic, and get down to business. I imagine myself being charmingly caressed and supported (bodily, of course). I am delightfully passive and dependent in some strong man's arms, but I also imagine living a humdrum existence with him. A very common dream is partly memory amplified. I go over in my mind two or three love affairs, adding and guessing what might have happened, and ending up with a feeling of relief that I was not carried off my feet and tied up with a wretched, unsuited existence.

Case 4. My plans for the future have changed a great deal since I entered high school. Then, my ambition was to become an actress. I had no great appreciation of dramatic art, but the excitement and glamour of the stage appealed to me strongly. In my junior year of high, a very wonderful English teacher made me feel that a life of service was more important than anything else. I adopted the idea of being "an angel of the slums," and felt that in order to gain my life I must first lose it. This ideal remained with me in a somewhat modified form until my junior year in college, when the fascination of zoölogy decided me to become a doctor. I do not know how I shall find the life of service, even yet.

I have never noticed any marked difference in the quality of my work at menstruation. It does not seem to affect my mental or physical condition in the least, as it does those of most girls, but I am a little weakened physically. After the first half day, I can see little change from my normal condition.

No one has ever given me definite information concerning sexual matters, and it was a long time after the first menstruation that I received any information at all,—probably I was about sixteen. Nearly all I know has been gathered from scattered reading, hearsay, and certain zoölogy courses. At times my lack of knowledge has given me some grave fears, and made me nervous in having anything to do with men. I have never, since I was a tiny child, cared as much for men as for women, but I have never felt any repugnance to them. If I ever met a man who came up to my ideal, and who loved me as I should want to be loved, I should marry him without hesitation. I never felt particularly favorable to the idea of having children. I must confess that it is repugnant to me in every way,—and then, children are such an uncertain lot. However, if I loved enough to marry, which is doubtful, no sacrifice would be too great.

I can recall no erotic dreams, and have heard very little about them from other girls.

Case 5. I read a great deal from seven years or so up to the time I went to college. Reading has given me most of my cultural interests and many of my ideals. In college, I liked English and history for the subjects themselves, and sociology and politics because of the teachers.

I am not sure as to the effect of menstruation on the quality of work done. The quantity is less, and there is more effort, I have no pain, but am languid and lazy, cry easily. I find no marked effect on the sexual emotions. Am apt to be discouraged or irritable the day before the beginning of the menstrual period.

After an experience with a playmate in mutual masturbation at nine or ten, I repented, and turned to better ways. I had two bitterly repented lapses at twelve and fourteen. At eighteen, I was more often tempted, but my lapses were few and far between, and from twenty-one to twenty-four I had a record free from masturbation. During this period of repression, the denied desire expressed itself in very vivid dreams. I would wake thinking the dream had been real, then realize it to be a dream with mingled feelings of shame and relief.

My day-dreams center around a home clearly visualized. I picture myself as the mother of a large family, but their father is a shadowy being. My dreams about special men are always concerned with going somewhere, dancing, etc.

Case 6. My dreams of the future have always been more or less influenced by favorite teachers, I believe. In high school, encouraged by a beloved teacher, I determined to go to college and prepare myself for a life of teaching mathematics, but once there chemistry and physics lured me, as I liked the teachers of those subjects. Of course, the subjects themselves opened up new and hitherto unexplored fields to my exploring mind, but without inspiring teachers, my interest would have waned, as it did in mathematics.

At the menstrual period I have marked attacks of mental depression. There is little or no physical pain, though I am more apt to have some pain than formerly, probably on account of increased sexual tension and nervous strain. Work requires an effort of the will, and causes extreme fatigue. I experience marked increase of sexual desire just before the beginning of the menstrual period, and again after the third day of that function. I also have very vivid erotic dreams at this time. These dreams began when I was twenty-one, and have recurred frequently ever since. Sometimes I awaken before the act is completed, but more often, an entire sexual orgasm occurs. The dreams are most apt to occur well toward morning, and on several successive nights, after which I am too weary to care for anything in the sexual line for a time.

Spring fever is a prolongation of the depression and restlessness and desire for love which accompany the menstrual function. I satisfy it by outdoor life or intensive flirtation.

My day-dreams were originally concerned entirely with

my ambitions for a career and a life of social service. I had never known of physical sexual passion until my junior year at college, when I heard a lecture on sex hygiene. At about the same time, in the course of dances, I began to feel distinct bodily thrills from the pressure against my breast as I was held closely in a partner's arms. Even yet I could not realize that men definitely attracted me. Then I learned about birth control, and realized that marriage must involve frequent sexual relations. As the conscious sexual desire increased, and I began to want the experience I was having in dreams in actual life, I day-dreamed of having masculine love. This reënforced my physical longings, and made me sure I wanted marriage, if it did not necessitate my renouncing all other work.

Case 7. I was put in the convent when a child and came out at seventeen. During summer vacations I made friends with other girls, and always hated to go back to the convent school and leave them, for I loved them. When I was sixteen, one of the girls gave me a novel; I stayed up all night to read it. Oh, how I wanted to be loved! I wondered if I would ever meet a man to love me like the hero in that book. The same week I went back to school, and according to rules had to go to confession. The novel reading was my biggest sin. I was so afraid the priest would scold me. Instead he smiled. Yet he said, "My child, there are bad books, and you who are pure at heart must never know them. The world is full of bad men, too, you should stay here in the convent, and devote your life to prayers and sacrifice." All that year he kept trying to persuade me to stay in the convent, but I wanted to see the outside world. I wanted love, though I knew so little what it meant.

The summer I was seventeen I left the convent for good, and began to work in my father's store. One day,—the very day I put my hair up for the first time,—a salesman asked me to go for a spin in his big car. I felt I was really grown up at last. I told him I was nineteen, it sounded older than seventeen. I said, "Wait a minute till I tell Father." He didn't seem to like that. Well, dad didn't like it either. He sent me home, and the salesman never came back to the store again. My sister told me not to be too nice to strange men. I wanted to know why, so I answered an advertisement and got a book called *Sexual Science*. It was a medical work, and I read it whenever I had a chance. My sister found it and took it away from me. Then I got library books on anatomy, etc.

At eighteen I began my nurse's training. At nineteen I got my first private case, a man patient, but I was too busy to think of his sex. At twenty-one I saw the first circumcision case in the operating room. It was the first time I realized consciously the anatomical difference between the sexes. The doctors teased me because I blushed so much.

It was after this that I began to have such vivid sexual feelings. A few days before and after menstruation, how I longed to be loved. I flirted with the doctors at those times, but at the last minute I'd back out,—I was scared,—and my religion came in, too. They would be provoked, but always let me go, because I was still so innocent.

I am now twenty-three, and deeply in love with another Catholic, who has always respected me as the doctors never did. I have often dreamed of having sexual intercourse with him after he has been caressing me.

I know now that I am the passionate type, and I used to think I was very bad to be so, and bound straight for hell. Lately I have come to understand that it is natural for women to have sexual feelings and my mind is more at ease, but for a long time I thought I was really going to be bad as the nuns said.

Even these few concrete cases show as no amount of abstract discussion could hope to do the strength and vividness of the new affective life upon which the girl enters at pubescence. But the all-important point is the tendency of the sexual impulse to pass over into other forms of emotion, so that the girl is actuated more powerfully by fear, anger, or more especially the religious and æsthetic emotions than at any other time during her life. Frink notes this tendency of the sexual energy to reënforce other emotions in his studies of pathological cases, and points out that no physiological difficulty is involved in this transformation since the same metabolic changes are common to all other emotions as to sex tension. It is this transformation of the emotional energy which suffuses the young girl with a sense of shyness closely akin to fear, or gives her the repellent boldness which makes her appear to be devoid of all sentiments of modesty and humility. Often this unstable emotional state fluctuates between the extremes of joy and sorrow, so that the transition from the supreme ecstasy of happiness to the lowest depths of despondency may be the instantaneous result of the most trivial occurrence. With this affective transmutation is correlated congruous efferent outlets so that the sexual impulse, denied its primary expression, seeks other pathways, sometimes abnormal and injurious, but more often of great use and beauty for the individual and society.

Although the thought of motherhood is not rigorously repressed from consciousness like the idea of sexuality, it is not so easy to detect the presence of any deep maternal instinct in the make-up of the adolescent girl. Anticipations of motherhood are indeed inculcated in almost every girl as a matter of social tradition, but for this very reason it is difficult to be sure just how much of the enthusiasm and love for children which she professes is spontaneous, and how much is due to the unconscious motive of desire for social approval. Dreams of childbirth, which are perhaps more common among girls than the purely erotic dream, are certainly unmistakable evidence of the existence of such an instinct during adolescence, and the psychoanalysts admit that the basis of many a symbolic dream is the secret desire for children rather than suppressed sexual wishes.

In visions of a home and children, again, the day-dreams of the adolescent girl find a fertile theme; indeed her fancies are quite as much occupied with painting pictures along this line as with the visualization of the man who is to share this happy future. As Dr. Peters has found in her work with adolescent girls, the ideal man is more often the ideal father than the perfect lover, and the eugenic motive is taking an ever increasing part in the young girl's conception of her "Prince Charming." That the modern girl is beginning to choose for her husband the man whom she wants to see as the father of her children at least augurs well for the future of the race, and it would also seem to indicate the first faint stirrings of the maternal impulse.

Kohl suggests that the maternal motive prompts the mothering of younger brothers and sisters, and also appears in the love of strange little children and baby animals. All these traits are very apparent in the adolescent girl. The adolescent passion for secrets is recognized by G. Stanley Hall as genetically akin to nest-building and home-making, which were activities carried on with the utmost caution during the long phylogenetic history of the race. That there should be even these suggestions of a maternal instinct during adolescence is remarkable when we consider that at best it can only be faintly prophetic of the powerful impulse to come, since it lacks the complete physiological background which only motherhood itself can give.

THE LOVE PROBLEM OF THE STUDENT [1]

By C. G. Jung

LOVE is always a problem, whatever the age of life we
are concerned with. For the phase of childhood the love of
the parents is the problem; for the aged man the problem
is, what has he made of his love. Love is one of the great
forces of fate that reaches from heaven to hell. We must, I
think, understand love in this way, if we are to do any sort
of justice to the actual problems it involves. This problem is
one of immense scope and intricacy; it is not confined to this
or to that special province, but involves every aspect of
human life. (It is an ethical, a social, a psychological question, to name only a few of the aspects of this many-sided
phenomenon.) The invasion of love into all the aspects of
life that are general—that is, collective—is, however, a relatively small difficulty in comparison with the fact that love
is also an intensely individual problem. For, regarded from
this point of view, it means that every general criterion and
rule loses its validity, just as in the matter of religious conviction which, though perpetually recodified through the
course of history, yet, as an original phenomenon, is always
an individual experience, bending to no traditional ruling.

Moreover, the very word "love" is itself no small handicap
to a clear discussion. What indeed has not been called "love"!
If we begin with the highest mystery of the Christian religion, there is the *amor Dei* of Origen, the *amor intellectualis
Dei* of Spinoza, the love of the idea of Plato, the *Gottes-
minne* [2] of the mystics. When we come to the human sphere
there is Goethe's:

[1] From *Contributions to Analytical Psychology*. New York: Harcourt, Brace and Company, 1928.
[2] Romantic love of God.

> Entschlafen sind nun wilde Triebe
> Mit jedem ungestumen tun,
> Es reget sich die Menschenliebe
> Die liebe Gottes regt sich nun.[3]

Then there is the love of one's neighbor, both in its Christian and Buddhistic characters of compassion, philanthropy, and social service. Next there is love of country, and the love for other ideal institutions as, for instance, the church, etc. Then comes parental love, above all, mother love, then filial love. When we come to conjugal love we leave the purely spiritual realm behind, and enter that between-world that stretches between mind and instinct, where on the one hand the pure flame of Eros sets fire to sexuality, and where, on the other, ideal forms of love, such as parental love, love of country and love for one's neighbor, become contaminated with lust for personal power and the will to possess and command. But in saying this we do not mean that every contact with the sphere of instinct necessarily involves deterioration. On the contrary the beauty and truth of the power of love will prove the more perfect, the more the instinct can embrace it. But in so far as instinct dominates love, the animal will come to the surface. The love of bride and bridegroom can be of the kind that Goethe has in mind when he says:

> Wenn starke Geisteskraft
> Die Elemente
> An sich herangeraft,
> Kein Engel trennte
> Geeinte Zwienatur
> Der innigeon beiden
> Die ewige Liebe nur
> Vermags zu scheiden.[4]

[3] They sleep, the wild impetuous instincts
With every unrestrained deed.
Human love doth stir and quicken
The love of God now breaketh seed.
    [4] When spirit irresistible
    Grasps and holds within itself

But it is not necessarily such a love. It may also be that love of which Nietzsche says: "two animals have recognized each other." The love of the lover goes even deeper. Here the dedication of the betrothal, the pledge of common life are lacking. But in compensation that other beauty, the beauty that clings to what is fateful and tragic, can transfigure this love. However, as a rule, instinct predominates with its dark, slow fire, or its flickering flares.

Yet even here the word "love" has not reached its limits. We speak of "love" to cover the sexual act on all possible levels, from officially sanctioned, wedded cohabitation to physiological necessity which the latter makes or is forced to make of love.

We speak also of love of boys (*knabenliebe*), by which we mean homosexuality, which, ever since the classic period of Greece, has been stripped of the appearance of a social and educational institution, and, in so far as men are concerned, ekes out a wretched and anxious existence as a so-called perversity. In Anglo-Saxon countries, on the other hand, homosexuality among women appears recently to have acquired more significance than Sapphic lyricism, inasmuch as it seems to serve the ideas of women's social and political organization as an advantageous undercurrent, much in the same way as the formation of the Greek city had to thank male homosexuality for an essential reënforcement of energy.

Finally the word "love" must be stretched still further, to cover all the perversions of sexuality. There is an incestuous love, an onanistic self-love, which has won the name narcissism. Besides these, the word love has to include every morbid sexual abomination as well as every greed, that has ever degraded man to the level of the beast and the machine.

> The elements,
> No angel severeth
> The twin natures thus joined
> In their inmost being.
> Only love eternal
> Can achieve this sundering.

Thus we find ourselves in the unprofitable situation of beginning a discussion about a matter and a concept of absolutely unlimited extent and indefiniteness. One feels inclined, at least for the purposes of today's discussion, to restrict the concept of love to the problem, for instance, of how youth in its student days has to come to terms with and behave towards sexuality. But this restriction is precisely what is impossible, since all the aspects I have mentioned above must be included in this problem, and because all the significations of the word "love" are also contained as active factors in the love problems of the student.

We can, of course, agree to discuss the average problem, namely, the queston as to how the so-called normal man has to conduct himself under stated circumstances. Disregarding the fact that the normal man does not exist, there is, nevertheless, similarity enough among individuals even of the most diverse kind, to give us that common ground which could warrant the notion of average possibilities. Here, as always, the practical solution of the problem is conditioned by two factors: on the one hand by the demands and capacities of the individual, and on the other by the circumstances of the environment.

A certain obligation falls upon the opener of a discussion to present a general survey of the problem. Naturally this demand can be satisfied, only if, as physician, I restrict myself to an objective account of things that actually occur, and abstain from that stale, moralizing talk which tries to cloak this subject in a piebald garment of bashfulness and hypocrisy. Moreover, I am not here to tell you what you ought to do. That must be left to the man who always knows what is best for other people.

In the title for our discussion, namely, "The Love Problem of the Student," I must assume that this wording—love problem—refers to the mutual relation of the two sexes one to the other, and therefore must not be construed to mean sexual problem of the student. This provides us with an essential limitation of the subject. The sexual question would come into the discussion then, only in so far as it concerns the problem of love, or relationship. Hence we can exclude from the discussion all those sexual phenomena that do not concern the problem of relationship, namely, sexual perversions (with the exception of homosexuality), onanism, as well as the sexual traffic with prostitutes. We cannot exclude homosexuality, because very often it is a problem of relationship. But we can exclude prostitution, since as a rule it does not involve relationship; the rare exceptions only serve to confirm the rule.

The average solution of the love problem is, as of course you know, marriage. But experience shows that this average truth does not hold good for the student. The immediate cause of this is the fact that from economic reasons the student cannot, as a rule, set up housekeeping. We must also remember the youthful age of most male students, which will not yet bear the degree of social fixation that marriage demands. This is largely due to his unfinished studies, but also to the need of freedom and the liberty to move from place to place as this freedom may decide. There is furthermore the psychological immaturity, the childish clinging to the home and family, the relatively undeveloped capacity for love and responsibility, the lack of any breadth of experience of life and the world, the typical illusions of youth and so forth. There is also a reason that should not be underestimated in the wise reserve of the woman; that is, the girl student in the present instance. Her first aim is to complete her studies and to take up a calling. Therefore she abstains from marriage, especially from marriage with a student who so long as he remains a student is for the very reasons just named none too desirable from the point of view of marriage. Another essential cause of the infrequency of these student marriages is the question of children. As a rule when a woman marries she wants a child; whereas the man can manage well enough for a time without children. A marriage without children has no especial attraction for a woman; hence she prefers to wait.

Recently marriages among students have certainly become rather more frequent. This is due partly to certain psychological changes in our modern consciousness, and partly to a more general dissemination of contraceptive means by which a voluntary postponement of conception is made possible. The psychological changes which, among other things, have brought about the phenomenon of the student marriage come from the general mental upheavals of the last decade, the total significance of which we, as contemporaries, are scarcely able to grasp in all its depths. We can only substantiate the fact that as a consequence of a more general spread of scientific knowledge and a more scientific way of thinking, a change in the very conception of the love problem has taken place. For natural science has made it possible to link up man as the species *homo sapiens* to the whole natural system. This change has not merely an intellectual, but also an emotional aspect.

This vitally new perspective influences the feeling of the individual because he feels released from the chains of that metaphysical determination with its moral categories which was characteristic of the world consciousness of the Middle Ages. He is also delivered from the taboos which those chains had wrought in man's attitude to nature, namely, the moral judgments which in the last analysis always have their roots in the religious metaphysic of the time. Within the national moral system everyone knows well enough why marriage is "right," and why other forms of love are to be condemned. But outside the system, upon the wide playground and battlefield of the natural earth, where a man feels himself to be the most gifted member of the great family of animals, and where perchance he has again forgotten that medieval contempt of the animals which deprived them of human kinship, here he must begin to orientate himself anew.

The loss of the old standards of value means virtually

moral chaos. We feel a doubt about hitherto accepted forms, we begin to dispute about things which long have sheltered behind a moral prejudice. We make intrepid investigations of actual facts, we feel an irresistible need to get clear about the fundamentals of experience, we intend to know and to understand. The eyes of science are fearless and clear; they do not flinch from adventuring into moral obscurities and dirty backgrounds. The man of today is no longer just content with a traditional view; he must know why. This spirit of investigation leads him to new standards of value.

One of these modern points of view is the hygienic valuation. Through a franker and more objective discussion of the sexual question a knowledge of the immense mischief and dangers of venereal disease has become far more general. The duty of consciously maintaining one's own health has superseded the guilty fears of the old morality. This moral sanitation has, however, not yet progressed to the point when the public conscience demands that the same civic measures be taken for dealing with venereal diseases as with other infectious diseases. For venereal diseases are still "improper" maladies, as opposed to smallpox and cholera, which are morally fit for the drawing-room. In a later and better time mankind will ridicule these distinctions.

Apart from the fact of venereal diseases, the widespread discussion of the sexual question has brought the extraordinary importance of sexuality in all its psychic ramifications into the field of social consciousness. A good portion of this work has been achieved by the much abused psychoanalytic research of the last twenty-five years. It is no longer possible today to brush aside the stupendous psychological fact of sexuality with a bad joke or with a slow moral indignation. We begin to place the sexual question within the constellation of the great human problems, and to discuss it with a seriousness commensurate with its importance. The natural result of this has been that much that was formerly held to be established fact has become open to doubt. There is a doubt, for instance, as to whether officially licensed sexuality is the only form of procedure that is morally possible, and whether every other form should be rejected *en bloc*. The arguments for and against gradually lose their moral edge; practical points of view force themselves into the discussion, and finally we begin to discover that traditional legitimacy is not *eo ipso* equivalent with moral elevation. The marriage problem with its usually somber background has become the object of romantic literature. Whereas the romance of the old style concluded with a happy betrothal or a wedding, the modern romance often begins after marriage. In these literary productions, with which everyone is acquainted, the most intimate problems are often handled with a lack of reticence that is positively painful. Of the veritable flood of more or less undisguised pornographic writings we need hardly speak. A popular scientific book, Forel's *Sexuelle Frage,* not only had an enormous sale, it also found not a few imitators. In scientific literature compilations have been produced, that not in scope alone, but also in the nature of the depths which they attempt to plumb, outstrip Krafft-Ebing's work *Psychopathia Sexualis* in a way which would not have been dreamed of thirty or forty years ago. These general, and also generally known, phenomena are a sign of the times. They make it possible for the youth of today to apprehend the problem of sexuality in its whole range much earlier and more radically than was ever possible before the last two decades. There are not lacking those who maintain that this early preoccupation with the sexual problem is unwholesome, and that it is a symptom of degeneration peculiar to large cities. I remember an article which appeared fifteen years ago in Ostwald's *Annalen der Naturphilosophie,* in which an author actually said: "primitive peoples like the Eskimos, Swiss, etc., have no sexual question." It scarcely needs much reflection to understand why primitives have no sexual problems; beyond the concerns of the stomach they have no other problems to worry about.

The latter are a prerogative of civilized man. Although in Switzerland we have no great cities, such problems nevertheless exist. Hence I do not hold that discussion of the sexual question is unhealthy, or in the least degenerate: rather do I see in this problem a symptom of the great psychological revolution of our time. On the contrary it seems to me that the more we discuss this question seriously and fundamentally the better, for this problem is surely a pregnant one for the life and happiness of mankind. The fact that many pursue such discussions to the point of abuse does not spring from the nature of the problem, but rather from the inferiority of the people who abuse it. Abuse after all is common to every time and to every kind of activity.

It is doubtless the serious preoccupation with this question that has led to the hitherto unknown phenomenon of the student marriage. It is a phenomenon of such very recent appearance that from lack of sufficient data it is difficult to form a judgment about it. Early marriages there have been in abundance in former times, marriages also that have seemed very unbalanced from the social standpoint. Thus in itself student marriage is something perfectly possible. But the question of children is another matter. If both parents are studying, children surely must be excluded. But a marriage that is kept childless by artificial means is always somewhat problematical, since children are a cement that holds where nothing else could. And it is the concentration upon the children which in innumerable cases sustains that feeling of common life which is so essential for the stability of relationship. Where children are lacking the interests of the married pair are directed upon each other, which in itself might be a good thing. But in practice, unfortunately, this preoccupation with one another is not always of a very amiable character. Each is inclined to hold the other responsible for the lack of satisfaction felt by both. Probably under these circumstances it is better that the wife should also be studying; for otherwise she is apt to suffer from the lack of an object. Moreover, many women when once married cannot tolerate it without children, and become themselves intolerable. But when the wife is also studying, she has at least a life outside of her marriage that is sufficiently satisfying. A woman who is focused on the child, and with whom the meaning of marriage is concerned more with the child than with the husband, should certainly think twice before undertaking a student marriage. She should also beware of the fact that the maternal feeling often appears in an imperative form only when marriage is an accomplished fact.

Concerning the prematureness of the student marriage we should note a fact that is relevant to all early marriages, namely that a woman of twenty is as a rule older than a man of twenty-five, in so far as psychological judgment is concerned. With many men of twenty-five psychological puberty is not yet completed. But puberty is an epoch of life that is liable to illusion and states of partial accountability. This springs from the fact that the boy, up to the age of sexual maturity, is as a rule quite childish, whereas the girl develops much earlier the psychic subtleties that belong to puberty. Into the childishness of the boy sexuality often breaks with a stormy and brutal entrance; whilst with the girl, in spite of the onset of puberty, it continues to slumber until the passion of love awakens it. There are, however, a surprising number of women in whom effective sexuality, even in spite of marriage, remains long in the virginal condition, first becoming conscious perhaps only when she falls in love with a man other than the husband. This is the reason why very many women have no understanding at all of masculine sexuality; because to a very great extent they are unconscious of their own. It is different with the man; upon him sexuality forces itself as a brutal fact, filling him with the storm and stress of new struggles and needs. There is scarcely one who escapes the painful and anxious problem of onanism; whereas a girl is often able to masturbate for years without knowing what she is doing.

The inrush of sexuality in a man brings about a powerful change in his psychology. He now has the sexuality of an adult man, yet with it the soul of a child. Often like a devastating tide of filthy water, a flood of obscene fantasies and the disgusting puberty talk of his schoolfellows is poured over every tender, childish feeling, in some cases stifling it forever. Unsuspected moral conflicts arise, temptations of every kind lie in wait for the youth and engross his fantasy. The psychic assimilation of the sexual complex is the cause of immense difficulties, even though he may be unaware of the problem.

The onset of puberty also involves a considerable change in the body and its metabolism, as is seen, for example, in the acne of puberty, a common pustular eruption of the face and neck.

In a similar manner his psyche is disturbed and thrown somewhat off its balance. At this age the youth is full of illusions, which are always the expression of a certain loss of equilibrium. For a long time illusions make stability and mature judgment impossible. His taste, his interests, his life projects undergo many changes. He may suddenly fall mortally in love with a girl, and a fortnight later be no longer able to conceive how it could ever have happened to him. To such a degree is he subject to illusions, that he actually needs these mistakes before he can become at all conscious of his own taste and individual judgment. At this age he is still experimenting with life. And he must experiment with it, so that he may learn how to form correct judgments. But no experiments are made without failure and mistakes. Hence it comes about that few men have not had sexual experience of some kind before they are married. At the time of puberty there is a leaning towards homosexual experiences, which are much commoner than is usually admitted. Later there are heterosexual experiences, not always of a very beautiful kind. For the less the sexual complex is assimilated to the whole of the personality, the more will it remain independent and instinctive in character. Sexuality is then purely animal, recognizing no psychic distinctions. The most inferior woman may be good enough. It suffices that she is woman with typical secondary sex attributes. But a false step or two of this sort does not necessarily give us the right to draw conclusions as to the definite character of the man, since the act can occur at a time when the sexual complex is still divorced from psychic influences. Nevertheless frequent experiences of this kind have a bad effect upon the formation of personality, inasmuch as they tend to establish sexuality habitually upon too low a level, so that it becomes incompatible with the moral personality. The result is that, morally, such a man although outwardly a so-called respectable married man, is a prey to sexual fantasies of a low kind, or else he represses them and on some festive occasion they will come leaping again to the surface in their primitive form, much to the amazement of the un-suspecting wife, assuming, of course, that she observes what is going on. Not infrequently in such cases there is also a premature coldness of feeling for the wife. Often the wife is frigid from the beginning of marriage, because her sensation does not respond to this kind of sexuality in the husband.

The weakness of a man's judgment at the time of psychic puberty should prompt him to reflect very deeply before risking a premature choice of a wife.

Let us now pass on to consider other forms of relationship between the sexes that are customary during the student period. There exist, as you know, chiefly in the great universities of other countries, characteristic student liaisons. These relationships have a certain stability and even a certain psychic value, i.e., they exist not only for the sake of sexuality, but also, in many cases, for the sake of love. Instances sometimes occur where a liaison goes on later into marriage. This relationship stands, therefore, considerably higher than prostitution. It is usually limited, however, to those students who were circumspect in their choice of parents. As a rule it is a question of the money-bags, since most of these young women are dependent upon the financial help of their lovers; not that one could say, however, that they sell their love for money. Often such a relationship means for the young woman a beautiful episode in an existence otherwise poor and empty of love. For the man it may be his first intimate acquaintance with a woman, and a memory upon which he looks back in later life with emotion. But often there is nothing valuable in such a connection, partly as a result of crude sensuality, thoughtlessness, and lack of feeling on the man's part, and partly as a result of foolishness, fickleness, and light-mindedness on the part of the girl.

Always, however, there hangs over these relationships the Damocles sword of transitoriness, which hinders the realization of higher values. They are only episodes, experiments of a very limited validity.

The injurious effect of such connections on the formation of personality is due to the fact that the man gains the woman too cheaply. Consequently the value of the object is depreciated. It is too easy for the man to dispose of his sexual problem in such a convenient and irresponsible way. He becomes spoiled and luxurious. Furthermore, the fact that he is sexually satisfied deprives him of a certain impetus which a young man can scarcely dispense with. He becomes blasé. He can wait, and in the meantime can calmly review womanhood passing before him until he discovers the congenial *parti*. Then when the wedding comes along the liaison is thrown over. This procedure is hardly profitable to the character; moreover, the lower type of relationship tends to establish sexuality on a low level of development, which can easily produce subsequent difficulties in marriage. Or if the fantasies on this level are repressed, neurotics are the outcome or, worse still, moral zealots.

Homosexual relations between students of either sex are by no means uncommon. So far as I am able to gauge this phenomenon, I would say that these relationships are less common with us, and upon the continent generally than in certain other countries where the students (male and female) live in colleges. I am now speaking not of actual homosexuals who, as pathological figures, are incapable of a real friendship and, therefore, find no particular sympathy among normal individuals, but of more or less normal young people who feel such an enthusiastic friendship for each other that they express their feeling also in a sexual form. In such cases it is not just a matter of mutual masturbation, which in the earlier phases of school and college life is the order of the day, but rather of a higher, more spiritual form that deserves to be called "friendship" in the classical meaning of the word. When such a friendship exists between an older man and a younger its educational importance is undeniable. A slightly homosexual teacher, for instance, often owes a brilliant educational capacity to his homosexual disposition. Thus the homosexual relation between the older and the younger can be of mutual advantage and have a real value for life. An indispensable condition of the value of such a relation is the loyalty and permanence of the friendship. But only too easily is this the one condition that is omitted. The more homosexual a man is, the more is he liable to disloyalty, and to become a mere seducer of boys. Even where loyal and true friendship prevails undesirable consequences for the growth of personality may easily ensue. A friendship of this kind naturally involves a particular cult of the feelings, hence, of the womanish element in a man. He becomes *schwärmerisch*, soulful, æsthetic, "sensitive," in other words effeminate. And this womanish bearing does not fit a man.

In the friendship between women similar advantages can be brought out; only here the difference of age and the educational factor play a smaller rôle. Its main value lies in the interchange of tender feelings on the one hand, and of ideas on the other. As a general rule it is the high-spirited, intellectual, rather masculine type of woman who is seeking in such a relation a defense against and a superiority over man. Her attitude to man often takes on the character of a disconcerting assurance and a certain delicate defiance. The effect upon her character is to emphasize the masculine traits and to diminish womanly charm. Often a man discovers her homosexuality by observing that such a woman leaves him as cold as an ice house.

The practice of homosexuality does not in normal cases prejudice a later heterosexuality. Indeed occasionally both can exist side by side. I have seen a most intelligent woman who lived her whole life in a homosexual relation, and at fifty entered into a normal relationship with a man.

Among the sexual relations of the student period another peculiar form must be mentioned, which also falls within the orbit of the normal, namely, the relation of the young man to the elderly woman, who if possible is married or at least widowed. You will perhaps remember Jean-Jacques Rousseau and his relation to Madame de Warens. This or a similar kind of relation is what I am referring to. Usually in these cases the man is of a timid nature, unsure of himself and inwardly anxious, in short, childish. He naturally seeks a mother. Many women like nothing better than a rather helpless man, especially when they are considerably older than he; in fact they do not love the strength, the virtue, or the merit in a man, but his weaknesses. They find his infantilities charming; if he stammers a little he is enchanting; or perhaps he is lame, and this excites maternal compassion and a little more besides. As a rule the woman seduces him, and he wraps himself in her maternal atmosphere.

Not always, however, does a timid youth remain half a child. It may be that just this surfeit of maternal solicitude is the thing his undeveloped virility needs in order to bring it to the surface, and the relationship with such a woman will enable him to educate his feeling into full consciousness. He learns to understand a woman who has had experience of life and the world, and who is conscious of herself. Thus he obtains a rare opportunity of a glimpse behind the scenes of the world of men and women. But this advantage is gained only by the man who soon outgrows this type of relationship; for should he stay in it her mothering would ruin him. Maternal tenderness is the most mischievous poison for the man who must prepare himself for the hard and pitiless struggle of life. If he will not let go of her skirts he will eventually become an invertebrate parasite—for as a rule she has money—and gradually sink to the level of parrots, lap-dogs, and old dames' cats.

The natural course of our discussion now leads us to that form of relationship which yields no solution of the sexual question, namely, the asexual or "platonic" relationship. If an exhaustive statistic of student relationships could be made, it would probably show, if my judgment be correct, that with us in Switzerland the majority of students favor platonic relations. Naturally, this raises the question of sexual abstinence. One often hears the view that abstaining from sexual intercourse becomes injurious to health. This view is wrong, at least for the student phase of life. Complete abstention has an injurious effect upon the health, only when the age is reached when the man could win a woman, and when, according to his individual way, he should win her. The extraordinary intensification of the sexual need that so often accompanies this particular psychological constellation has the biological aim of clearing forcibly out of the way certain scruples, prejudices, and hesitations. This is at times most necessary, for the need to decide in favor of marriage with all the doubtful possibilities connected with it, has made many a man shy. It is only natural, therefore, that nature tries to push him over the obstacle. Resistance against and abstention from sexual expression under such circumstances may certainly have injurious effects; but this need not be the case of course if no physical or psychological probability or necessity presents itself.

This question has a certain similarity with the question of the injuriousness of onanism. Under circumstances where either from physical or psychical causes normal intercourse is impossible and it is used merely as a safety valve, masturbation has no ill-effects. Those young people who come to the doctor suffering from the harmful results of masturbation are not by any means excessive onanists—the latter as a rule need no physician because they are not at all ill—but their onanism has bad results because it involves psychic complications. On the one hand through the stings of conscience, and on the other through a riot of sexual fantasies. This latter form is particularly common with women. Onanism that involves psychic complications of this kind is harmful, but not the ordinary uncomplicated masturbation due to necessity. But when onanism is continued into that age of life when the physical, psychical, and social possibilities of normal intercourse are present, and masturbation is indulged in in order to evade the necessities and responsible decisions of mature life—then it is harmful.

Platonic relationship is very important in the student period. Its commonest manifestation is flirting, which springs from an experimental attitude that is quite appropriate at this age. It is voluntary and, by virtue of a tacit but general understanding, it is without obligations. That is both its advantage and its disadvantage. The experimental attitude makes it possible for an acquaintance to be formed without immediately fatal results. Both sexes exercise their judgment and dexterity in reciprocal expression, accommodation, and defense. Innumerable experiences that often prove uncommonly valuable in later life can be included in the category of flirting. But, on the contrary, the absence of obligation often tends to seduce a man or a girl into the practice of habitual flirtation, and then they grow shallow, superficial, and heartless. The man becomes a drawing-room hero, a heart-breaker, never dreaming what a dull insipid figure he presents. The woman becomes a coquette whom a serious man instinctively feels is not to be taken seriously. Hence flirting *à tout prix* is not to be commended.

A phenomenon that is as rare as flirting is common is the genesis and conscious cultivation of a serious love. We might term this phenomenon simply the ideal case, without thereby committing ourselves to traditional romanticism. For the formation of the personality the timely awakening and conscious cultivation of a deep, serious, and responsible feeling is undoubtedly of the highest value in every respect. For the young man such a relationship can be the most effectual shield against all side-tracks and temptations, against all physical and psychic hurts, and can also be a powerful spur to industry, proficiency, loyalty, and reliability.

There is, however, no value so great that it has not also its unfavorable aspect. A relationship that is so ideal easily becomes exclusive. There is before his eyes ever the same object and the same goal. Through his love the young man is too much cut off from the acquaintance of other women; and the girl does not learn the art of erotic achievement, since she already possesses her man. And the possessive instinct of the woman is a dangerous thing. It may easily happen that the man, regretting all those experiences with other women that he omitted to have before marriage, decides to make up for them later.

It must not be concluded from the above that every love relationship of this kind is ideal. There are cases which are exactly the opposite, where, for instance, a sweethearting begun in schooldays is somehow prolonged by force of habit and for no other intelligible reason. From inertia, lack of spirit, or awkwardness they simply cannot get free of each other. Perhaps the parents on both sides find it quite suitable, and inasmuch as thoughtlessness and habit gave it birth, so passivity rules it to the end. They put up with it as a *fait accompli,* and simply endure it. Then the disadvantages accumulate without a single advantage. Whatever benefit may be assumed for this state of things is only apparent, since as regards the formation of personality it is merely an unhealthy ease and passivity that entirely frustrates the realization of valuable experiences and the exercise of manly or womanly gifts and virtues. Moral qualities are only won in freedom, and are only proved in situations that are morally dangerous. The thief who refrains from stealing because he is in prison is not a moral personality. The parents of such children may indeed blink fond eyes upon this touching marriage, and add the respectability of their progeny to the tale of their own virtues, but this "virtue" is only a phantom, not moral strength, but immoral complaisance.

With this very brief survey let us turn from the field of living phenomena to the chapter of desiderata and utopian possibilities.

Nowadays we cannot discuss the love problem without also speaking of the utopia of free love, including trial marriage. To anticipate somewhat I must say that I regard these ideas as in the nature of wish-pictures, or attempts to make easy something that in actual life is invariably difficult. Our time is certainly prolific in these attempts. Were there not more than 100,000 Swiss citizens who imagined that the dividing up of property would achieve the goal; whereas every man knows that only the initiative, the conscientiousness, and the responsibility of the individual maintains the race. Just as there grows no herb which can keep away death, so there exists no simple means which can make a hard thing, as life assuredly is, an easy matter. We can only overcome the force of gravity by a corresponding application of energy. Thus the solution of the love problem challenges the whole of a man. Satisfactory solutions are found only when a totality is given to the work. Everything else is only patch-work and in the long run unserviceable. Free love would only be thinkable if every man achieved morally his maximum accomplishment. But the idea of free love is not invented for this end, but in order to make what is difficult appear easy. To love belong the depth and loyalty of feeling, without which love is not love but mere caprice. True love will always engage in lasting, responsible ties. It needs freedom only for the choice, but not for its accomplishment. Every true, deep love is a sacrifice. A man sacrifices his possibilities, or, to put it better, the illusion of his possibilities. If this sacrifice is not made his illusions hinder the realization of the deep and responsible feeling, and accordingly the possibility of experiencing real love is also denied him.

Love has more than one element in common with religious conviction; it demands an unconditioned attitude and it expects complete surrender. Only that believer who yields himself wholly to his god partakes of the manifestation of divine grace. Similarly, love reveals its highest mysteries and wonder only to him who is capable of unconditioned surrender and loyalty of feeling. Because this is so hard, few indeed of mortal men can boast of achieving it. But just because the most devoted and truest love is also the most beautiful let no man seek that which could make love easy. He is a sorry knight of his lady who recoils from the difficulty of love. Love is like God: both give themselves only to their bravest knights.

In much the same terms must trial marriage be criticized. The very fact that a man enters marriage on trial means that he makes a reservation; he wishes to insure himself against the chance of burning his fingers; he means to risk nothing. But thereby he frustrates in the most effective way possible the realization of a real experience. You cannot experience the terror of the polar ice by perusing a book of travel, nor can you climb the Himalayas in the cinema.

Love is not a cheap matter; let us therefore beware not to cheapen it. All our evil qualities, our egotism, our cowardice, our so-called worldly wisdom, our greed—all these things would like to persuade us not to take love seriously. I must even regard it as a misfortune that nowadays the sexual question is spoken of as something distinct from love. The two problems should not be separated, for when there is a sexual problem it can only be solved by love. Every other solution would be a harmful surrogate. Sexuality released as sexuality is brutish. But as an expression of love sexuality is hallowed. Never ask therefore what a man does, but how he does it. Does he act from love and in the spirit of love, then he serves a god, and whatever he may do, it is not our business to judge, for it is ennobled.

I trust these remarks will have made it clear that I make no sort of moral judgment about sexuality as a natural phenomenon, but prefer to make moral judgments dependent upon the way it is expressed.

VIII

SEX IN LITERATURE

CONTEMPORARY SEX RELEASE IN LITERATURE [1]

By V. F. Calverton

THE twentieth century crosses a new phase in the cultural history of the modern world. The World War brought to an end the illusionment of bourgeois idealism. World leadership has become entirely a matter of economic resources and power. The shift of supremacy has been determined by these factors. England, which formerly replaced Italy as the center of world power because of its position of vantage in the commercial world, has reluctantly relinquished its supremacy to the United States which, with its superior natural resources and superior position of vantage because of the development of ocean traffic in the Pacific as well as the Atlantic, has become the dominating dinosaur in the modern menagerie of world control.[2] The Far East is at present a shadow that time threatens to spread into a giant. Imperialism has engulfed democracy into the maw of the ridiculous.

The bourgeoisie, still the ascendant in society, is undergoing, despite its bellicose expansion in unexploited countries, a process of decay. Its philosophy, shot through with contemporary contradictions, is deteriorating into a myth impossible because absurd. The heyday of the bourgeoisie in the nineteenth century overflowed with the richness of promise and the prophecy of poet. The proletarians and æsthetes of the last years of the century, however, exposed and satirized its slipping pretensions. The twentieth century has transformed the exposure and satire into inescapable logic.

The bourgeois philosophy was built upon the theory of

[1] From *Sex Expression in Literature*. New York: Horace Liveright, 1926.
[2] Cf. Horrabin, *Economic Geography*. Also Trotsky, *Whither England?*

laissez-faire economics and the pragmatic concept of individualism. The very development of the social contradictions in capitalism has stultified their practice and defense. Even economists as conservative today as the asinine Carver recommend restricted *laissez-faire,* and all radical economists advocate its abandonment. The development of corporations and monopoly, the advance of the trustified state of industry, have revealed the fallacies of the *laissez-faire* doctrine. The very nature of the trust annihilates competition. Competition then takes place between trusts. National trusts struggle with other national trusts in an endeavor to capture foreign markets and exploit natural resources.[3] The trust becomes a tremendous collective enterprise in which everyone connected with the organization coöperates except in the profits. Competition is kept alive only between large units, between the trusts themselves. The petty bourgeoisie, the owners of small businesses, are slowly and excruciatingly extinguished. The trust exploits the public—and so we have anti-trust laws which are like the gestures of a comedian who cries to the audience to stop laughing at the contortions that he is inevitably continuing and perfecting. In brief, the trust destroys the free competitive market, that the older economists had postulated as necessary to the evolution of *laissez-faire* economics, and in the exigency to control the trust, restrictions are intruded that are contrary to the *laissez-faire* doctrine itself. Thus, the economic philosophy of the bourgeoisie, with the new developments in its industrial life, has become anachronistic and untenable.

In the very criterion of bourgeois production—efficiency—inheres another contradiction that has hastened the decay of the system. Efficiency demands effective, unwasteful organization. Competition means waste. Many firms, with different overhead expenses, battling blindly with a market that is as fickle as fate, is evident waste and social extravagance.[4]

[3] John Bakeless, *Origin of the Next War.*
[4] Stuart Chase, *Waste.*

The corporation and trust avoid this useless expenditure. To attain greater efficiency, therefore, the competitive enterprises must give way to trustified, which again spells the finale of free competition in manufacture, sale and purchase. The eventual efficiency of it all, it is obvious, leads to a World Trust or Corporation.[5] But here again another contradiction is interpolated by social circumstance. Capitalism has deepened and aggravated nationalisms and promoted the national profits creed to such an extent, fortifying it with armies, navies, airplanes, submarines, and gases, that wars gleam and glare at every maneuver of national enterprise. And wars threaten to destroy the very unity that industry inevitably demands.[6]

With the evolution of these changes and contradictions in economic life, and the rapidly disappearing faith in the *laissez-faire* economics of the bourgeoisie, there has weakened and receded the bourgeois concept of economic individualism. The centralization of industry which we have just described, and the consequent centralization of wealth, which has made it possible for about 2 per cent of the people of the United States, for instance, to own approximately 65 per cent of the wealth, have darkened the old cry of the Jeffersonians into a protest of abiding futility. In simple terms, the individualism, the freedom-for-all doctrine, of the bourgeoisie, pertinent in the early days of capitalism, has now become a delusive fiction. The freedom of the individual today in economic enterprise is very often a freedom to starve—or become a wage slave. It is *big business* that is dominant. The little *entrepreneur,* as we have said, is mercilessly crucified. The individual worker is paralyzed if he stands in isolation and fights as an individualist. The heroics of the La Follette campaign in 1924 with their promise of a return to the days of '76 was as hopeless a gesture as the bombast of a Tam-

[5] Gillette, *The People's Corporation.*
[6] Angell, *The Great Illusion.*

many alderman. Collectivistic labor has replaced individual-istic. The original individualism of the bourgeoisie has led to the contemporary collectivization of the proletariat. In-dustry today, as we said in our reference to the trusts, is moving in the direction of collectivism in everything but the proceeds. This collectivization of labor has led to another contradiction in the philosophy of the bourgeoisie. Its in-dividualism has become an absurdity.

And from this collectivization of labor has come the or-ganized, swiftly solidifying proletariat, with a collectivistic attitude toward society. This organized proletariat has acted both as a source of social control and as a source of social destruction. Instrumental in the decadence of the bourgeoisie, it is also instrumental in fashioning new attitudes and new philosophies. A new literature has been influenced by its democratizing, revolutionary force.

From all of these contradictions and catastrophes of con-flict have come the inevitable decadence of the bourgeoisie and its philosophy of life. The evidence is upon us in such a vivid flood of detail that only the zany can deny it. Bourgeois morality is disintegrating so rapidly that it has been flung to the defensive by the impetuosity of a revolt that has risen into a movement in these recent years of parlous change. In sex life the bourgeois rigidities have broken into barren rhetoric. The upper tiers of the bourgeoisie, the plutocracy of our day, wallowing in wealth that is unearned and that multiplies without a turn of the wrist, has forsaken the old virtues for the older vices. The moral pollution of the upper hundreds has become a social axiom and a news-paper classic. The basis of this change in life *mores* of the upper bourgeoisie, a change which periodicals parade, novels illustrate and courts prove, is to be explained in terms of simple economics. The bourgeoisie of the eighteenth and nineteenth centuries was an industrious class, participating in the actual work which made its wealth. Its economic virtues, as we have shown, derived their force from the exigencies of its life. Today the upper bourgeoisie is a comparatively leisure class, living upon unearned incomes and participating little if at all in the labor of production. The actual work, once done by the owners themselves, is now achieved by superintendents, managers, foremen and efficiency experts. The upper bourgeoisie can now winter in Florida and summer in Maine while its wealth is squared in the mills of South Carolina or the mines of Mexico. As a result, the economic virtues of the older morality are remembered as a Sunday tradition but unpracticed as a week-day performance. In short, this group can afford to be immoral, as immorality is conceived according to bourgeois standards. So we have in our society divorce-dramas which transform the life of the upper bourgeoisie into a spectacular stage of newspaper comedy. It is the petty bourgeoisie, still suffering from economic uncertainty and beguiled by the illusion of suppressed desires, who keeps the old bourgeois morals alive with weakening but still aggressive vigor and indignation.

Another contradiction fatal to the old bourgeois morality finds its curious origin in the increase of insanity. Capitalism has created a life of rushing excitement and expansion, of incessant and disconcerting change, in which the individual often finds adjustment difficult and disastrous. Increasing insanity, under these conditions, becomes unavoidable. Alienists come into demand. Psychiatry clinics become a necessity. Psychiatry becomes a science. Psychiatric investigations and theories become inevitable. Thus, Freud, Jung, Adler, Stekel, Janet and others become prominent.

Sex was rediscovered by the psychoanalysts. The consequences of bourgeois morals were revealed in startling fashion. Something of the perfection of civilized virtue which the Victorians had made their boast was seen to fade into a putrid rationalization. Repressions became anathema. The Victorians had cultivated them; the moderns endeavor to avoid them. The dangers of repressions were seen to extend from the individual to the whole of society. Regardless of scientific caution, the Freudian theory was introduced into every field of analysis: philosophic, scientific and æsthetic. Even in literature, the novel, the story, the play, the Freudian concept prospered. While nations have been psychoanalyzed,[7] and the work of genius shown to be the result of erotic complexes,[8] analyses more mythical perhaps in much of their detail than scientific, the actual substance of literature has been changed, in many instances, to harmonize with the new psychology. The phallic symbolism of Beardsley's art is mild compared with some of the bold configurations of modern art and some of the stage presentations of erotic phenomena. The sex descriptions of Hardy are almost fastidious beside the sex descriptions of James Joyce, Sherwood Anderson and Theodore Dreiser.

Reflecting a state of society, dissecting a situation of social abnormality, Freud, with his overwhelming emphasis upon sex as the central factor in all life-processes, has become the vogue in cultural circles. Freud has become as famous as Shakespeare and certainly more read. In fact, he has become a myth.

This reaction toward Freud is all part of the general revolt against bourgeois morals that has so excitingly enthralled our youth and so virulently enraged our fathers. A product of the very society which his psychology is hastening on the toboggan of decay, Freud's declaration that what we need today is not more morals but more knowledge is significant of a new attitude that is essentially salutary in its release from the repressive *mores* of the bourgeoisie. Only with the decay of the bourgeoisie, of which it is a reflection, could such an interpretation of life as the Freudian become at all popular and acceptable.

[7] Oppenheim, *Psychoanalysis of America*. Kansas City: Haldeman-Julius.
[8] Kempf, *Psychopathology*. Section on Darwin. Also Freud, *Leonardo da Vinci*.

The economic independence of woman is another important factor in the evanescence of bourgeois virtue. In the eighteenth and nineteenth centuries woman was not only economically dependent upon her husband, but work for her was taboo by custom except in the lower classes, and legal procedure afforded poor protection for her possessions. Domestic devotion was perpetuated by economic security. The developments in contemporary society, however, have changed the situation. The economic dependence of woman is rapidly disappearing. The political freedom, legal security and economic independence of the new woman have turned Ibsen's *The Doll's House* into an unthrilling anachronism. One can still recall the time when *The Doll's House* was the dramatic handbook of the feminine revolutionist. Today its theme, its object, are no more radical but commonplace. The bondage under which woman lived and suffered, the hothouse atmosphere which she was forced to breathe when confined by the dictates of bourgeois conventionality, have practically disappeared except among the orthodox vestiges of the old order. Nora is no longer a study in the future, no longer a promise—but an actual fulfillment. The fragments of the old morality that Nora flung aside with such audacity and command, with the new woman of today have been subtly merged and lost in the rising concept of a new morality or been triturated into nothingness. The revolutionary is steadily fading into the bromidic. The strange has become ordinary, the unusual common. The movement for the political emancipation of women has spread almost over the entire civilized world. Her economic advance we have adverted to in earlier sentences. This growing freedom on the part of the new woman is a result of the hastening concentration of industrial production which has swung woman into its gigantic orbit and driven her to the economic as well as political defensive. Only in countries where industry is yet in embryo, in countries like Mexico and the tropical republics, has the condition of woman remained unchanged. So,

Nora's heroism is no longer a breath-seizing dénouement. Sex life has advanced in the decades that have split the day of *The Doll's House* and ours.

The family, as a whole, has changed. The attitudes of children toward their parents have gone through a score of searing mutations. Modern fiction reflects this revolt. Filial impiety and rebellion are exalted in the modern novel. The sexual sybarite is described today neither to horrify nor distress. Illegitimacy of birth or promiscuity of love, the midnight manias of Parisian grisettes or the flying cries and antics of the basement bordello, have become the commonplace of fiction. Women parading the streets in knickers today would have been like phantoms from the world of harlotry to the *good-minded* Victorians. This new attitude toward sex, the sweep and swing of the new morality, are incontrovertible evidences of the decay of the old ethics and the old society.

In literature the contrasts in attitudes of last century and this can be illustrated excellently by reference to two novels: George Eliot's *Adam Bede* and W. L. George's *Bed of Roses*. In *Adam Bede* we have sexual dereliction treated with a candor that was always characteristic of the Victorian approach to the delicacies of sex. Hettie's sin is considered profound if not irremediable. Victoria Fulton's maneuvers, on the other hand, are considered in an utterly different spirit. The economic drive to prostitution is recognized, admitted and described. The intimacies of Victoria's sex life are not evaded by the glib or somber phrase, or the sprinkling of asterisks, nor is a sermon appended to each or any of her defections from established virtue. As in Zola there is a cognizance of social determinism, a realization of the effect of environment in deciding the nature of human response, its beauty or baseness, its grandeur or decay.

With the viceless Victorians a girl could not kiss until engaged, venture far from the fireside with a man unless chaperoned, embrace until married, or bear child until the proper months had hallowed the preacher's gesture. But today, coetaneous with the emergence of the new woman, has come a new youth which is in active rebellion "against our system of taboos, tribal superstitions, intolerances and hypocrisies." [9] Judge Lindsey in his recent book, *The Revolt of Modern Youth,* has made a careful and illuminating study of the nature of social and sexual relations between the youths of today, and it is because his conclusions are based on fact, on actual contact and observation, that they are so signal. Correctly observing that the revolt of youth today has "the whole weight and momentum of a new scientific and economic order behind it," Judge Lindsey enters into a serious investigation of facts as he has known them before he sets forth his conclusions. With the automobile, the telephone, the dance halls, the shores, all part of the age of flappers and jazz, the innocence of ignorance has dissolved. In the youth world of today a girl can

go automobile riding (with boys) at 13 . . . drink freely when 18 and participate in lovemaking at any time. Kissing, petting and other tentative excursions into sex experience are taken for granted.

In other words, the Victorian girl has become obsolescent. As to the actual character of sex experience, Judge Lindsey's conclusions are again striking if not startling. After an examination of cases and averages, it seems a conservative estimate to state that 50 per cent of high-school boys have sex relations either with their girl friends or prostitutes. Among high-school girls the figures are even more interesting as a index to our changing morality. More than 90 per cent indulge in kissing and hugging, at least 50 per cent of this 90 per cent indulge in other sex liberties, which "by all conventions are outrageously improper," and 15 per cent to

9 Ben B. Lindsey, *The Revolt of Modern Youth.*

25 per cent of the original 90 per cent "eventually go the limit." [10]

Compare this status of morality with the status of morality of the Victorian girl and a picture is presented that is unforgettable for its stark and vivid contrast.

Out of all of these chaotic changes and contraditions in social system and social ethics, has come the new literature with its new freedom and its new morality. Victorian smugness has become a despicable deceit—except with the Frank Cranes and Henry Van Dykes who decorate it with starched metaphor and stale simile. Victorian realism has become contemporary sentimentalism. The æsthetes of the 1890's had begun to break away from the Victorian tradition; the æsthetes of the teens and twenties of our century have completed the rebellion.

However we may regard the psychology of Freudianism, the problem of sex in modern society is of incalculable significance. The Victorians in trying to ignore and suppress it committed a grave error. There can be no genuine realism if the sex motif be eliminated from the substance. To again admit the sex motif meant a return to the candor of description which bourgeois literature had eclipsed. It did not, nevertheless, revert to the candor of sex representation that had given Elizabethan literature such passionate energy and power. Civilization has changed. Individualism has spread. Sex antics have complicated. Eccentricity has been cultivated, and insanity has increased. Repressions have diverted impulse and twisted it into strange shapes and drives. Madness has become allied with genius and the morbid with the profound. Sex expression in the new literature, therefore, is not the bold gay affair that it was in the hands of the old dramatists, but has added to its ingenuousness and zeal, in line with the new civilization which it mirrors, a fascination for the interstitial manifestations of erotic affection and be-

[10] It is important to remember that, as Judge Lindsey says, his cases are "drawn from all levels of society."

havior. Bourgeois life and literature had endeavored to stifle natural tendencies and urges. The outbreak against this reaction was necessarily extensive and violent. While genuine realism cannot escape sex, it can be ruined by preoccupation with the theme to the exclusion of everything else, as in the absurdities of *Many Marriages,* and thus turned from the intense to the insipid. After all, as we have seen, sex expression in literature is an expression of social life, of class tendencies and group economics, and an enduring realism should aim neither to be hindered nor consumed by sex.

The protest against sex freedom in contemporary literature has seemed amazingly childish and sacrosanct. Fortunately, it is a losing protest. The age is in conspiracy against it. The changing economic conditions, which we described in earlier paragraphs and chapters, with the resultant decay of bourgeois morality, have produced a different reading public as well as a different author's psychology. Many of the ladies of the last century, who would not read Mrs. Aphra Behn, were they living today would read Mr. Sherwood Anderson or Mr. Theodore Dreiser, or if interested in popular fiction devour the novels of Beatrice Burton and Elinor Glyn. While the bourgeoisie, through their censorship and vice committees, may still suppress books dangerous to their morals, the advance of the new literature continues notwithstanding. American and English literatures of today have been captured by the insurgents. The new literature is synonymous with the new morality.

The conflict between the old school and the new, the mentally lapidified vestiges of the old order and the actively courageous defendants of the new, has been no mild or listless affair. The old scare-faces are still voraciously eager for attack. They are still intent upon purifying literature of value. Books are still banned and their plates confiscated by the contemporary Endicotts. But the battle, as we said, is going the other way. The brave essay of Mr. Mencken, *Puritanism a Literary Force,* the singular dissections of the bourgeois attitude by Harvey O'Higgins' *The American Mind in Action,* the piercing study of Randolph Bourne, *The Puritan's Will to Power,* and a score of other studies and analyses, reflecting the trend of the new motif, have not been without influence. Zola may still be objected to by the sex-starved spinsters of the purity league, the *Dial* excluded from the files of a public library, but the cynosures of American and English literature today are anti-bourgeois in morality if not in economics. The defense of the bourgeoisie grows more aggressive as it is driven to the corner, and hence its vigorous attempts at suppression today are but natural continuations of its old tradition, intensified, however, by the stress of situation that is steadily and sharply converting its protest into futility.

The actual developments in this struggle for freedom from the fetters of a decaying social class are abundant with farce and tragedy. Extending from the famous case of the man who was arrested for sending a passage from the Bible through the mails and the notorious instance of a volume of Ovid being interrupted by the Post Office at Baltimore while on its way to the hands of a tame professor at Johns Hopkins University, to the actual prosecuting of authors and imprisonment of publishers,[11] the melodrama of suppression has furnished the reading public with exciting diversion and thrill. The forensics involved have been flavored with a mingling of casuistry, cleverness and stupidity. In no other testimony is the clash of social and moral attitudes more nakedly revealed

Although the new intransigeants have leaped into the literary limelight, it should not be thought that their new literature has not suffered from the ferocity of the virtuous. In the gallant game of suppression and destruction, Anthony Comstock has been most dutifully illustrious. In his zeal for virtuous banality he destroyed

[11] Henry Vizetelly, for instance, was imprisoned at the age of seventy-three for publishing Zola's works.

. . . something over fifty tons of *vile* books; 28,425 pounds of stereotype plates for printing such books; 3,984,063 obscene pictures; 16,900 negatives for printing such pictures; 3,646 persons have been arrested and of these 2,682 have been convicted or pleaded guilty, and 2,180 have been sentenced. If the matters which have been seized were to be transported this would require sixteen freight cars, fifteen loaded with ten tons each, and the other nearly full. If the persons arrested were to be transported, sixty-one passenger coaches would be needed, each with a seating capacity of sixty persons, sixty cars filled, and the other nearly full.[12] (Italics mine.)

In this holocaust have suffered works of genuine merit and authors of genuine distinction.

Comstock's defense-rationalization was notable for its ludicrousness:

It is a question of Peace, Good Order and Morals and not of Art, Literature or Science. Art for art purposes in art gallery, medical works for medical and scientific men, and standard literature for literary persons and students, does not mean that the nude in art, anatomical plates from medical works, nor bawdy and obscene extracts from standard authors have a right to be placed before immature minds, when such exhibition, sale or indiscriminate circulation tends to endanger the morals of the young.[13]

Mr. John S. Sumner, Comstock's worthy successor, acting as the secretary to the New York Society for the Suppression of Vice, continues the same wail in his statement of the purpose of the society:

As the general work of the Society, this corporation was organized in 1873 to enforce the laws seeking to suppress traffic in obscene, lewd, lascivious, indecent, filthy, and disgusting books or publications, and for other purposes. This

[12] Charles Gallaudet Trumbull, *Anthony Comstock, Fighter*, p. 239.
[13] Anthony Comstock. Quoted from p. 73 of the Report of the Emergency Committee organized to protest against suppression of *Jurgen*.

law does not make exception as to the publications of any particular class. That is, it does not distinguish between the writings of John Doe, who has no reputation, or Richard Doe, who is a distinguished author; nor have the courts in interpreting this law, permitted the intent of the author, expressed or implied, to influence them in their decisions. If the language of a book is lewd, or if it is suggestive of lewdness, it is a violation of the law, regardless of the literary or artistic character of the published matter. Some of the court decisions have held that a writing of an obscene character was more dangerous when couched in fine language than when set forth in crude form, and this is undoubtedly true.[14]

The opposing stand of Mr. Horace Liveright, a publisher, in his attack upon the censors in the defense of the insurgents, is striking in its denial of the bourgeois contention:

Certain fiction, which seems to be the principal object of attack today, expresses itself according to the contemporary interpretation of science, abnormal psychology, psychoanalysis, and other methods of study of human behavior. Art and mind are always in process of change; a new age has a new literary and philosophic expression. But this affects only the intelligent-minded; never the ignorant. . . .

We may become depraved by, or vicious by, economic or physical conditions, but certainly not by literature.

There is nothing pornographic in any work of literature or even such books as can be classified as literature. Pornographic books have been issued but they are manufactured by obscure printers in Europe and America, and are sold by peddlers; they are not issued by publishers or reliable printers.[15]

It should be realized, at this point, that the censorship of books has gone through a process of social evolution. Its origin was purely political. Utilized as a method of combating books and publications subversive to the sovereignty of

[14] Page 10 of the Report.
[15] Horace Liveright, "The Absurdity of Censorship," *Independent Magazine*, March 17, 1923.

the ruling power, it was employed at the time of Elizabeth and speedily became a device sanctioned by the repetition of expediency. Its legal justification in England, for example, depends upon two acts, one passed in 1737 and the other in 1843, the second of which crowns the censor as the direct licensing authority for London and endows him with the means of enforcing his decisions. In the eighteenth century it was Sir Robert Walpole, who, irritated at the satire of Fielding and Gray, effected the first gesture in this game by trying to stop the exposures of his corruption. Today with the disintegration of the ethics of the bourgeoisie, the center of attack has shifted soil from the political to the moral. Censorship now affects to be a moral cathartic. Politically, in England and America, to be sure, the bourgeoisie is still in control, but the proletariat, at least in England, is steadily gaining ground, and when the test of situation demands, as in the instance of the World War, censorship of economic and political polemics will become as severe as ethical. In the advance of literature, however, it has been the ethical proclivities of the censor that have proved more dangerous and drastic.

Before penetrating further into the attitudes of the two groups, let us note some of the actual achievements of these endeavorers in the cause of virtue. The trial of Flaubert, the burning of Swinburne's poems, the incarceration of Zola's publisher, have become so memorable that they are classic. While Shaw's play, *Mrs. Warren's Profession,* was censored, it met with a curious moral defense in many places. In the *Edinburgh Review,* for instance, in 1905, one of its writers declared:

A play with finer moral determination than *Mrs. Warren's Profession* has not been produced in Europe during the last twenty years.

Shaw himself maintained in manner as clever as it was provocative:

I write plays with the deliberate object of converting the nation to my opinions. My reputation has been gained by my persistent struggle to force the public to reconsider its morals.

The case of *The Shewing Up of Blanco Posnet* is more singular. This Shavian play was censored in 1909. In this, as in all other instances of moral censorship, the stupidity of the bourgeois attitude is painfully apparent. Here are a few of the speeches censored:

Elder Daniels. Oh, is that the way to speak of the ruler of the universe—the great and almighty God?

Blanco. He's a sly one. He's a mean one. He lies low for you. He plays cat and mouse with you. He lets you run loose until you think you're shut of Him; and then, when you least expect it, He's got you.

El. D. Speak more respectful, Blanco—more reverent.

B. Reverent! Who taught you your reverent cant? Not your Bible. It says He cometh like a thief in the night— aye, like a thief—a horse thief.

El. D. Oh!

B. And it's true. That's how He caught me and put my neck into the halter. To spite me because He had no use for me,—because I lived my own life and would have no truck with His "Don't do this," and "You mustn't do that," and "You'll go to Hell if you do the other." I gave Him the go-bye and did without Him all these years. But He caught me out at last. The laugh is with Him as far as hanging me goes.

And here, by way of contrast, are a few that were allowed to go unscathed:

Blanco. I accuse the fair Euphemia of immoral relations with every man in this town, including yourself, Sheriff. I say this is a conspiracy to kill me between Feemy and Strapper because I wouldn't touch Feemy with a pair of tongs. I say you daren't hang any white man on the word of a woman of bad character. I stand on the honor and virtue of my American manhood. I say that she's not had the oath, because her lips would blaspheme the holy Bible if they touched it. I say that's the law; and if you are a proper United States Sheriff and not a low-down lyncher, you'll hold up the law and not let it be dragged in the mud by your brother's kept woman.

and

The Sheriff. . . . We don't wish to be hard on any woman; and most of us have a personal regard for Miss Evans (Feemy) for the sake of old times. . . .

Feemy. Worse people than I has kissed that Book. What wrong I've done, most of you went shares in. I've to live, haven't I?

Shaw's comment on the censorship in his Preface to the play is vivid:

He (the censor) licensed the play, but endorsed on his license the condition that all the passages which implicated God in his history of B. P. must be omitted in representation. All the coarseness, the profligacy, the prostitution, the violence, the drinking-bar humor into which the light shines in the play are licensed, but the light itself is extinguished.

But with all of this stupidity, this narrowness of class bias and sentiment, the censorship in the case of *The Shewing Up of Blanco Posnet* was mild in its mutilations as compared with the treatment of other plays and novels. The Town Councilors of Belfast, for example, destroyed the works of Nietzsche, and at Doncaster someone discovered a copy of *Tom Jones* which was at once denounced and destroyed by burning.[16] In New York the onslaught upon Sholom Asch's play *The God of Vengeance* was another tragic fiasco. On the testimony of two detectives who witnessed the performance:

The producer . . . and eleven actors in the case, including the distinguished Rudolph Schildkraut, (were) convicted by a jury of the Court of General Sessions of violating the penal laws of the State of New York. Judge McIntyre . . .

[16] *English Review*, February, 1913.

fined the producer and Mr. Schildkraut $200 each. He might have sent every member of the cast to Sing Sing for three years.[17]

Other cases neither so notorious in absurdity nor so violent in extremity are not less significant. Sudermann's *Song of Songs* and Mr. Niel Lyon's *Cottage Pie* were both suppressed in England [18] and both Zangwill's play *The Next Religion* and Eden Phillpotts' *The Secret Woman* [19] were banned by the censor.[20] Laurence Housman's *Bethlehem* and *Pains and Penalties* also were both banned from the stage.[21] Mr. Garnett's *The Breaking Point* and Granville Barker's *Waste* suffered a similar catastrophe. And thus the censors attempted to purify the stage for the perpetuation of bourgeois virtue and the cause of emasculated drama.

With the novel the tragedy deepens. In 1909 the tame temptations of *Ann Veronica* were denounced. In the *Spectator* Mr. Wells' novel was classified as "A Poisonous Book" and its teaching described as "pernicious." The reviewer's account of the depravity of the novel is fine farce:

The indignation which the book inspires in us is due to the effect it is likely to have in undermining that sense of continence and self-control in the individual which is essential to a sound and healthy state. The book is based on the negation of woman's purity and of man's good faith in the relations of sex. It teaches, in effect, that there is no such thing as a woman's honor, or if there is, it is only a bulwark against a weak temptation. When the temptation is strong enough, not only is the tempted person justified in yielding, but such yielding becomes not merely inevitable but something to be welcomed and glorified. If an animal yearning or lust is only sufficiently absorbing, it is to be obeyed. Self-sacrifice

[17] "Drama and Detectives." *Nation,* June 6, 1923.
[18] *English Review,* February, 1911.
[19] The novel, *The Secret Woman* (of which the play is a dramatization), it is amusing to observe, was not banned.
[20] *English Review,* March, 1912.
[21] *The Spectator,* December 2, 1911.

is a dream and self-restraint a delusion. Such things have no place in the muddy world of Mr. Wells' imaginings. His is a community of shuffling stoats and ferrets, unenlightened by a ray of duty or abnegation.

But while it is human to err and Christlike to pity and forgive, the great duties and prohibitions of life remain, and woe to those who cover them with the slime of their faint-scented sophistries. [22]

In the same year the Times Book Club refused to supply Henry James' *Italian Hours* to a subscriber "on the grounds that it was not likely to promote the library's reputation as circulators of wholesome literature." [23] D. H. Lawrence's *The Rainbow* was destroyed by order of court, and Lawrence wrote no other novel for five years. Arnold Bennett's novel, *The Pretty Lady,* due to the author's alertness to fight, escaped this miscarriage of moral zeal. Bennett's description of the situation is delightfully frank and encouraging:

With reference to your Emergency Committee Protest, my view is that the police alone should have the right to prosecute an author. To give to any private society the right to prosecute on public grounds is bound to lead to grave injustice. In England the number of private prosecutors is now almost nil, and I believe that no effective private prosecution can be begun without the consent of the Attorney-General. Two private societies in England took very strong objection to my novel—*The Pretty Lady*—not on moral but on sectarian religious grounds! They demanded the suppression of the book. As soon as they discovered I was a fighter they let the matter drop.[24]

In New York the Society for the Suppression of Vice took action against *A Young Girl's Diary,* D. H. Lawrence's *Women in Love,* and Schnitzler's *Casanova's Homecoming;* the last two were privately printed, but the society assailed

[22] *The Spectator,* November 20, 1909.
[23] Charles Tennyson, "The Libraries Censorship," *Contemporary Review,* April, 1910.
[24] Arnold Bennett, "Reply to a Letter." Page 48 of the Report.

them, notwithstanding.[25] *Jude the Obscure, The Damnation of Theron Ware, Hagar Revelly, Homo Sapiens, Trilby, Edna, A Summer in Arcady, Susan Lenox*—all were victimized in one way or another by the virtuosi of virtue. Other books that afforded further expression for the sadism of the society were Dreiser's *The Genius,* Guido Brun's *Edna, the Girl of the Street,* and *Madeleine.*[26] The Vice Society of Cincinnati, for instance, found that *The Genius,* alas, contained seventy-five lewd passages and seventeen profane.[27] F. L. Rowe, secretary of the Western Society for the Suppression of Vice, stated one of the developments in the case as follows:

Reverend John Herget, of Ninth Street Baptist Church, became acquainted with the book when he was called to the telephone by an unidentified person who complained. We immediately procured a copy of the present issue and find it filled with obscenity and blasphemy. We have succeeded in having it removed from practically every bookstore in the city.[28]

A gratifying reversal that the New York Society met with occurred in its conflict with Mr. Raymond Halsey of the McDevitt-Wilson Co. Mr. Halsey was arrested for publishing *Mlle. de Maupin;* the case was dismissed, Mr. Halsey sued, and the Society was forced to pay $2,500 in damages and costs.[29] The case of *Jurgen* was less fortunate, although after two years the ban was lifted, and Mr. Cabell's books today sell more widely and continuously than they ever did before the suppression of his novel. *Jurgen* was published on September 27, 1919. All plates, copies, and sheets of *Jurgen* were seized on January 14, 1920. An Emergency Committee was formed to protest against the suppression. Many of them

[25] "With Intent to Corrupt." The *Nation,* July 26, 1922.
[26] Report of the Emergency Committee.
[27] Report of the Authors' League.
[28] Cincinnati *Enquirer*—September 14, 1916.
[29] Page 26 of the Report.

unfortunately revealed an unabashed bourgeois twist of tongue. The members of the old school, the Paul Elmer Mores [30] and vestigial Howellsians, steadily stood by the bourgeois tradition. The new school, however, has continued courageously its fight for a free literature.

With the magazines, three recent episodes are notorious. In 1920 the *Little Review* was convicted of obscenity on the complaint of the New York Society for the Suppression of Vice. Early in 1926 the *American Mercury* was attacked in Boston by the Watch and Ward Society and forbidden sale to customers, and a few months later in the same year the *New Masses* was prohibited from the mails by the United States Postal Service. The *American Mercury* was assailed for a simple story of prostitution in a small village in which the protagonist passed under the exciting name of Hatrack, which, since the test trial in Boston, has become an appellation of enchanting suggestiveness and salacity.[31] Among other things the *New Masses* was banned from the mails for the publication of several unrevolutionary, untitillating, uninspired poems by a Yale professor. Of course, the brave stand that the *New Masses* has taken against the capitalist system will strengthen its logic but weaken its privileges— in the eyes of the censors, postal and private.

In Los Angeles another scene in the drama of virtue was recently enacted. At the close of the performance of Eugene O'Neill's play *Desire Under the Elms*, on February 18th of this year, all of the actors were seized by the police on the charge of having presented a play dangerous to the morals of the American people. The actors were detained under

[30] Paul Elmer More's letter is typical of his ilk; "I am not at all in sympathy with a group of writers who would take any protest against the Society as a justification of what they are pleased to call art. The harm done by the Society seems to me very slight, whereas the harm done by the self-styled artist may be very great."

[31] Canoes have been named Hatrack, automobiles dubbed with the title, and parties dedicated to her honor. Thus a story that would have passed unobserved has become a fillip to the national palate. In addition, Mr. Mencken won the case when it was tried in Boston.

arrest until four-thirty the next morning, their fingerprints having been taken as a precaution against their escape, and not allowed to go at liberty until a bail of $850 had been provided. A jury trial ensued, in which the outraged moralists testified that their ears had been offended by such profanity as "damn," "hell," and "whore," and their consciences embarrassed by the presentation of a plot feeding upon filth and degeneracy. The defendants—clubwomen, the wife of the dean of the University of Southern California, the dramatic critics of the Los Angeles newspapers, and a girl and a boy—all stated that:

to them the play was not immoral—far from it. It was a literary and dramatic *tour de force*. It taught a strong, wholesome, moral lesson: the wages of sin is death. When they came from the theater they felt cleansed, morally elevated.[32]

After deliberating for almost nine hours, eight of the jury were for conviction, four for acquittal.

The play continued and Los Angeles was demoralized by a run of over ten weeks which the citizens demanded by their prosperous attendance.

In their attitude toward these devastating violations of artistic intelligence, the bourgeois literati are in vapid acquiescence. Hamlin Garland, in sentiment conspicuous for its moral myopia, expresses their attitude:

Since the war the number of our writers who are imitating the French, the Norwegian, and the Russian have notably increased. Half the plays on our stage this year are said to be adaptations of farces from Vienna or Paris, and several of our younger novelists are bringing to our fiction that eroticism which has so long been the peculiar province of the "French novel." In others the brutal plainness of speech of certain Scandinavian writers and the pessimistic animalism of modern Russian novelists appear, while many of the English novelists imported by our publishers are of the decadent quality of Matisse and Archepenko. Design is lost. The

[32] "Los Angeles Must Be Kept Pure," *Nation*, May 19, 1926.

sense of humor which should be a corrective is absent. It would seem that we are importing the vices and not the virtues of Old World art.

Per contra, among the younger writers I sense a quality akin to the jazz band, the modern dance, and the moving picture, and while I am willing to grant that each generation must have its chance to state itself in its own way, I find myself revolted by an overinsistence on sex themes and by a kind of sad ego-mania in these writers. Their characters whine and complain and shirk. As poets they are obsessed with their own petty concerns. As novelists they have small sense of humor or proportion, and for the most part they are lacking in sound craftsmanship. After reading a few of them *I am filled with disgust of their futility, and I return to Howells with a sense of getting back to broad culture, sanity, humor, and good workmanship.*[33] (Italics mine.)

Booth Tarkington is scarcely less explicit or less puritanical:

I read so few of the modern novels that I really shouldn't make any generalization, but of those I had read, many seem to be in bad taste. When the book is written by one of my contemporaries, I feel that he has succumbed to this craze for erotic literature simply because he knows he will make more money by that kind of book. When it's written by a young writer just starting out, it's more likely to be a deliberate seeking of the salacious because that is the easiest way to get a book published. And a young author is so passionately self-assertive, so indignant about his art, any criticism seems terrible to him.

Establishing a censorship would certainly check the tendency, but the real solution to my mind lies in awakening the good taste of the public. I don't think real people read all this trash. The problem is to make the twenty million disregard it, too. That was the solution after the Elizabethan age. Literature has never been as raw as it was then. It wasn't Puritanism that put a stop to the publishing of in-

[33] Quotation from the *New York Times* in the *Literary Digest*, January 19, 1924.

decent books then. It was that they offended good taste, and a wave of repugnance for them spread until they were not read by anyone who counted, and that is what will have to happen here. (Italics mine.)

Henry Holt, in a letter to the *New York Times,* betrayed the same prejudice; Bliss Perry, in a speech before the Boston Watch and Ward Society (1923), warned his audience that "the American public is now facing a clear and present danger through unclean books"; H. W. Boynton, in an article in the *Independent,* contended that "most of the recent American and British novels which are most offensive to people who think dignity and continence have something to do with art, are plain mongrels," [34] but the triumphant climax was left for Henry Van Dyke, the anachronistic Galilean who in his disdain for both the insurgents and the foreigners gave utterance to a flash of wisdom that it would be tragic not to quote:

What do I care for the ever so realistically painted marionettes in the fiction of Messrs. Gawky, Popoff, Dropoff? . . . or the dismal, despicable figures who are pulled through the pages of *The Way of All Flesh?*

Among the magazines the attitude of the bourgeoisie is represented with admirable precision, penetration and candor by an editorial in the *Ladies' Home Journal:*

We are told that the only great poets of the day are those who are writing epics on sex perversion.
We are told that the only worthwhile novelists are those who are dramatizing the romances and tragedies of middle-aged men and women who are seeking a rejuvenation so as to prolong their carnal indulgence.
Drunkenness, lust, murder, refinements of brutality, avarice, covetousness, should be analyzed and explained in an infinity of detail in order that they may be justified or glorified. Demonology is preferable to Christianity as a background for fiction. Know Your Neighbor for a Beast should

[34] "Native Versus Alien Standards," *Independent,* March 17, 1923.

be substituted for the Golden Rule. The decalogue was
meant for morons. (A moron is anyone who disagrees with
a prophet of expressionism or the modernist trend in literature.) The Beatitudes are a poetic fancy, but of poetry old
style and not today's. . . .

But it is the higher culture, say the book critics—particularly the daring ones fresh from college—the professors of
literature, and all the ultra-ultras of free verse and free love.
It is the opposite of soothing syrup and moral purpose fables;
it causes one to think the profound thoughts of gifted
idiots. Once you catch the tempo—a brief correspondence
course will put you in rhythm—it is worth more than a
lifetime of experience, contacts, travel and serious study.
Cross out forever your Aristotles and Platos, your Bacons
and Newtons, your Goethes and Shakespeares, your Comtes
and Spencers and Emersons, your Darwins and Huxleys,
your Henry Jameses—dodoes of the past—and swarm behind the banners of our Bertrand Russells and Havelock
Ellises. And there is a fine fat vogue for it, say the publishers who specialize in it.[35]

It is striking to note that while the Board of Temperance,
Prohibition and Public Morals of the Methodist Episcopal
Church discovered that "in years past when there has been
dirt upon the American stage it has been American dirt," and
that "at present shows on the New York stage are as foreign
to America as anything which could be tolerated in Suez,"
the censors rarely carry their attacks upon the New York
stage beyond the forms of verbal denunciation. The same
play that was attacked in Los Angeles, *Desire Under the
Elms,* and also such bawdy dramas as *Lulu Belle* and *The
Shanghai Gesture,* were all passed upon by the censorship
juries. As one writer expressed it:

The Society is blind enough on ordinary occasions, but it
knows a vested interest when it sees one. And so with regard
to the theater. If the Broadway stage is not organized to
stir and encourage the sexual emotions, then nothing on

[35] "The Filth Uplifters," August, 1924.

earth is. But here the Society for the Suppression of Vice, though acute enough to smell out novelties, never touches the traditional and established forms of temptations.[36]

It is this same bourgeois attitude that has rendered the attitude of the British Museum so ridiculous. The volumes of Havelock Ellis' *Psychology of Sex* series have been excluded. G. W. Foote's *Illustrated Bible,* and Leo Taxil's *La Bible Amusante* have been buried without record, and pictures of *indecent* objects discovered at Pompeii and a valuable book about Greek folklore have been uncatalogued so that the public cannot secure them. Edward Carpenter's *Intermediate Sex* was tabooed, but later was included in the catalogue.[37]

Thus the struggle between the two groups has raced. The new morality is upon us. The new literature is upon us. The very evidence of the bitterness of the struggle is proof of the vitality of the new literature. While the bourgeoisie declaims and protests, Aldous Huxley writes his *Leda* and *Fifth Philosopher's Song,* Sherwood Anderson pens his sex-emancipated stories of fact and fiction, and Theodore Dreiser depicts the bared souls of passion-driven men and women. Floyd Dell finds in love an art and Cabell in sex a symbol. D. H. Lawrence poetizes the erotic and sublimates the factual. James Joyce transforms passion into a psychography which bewilders by its vividness and overwhelms by its intensity. Swinburne and Whitman, Flaubert and Maupassant, precursors of the protest that has now become a trend, are but pale passion flowers beside the red Priapian shoots of their successors. Readers who believe that passion is a part of life, and who once had to resort to the *Memoirs of Fanny Hill,* can now find in the new literature the reality that bourgeois literature lacked.

While Florenz Ziegfeld has just threatened to "join with

[36] "Again the Literary Censor." The *Nation,* September 25, 1920.
[37] "The Taboos of the British Museum," E. S. P. Haynes, *English Review,* 1913.

John S. Sumner, of the Society for the Suppression of Vice, in a move to purify the stage,[38] the *Follies* of which he is the exponent, and the musical comedy of which Americans boast, scarcely excite our attention through their resemblance to Victorian taste and tedium. While plays like *The Shanghai Gesture, Lulu Belle,* and *Seduction,* with all of their catastrophic patency, abound in candor that would paralyze the sensibilities of a Victorian, musical comedies like *Jessie James* and *Cocoanuts* surpass them in suggestiveness and salacity. The contemporary musical comedy, the artistic abortion of our era, is another outlet for the sex release of our day. Part of the Jazz Age, the musical comedy reflects the direction of our moral attitudes and social satisfactions. Although the new literature has become a movement and its followers become many, the musical comedy has become a passion and its devotees become countless. The clean sex release found in the new literature is translated into a smirking, insinuating pornography in the musical comedy. The bold, fearless approach to the problems of sex by the new literati stands forth in contrast to the tantalizing innuendo, the covert allusion, the Parthian pornography of the musical comedy. In the freedom of the new literature, with its break from the traditions of the bourgeoisie, is an essence of reconstruction; in the furtive insinuation and risible sexuality of the musical comedy is nothing but the putrescent core of decay.[39]

The sex freedom of the new literature is a step toward its final emancipation. The anti-bourgeois attitude in morality is gradually being driven toward an anti-bourgeois attitude in economics. The nineteenth century, as we have seen, with the rise and struggle of the proletariat had brought with it the proletarian sentimentalists and a proletarian trend in

[38] Baltimore *Sun,* July, 1926.
[39] Of course, there are exceptions among musical comedies, although the rule is rather rigid. *Apple Blossoms* is one of the exceptions.

literature.[40] This proletarian trend was evidence of the beginning of a conflict that was to be neither short nor sweet. Where bourgeois characters had been featured and extolled in the bourgeois literature of the generations that had followed the ascendancy of the bourgeoisie in England, the proletarian sentimentalists turned toward characters of the proletariat for their heroes and idols. This tendency was emphatically prominent in the Gaskell-Kingsley school. With the twentieth century the trend has lost something of its sentimentality, although it still has to acquire definiteness and decision.

At the present time, due to the recent recoil from the effects of the bourgeois suppression of the last century and the bewildering ecstasy of the new freedom, there is a preoccupation with sex in literature that, in all likelihood, will diminish in the next few generations. With the gradual breakdown of the family, its compulsoriness of union and rigidity of organization, the mystery and confusion of sex are being annihilated in a process of clarification and coordination. With the weakening of the private-property régime a new ethic is born. Sex will be neither maximized nor minimized, neither exalted nor degraded, neither concealed nor advertised. Today sex is maximized and advertised, exploited and exhausted as theme and thesis—a natural tendency in time of class decay and social disintegration.

With the coming changes in society the young people will neither be consumed by sex nor confused by its manifestations, but, as in Russia today, they will

discuss sex relations, abortions and love with the candor of obstetricians.[41]

[40] We reiterate that this has nothing to do with proletarian art, which is art produced by the proletariat itself, for the sake of the proletariat.

[41] Paul Blanchard, "Sex Standards in Moscow," *Nation*, May 12, 1926.

Sex will become a part of life but not the whole of life, an expression of life but not the art of life. The reticences which have surrounded sex will have surrendered to the realities that constitute it. The literary artist will deal with sex without ceremony or prudery, without affectation or timidity. But this newer freedom for literati and layman will come only from the freedom of a newer society.

HERMAPHRODITES [1]

By Robert Herrick

"So there are also men who write like women," I said to
myself, as I scanned the weekly effusion of a moderately
celebrated critic with an accustomed sense of futility in the
effort to discover solid ground beneath the surface of his
supple phrases, to evoke for my own satisfaction the piece he
was supposedly discussing. It couldn't be done! At least, I
could not create from so many exquisite words (borrowed
from all the arts and a few trades) the plain realities my
mind demands. As often these days, I must resign myself to
sniffing the agreeable perfume of the words or abandon the
thing altogether. I am aware that the critic gets much pleasure out of the weekly display of his *expertise* in saying as
nearly nothing as is possible with the flourish of many
pretty words, and doubtless some of his readers get a similar
pleasure—an exhilaration of thinking they are thinking—
perhaps even more than they might derive from the piece
itself. . . . Of course, I reflected, such times as these there
must be many men who consciously or unconsciously are
writing like women. Why not—when sex distinctions are
breaking down all around, when the two sexes are becoming
functionally merged and confused, so that no longer does the
sex denominator in the human fraction mean what it once
did, and all generalizations (including my own!) based on
sex appear emptier than do most other generalizations? "So
like a woman" has long since lost whatever point it may
once have had, because, alas, it is also like so many men
one knows.

Nevertheless, to my old-fashioned mind there are still dis-

[1] From the *Bookman*, July, 1929.

tinctions between male and female, even in letters, that
should be preserved for the healthy functioning of both sexes.

.   .   .   .

I recall a dinner given not so long ago to a visiting English-
woman, who had written a few talked-about novels and was
then engaged in discovering these United States and telling
the world what she found here. As she entered the drawing-
room accompanied by one of our younger writers, I was at
once struck by the contrast between the two: the woman
large and sturdy, with a dark down on her handsome upper
lip, while the man was slight, pale, dapper, the curve of hips
being accentuated by the tailoring habit of the day, a little
chin fading away from a small mouth. It would not have
taken much change in make-up or costume to shift the sexes
of the two. The American's voice when he spoke was soft
and languid, insinuating and caressing, while the English-
woman boomed forth her platitudes in serene confidence.
The conversation thereafter resolved itself largely into a co-
operative exhibition of these two, the visitor trying to sum
up all our vagrant culture (as gathered during her six weeks'
lecture tour) and the American writer supplying an em-
broidery of innuendoes and exclamation points. Both toyed
with phrases which they sought to make realities for the
company, although the ideas were apparently *in tenebris*.
. . . They were still at it when I left, plucking generalities
from thin air. That method is one of the chief marks of the
man who writes like a woman. He does not seek to convey
a specific thought, a four-square idea, but to create the impression in another's mind of some not quite attained cere-
bration in his own. This method is not due so much to a lazy
habit of mind, or a hazy temperament, as to an indirect manner of thinking. We all know the person, male or female, who
conducts a discussion as a prosecuting attorney might deal
with a dull or reluctant witness, putting his own suggestions
adroitly into another's mind. "Only on dark nights like this,

wouldn't you say, it is hardly safe to take that road?" . . .
"One has the feeling, that something not yet wholly realized
exists at least in essence, etc.?" . . . Plainly such minds
achieve thought—if it can be called such—by approximations, thrown forth at random on the chance that somewhere, somehow, they will attach themselves to a substance
and clinging to its support will start the weaving process of
creative thought.

The thing can be done! It is done admirably by the younger
women writers of the day and by some of their brothers
marked with the feminine character, in poetry perhaps more
than in prose, but abundantly in both. Journalistically, such
a style is called "suggestive"; in more æsthetic circles, "subtle." And few there be who have the rude courage to squeeze
this wordy performance tightly and analyze the drip-
pings. . . .

"This is partly a matter of the mind" (I quote almost at
random from the critic's article) "in the sense of an over-
seeing element in which all the parts of a work of art are
perceived and given to us in their due relation among themselves, so that the character and meaning of the whole is
solidly achieved, etc., etc." Squeeze it and see what you get!
Another glance gives: "How bright and delicious Shakespeare
can be, so often better—however strong our wills to it—
than we could remember!" Delicious! The kitchen commen-
dation might well curdle in the poet's gut. Such an airy condescension is treating him worse than calling him the Bard
of Avon.

.   .   .   .

There is another type of critic, the table-thumping kind,
whose vehement and swiftly changing affirmations exhibit
that emotional instability commonly ascribed to women.
Each time my eye falls on one of his deliverances—he is a
favorite of publishers' jackets—he has discovered a new
astounding masterpiece, which can be exalted only by derid-
ing something old. For him literature to be good, like break-

fast rolls, must be baked this morning. Conscious that all may not accept his discoveries, he is truculent: he scorns the doubter in advance and covers him with verbal contempt. Criticism for this one seems to be a process of self-intoxication, for which the thing criticized serves merely as a point of departure for his ecstatic fury, as, alas, so often happens in love. "A great book, a rich and wise and beautiful and original and profound and sublime and immensely moving book, etc., etc." What more could one say of God? . . . The still small voice of truth does not penetrate such frenzy, nor the cool glamour of beauty. Heat is the sole medium of his passion and the more he writes—and he is voluble—the more heat he must give off, like a racing motor. He must, I am convinced, be married to a masculine woman; for I explain his vociferations, his frenzies of immediate convictions as due to his struggle to maintain the dominance of the male in a never-ending sex duel. In time his voice will grow less shrill, his truculent ardors fainter, as he loses out in the domestic contest and the woman smoothes him to her uses. He is fighting a losing battle like one slipping in heavy sand, and the daily article he pours forth so hotly is his means of self-defense. . . .

There are other varieties of the man-woman critic, more than I have time to mention. There is the humming-bird critic who pecks here and there capriciously like a woman with a whimsical appetite in a cafeteria, repeating again and again—"So it seems to me." He has much to say about "personality" and "individualism," the self. Does anyone who possesses an individuality talk much about it?

.   .   .   .

For the perfect example of the man who writes like a woman, however, I must go to England, as for almost every illustration of finish in letters, even today. I select Mr. Aldous Huxley, first, because he writes so well that any woman writer might be proud to be mistaken for him: he has perfected his manner meticulously for a number of years as the American writers of his type have not yet done. And, further, because his novel, *Point Counter Point,* comes so exactly to my purpose. That "slice of life" taken from post-war London begins nowhere and ends nowhere, like so many of the works of the younger writers (as though they felt it necessary to demonstrate the meaninglessness of time and space by giving a microcosm of futility!). Between the first and last pages of this book much is tucked deftly away—caricature, scandal, irony, reflection, stray bits of information, etc. There are many contemporary portraits, some done from life, it is said. This fact, of itself, both interests and intrigues, but above and beyond this, it is essential that the portraits shall have a life of their own—something else than identifiable traits—which in my opinion most of them just miss having. They are keen studies in perversity and stupidity and inanition, very, very clever studies often. But as the characters emerge from Mr. Huxley's caustic phrases they lack that touch of reasonable humanity without which their own mothers would fail to recognize them. They speak the proper idiom; they perform the trivial acts willed for them by their designer; but, like the electrical robots now being perfected by our mechanical geniuses to take the place of human robots, they would not deceive a child, skillful as their simulation of life is.

The women are much more believable and more thoroughly done than the men (also those men whose emotional range resembles that of the women!) which is one indication of the man who writes like women. Women, I am sure, must recognize these tarnished sisters, for only a woman soul could divine their hidden secrets, their griefs and indirect reflexes, and reveal them so remorselessly. As a rule the masculine portraits of women, even as great an instance as James' immortal Lady, are approximations (conventionalized, too) rather than fulfilled creations: the qualities of mind and soul may be there, but not the tricks, the little gestures, those subtle indirections which only women recognize and properly evaluate among themselves. All these Mr. Huxley has, as no other man novelist of our day that I know, has.

One of his female creations demands separate mention: Lucy, the incarnation of all that is vile in woman to date. Lucy is the one rounded, completely delivered character that I have found in the whole brilliant string of Mr. Huxley's books, and before her any mere man must stand aghast, appalled. Women, one might suppose, would flee the creator of Lucy as they would Medusa, but women are said not to mind the spiritually prying eye provided what it reveals makes them interesting. I doubt if any woman novelist at any time has so completely presented the Lucy kind of depravity as has Mr. Huxley. Kipling, in a fit of disgust, tried for Lucy in his line about "a rag and a bone and a hank of hair"; but that was an obscene daubing on a wall compared with the Huxley version. Over this ruthless masterpiece the author lays aside his accustomed manner of ridicule, caricature: he is in deadly earnest and admires his own creation too much to distort it. Lucy, terrible as she is—and fascinating to certain males largely because they are completely mystified by her—is not the kind most men writers would care to leave as their masterpiece.

The nearest approach to this female monstrosity is the Editor—more than half-woman on his weaker side—whom Mr. Huxley treats with a pursuing, relentless contempt, which saves him from the reader's disgust. Apparently his creator dislikes feminine traits in men—though why? . . . As for the others, men and women, they are shadow puppets, gayly, maliciously, cruelly thrown up on a drab screen: they make a rancid world, mocking reality close enough to be nauseating.

. . . .

It is not because Mr. Huxley is so exceptionally deft that I put him in the forefront of the tribe of man-woman writers. Subtlety is no sex attribute: witness that very fine and subtle work of art, *A Passage to India*. I know of nothing in recent

literature subtler than Mr. Forster's unpretentious story, nor
with a longer reach. It preserves an air of unpremeditation,
as though skillfully put together from trivialities. Simple as
it is outwardly, it goes deep into one of the great tragic mysteries of humanity—race antagonism and misunderstanding.
It presents for all time that baffling human complex of racial
arrogance, of men doing evil with a glow of noblest intention in their breasts, all unconscious of the wrong they are
doing. With equal justice it presents the petty aspects of
those who are wronged, who fail and must always fail to do
themselves justice no matter how excellent their cause may
be. . . . Of course, *A Passage to India* has an idea, a theme,
which is no longer in the mode, but that in itself is one of its
male characteristics. A man who has anything of importance
to say usually discovers some general idea or purpose around
which to group his material, no matter how inadequate or
false or imperfectly developed it may be: it is there like a
backbone in a torso. Spineless art, if not wholly a discovery
of women writers, is at any rate much practiced by them.

   A Passage to India is as subtle as the most sinuous product
of our introverted writers and has as well form and meaning,
and is beyond question male from the first page to the last.

    . . . .

   What do I mean by this sex tag, by a "male" style, "male"
imagination? I confess it is not easy to define these terms
as precisely as I should like: they must be felt. Just as any
handwriting expert is able to distinguish a woman's hand
from a man's in a specimen submitted to him—with an occasional mistake—so any expert in letters knows without being
told when a manuscript is written by a woman or a man.
I have read in my day thousands—perhaps tens of thousands
—of manuscripts and I rarely have had to turn to the
signature to discover whether a man or a woman was the
author. And where there would be any real doubt the product
was usually colorless, negative, negligible.

   This, obviously, does not imply that the creations of one

sex are preferable, better or wiser than those of the other.
Merely that they are different. Fundamentally different in
manner as well as spiritual content, as they should be to be
worth while, being the expression of two distinct organisms,
which nature has endowed differently although both use the
same media of expression and suffer, roughly speaking, the
same experiences. Each is excellent not in the measure that
it approaches a sexless norm, but in the measure that it
expresses most characteristically the basic traits of its own
nature. The critic should not judge according to the sex of the
writer nor make allowances nor in any way vary his standard.
But as he looks for one kind of performance from a Russian
and another from an American, let us say, because he knows
that the Russian has a distinct psychology, a separate racial
and cultural background, which must be reflected in his art,
totally different from those of the American, so one looks
for qualities in any writing proper to the sex of its creator.

Two pertinent instances of what I mean come to my mind:
the work of two authors approximately contemporary and
with approximately the same backgrounds, one by a woman
and the other by a man. No one could possibly believe that
the creator of *Lady into Fox* was a woman or of *Precious Bane*
a man. I do not know whether to admire Mrs. Webb's or
Mr. Garnett's art more: fortunately it is not necessary to be
comparative between two perfect achievements. I savor both.
I am grateful for both . . . and I am never troubled one
moment because neither one is trying to create in the terms
of the other. No man could feel our common world quite as
Mrs. Webb feels it in *Precious Bane* and in *Gone to Earth*. No
man (not even Mr. Huxley!) could reveal a woman's reactions to certain acute situations as justly as Mrs. Webb.
Nor could any woman achieve quite the strange imaginative
complexity of Mr. Garnett's delicate fancies in whose depths
lie concealed large ideas. If I might venture further I should
say that the man in this case has the stronger imaginative
flight while the woman has a more potent sensibility to all

physical phenomena. But I am content to have them as they are, separated by the chasm of sex, and each singing a common song in a different key.

.   .   .   .   .   .

The biologists tell us that there are species which are sexually interchangeable. Man does not belong to those species. He is a mammal, and the mammals conceive and create through the instrumentality of two distinct sexes, each equipped with appropriate organs, temperaments, psychology. It seems to be the fashion nowadays to ignore this rude basic fact, to confuse and swap the sexes. For political and social and economic purposes it may be helpful, temporarily, to forget the biologic distinctions: they have certainly been overstressed in the past to the discomfort and the disadvantage of one sex, the less (overtly) aggressive sex. But in art the distinction cannot be ignored, any more than in the creation of babies, and it might be well if our vociferous younger generation, male and female alike, remembered that as they cannot add a cubit to their stature by taking thought, so no cunning surface imitation will accomplish a real exchange of sex character. All that results is the hermaphrodite! . . .

Nor should anyone want to change sex character. The penalty in art as in nature is sterility, extinction. A feminized race in time becomes extinct. So too a feminized art.

SEX CONTROL [1]

By Morris L. Ernst and William Seagle

When morality triumphs, nasty things happen.

—REMY DE GOURMONT

THE triumph of Mrs. Grundy in the Anglo-Saxon world ceases to be inexplicable as soon as it is considered in terms of the three indexes of virtue. If the Age of Faith adopted the index of heresy, the Age of Divine Right, the index of treason, it was inevitable for the Age of Democracy to adopt the index of sex. The shift from the first index to the second has been made clear. It remains to show the transition to the Age of Sex Control.

It is customary to rail against the sex censorship. It is declared to be an insuperable obstacle to civilization. But we will be much nearer the truth if we say that it is one of the penalties of civilization. The paradox is that it came into existence as the first consequence of our enlightenment. Rightly regarded, the sex censorship is the measles of civilization. In evolving a politically free man, the life force made him a sexually inhibited one. In an ultimate sense, Galileo and Bacon are responsible for Lord Chief Justice Cockburn. The absurdities and inanities of the modern dread of the obscene have simply obscured the relationship.

When the conditions of political liberty and intellectual emancipation have been first fulfilled, we may expect the sex censorship to appear. It is no mere accident that the symptoms first made themselves visible in England. For almost three centuries, the closest parallelism is to be observed in the evolution of Continental and English censorship. Substantially

[1] From *To the Pure*. New York: The Viking Press, Inc., 1928.

the same social, economic, and political conditions made the mechanism of censorship almost identical and kept its focus at the same points. Then, at the end of the seventeenth century, the divergence begins. The preventive censorship of the Star Chamber, the Licensing Acts, disappear in England at the same time that they are still the normal mechanism of control on the Continent.

Indeed, England emerged from the barbarism of the Middle Ages so much earlier than the rest of Europe that whenever the history of liberty and democracy is discussed, we naturally turn first to England. It is customary to say that England took the lead in the emancipation of the serfs, in the formation of Bills of Rights, in the removal of religious disabilities, and in the establishment of representative government. The Anglo-Saxon speaks proudly of Magna Carta and the Petition of Rights. The early collapse of preventive censorship under the assaults of English libertarianism was an indication of this weakening of authority. The censorship was now administered under the criminal law in the punitive manner we know at present, and freedom of the press became the Englishman's ironic privilege of going to jail for his opinions. The right which an Englishman now had to a public trial and the verdict of his peers under a clear definition of the issues not only made it easier to escape a charge of sedition but made the crime itself unpopular.

When the evolution of criminal obscenity is discussed with reference to Continental countries, it is much easier to avoid confusion and obscurantism. But when we turn to England we discover that it is the usual custom to ascribe the whole business to Puritanism. It is the particular habit of literary critics to set Puritanism up as a windmill, and then like so many gallant Don Quixotes to charge straight at the monster. We are told again and again of the Puritan's hostility to joy, his suspicion of art, his tolerance of infidelity. Puritanism is shouted as a dreadful accusation which is expected to bring to their knees the weaker, more easily intimidated Puritans.

It is thus made to assume an objective reality which it is far from possessing. For Puritanism, which is offered as an explanation, is simply the label for a conclusion upon a very complex state of affairs. When it is used as a descriptive term for the sake of brevity, it serves a legitimate purpose. But unfortunately it has become perhaps the most frozen formula in the English language. It has resulted in our thinking that a peculiar kink exists in the English mind which separates it from all others.

When we say that the sex censorship is the creation of English Puritanism, all that we can properly mean is that the conditions which favored its existence appeared sooner in England than on the Continent. What is important to remember is that it was precisely the Puritans who had been largely instrumental in insuring English political freedom. Puritanism, which was bound up with the rise of modern capitalism, had need of such liberty to pursue its practical and worldly enterprises. But, again, it must not be forgotten that Magna Carta was the work in part of the barons and nobility who were in revolt against the excessive claims of prerogatives in the Crown. When we inject the economic necessities of Puritanism into the discussion, we need only take into account the fact that the creation of a large middle class led to popular education, which first resulted in an increased reading class, and then ultimately made for such a spread of enlightenment that a new sanction had to be discovered.

It is no paradox to say that the Puritan had little conception of the modern sex censorship of literature. What attention he paid to obscenity in books arose merely from his inability as an earnest and practical-minded man to distinguish between lewdness in books and lewdness in life. He was against sexual immorality in life because he knew that a profligate life led to the undermining of the virtues of sobriety, frugality and industry which were indispensable to his labors for civilization. Thus he was always concerned about the bad example which a lewd book or play might set. He had no objection to the depiction of vice and sin provided it was bound up with the proper indignation. His attitude toward obscenities consequently differed little from the prohibitionist's objections to intoxicating liquor in its effects upon a man's efficiency. It had as yet no connection with the censorship of ideas and did not constitute part of the political function. Hogarth exactly caught the Puritan motive when in one of his prints he pictured the wicked mechanic reading *Moll Flanders* while the good mechanic read the story of the apprentice who became Lord Mayor of London. This conception of the art of life which early displayed itself in a host of sumptuary laws so far antedates the evolution of criminal obscenity that no other conclusion is possible than that more than the Puritan state of mind was involved.

The critics who treat literary decency by a biometric formula in accordance with which it rises and wanes in relation to "Puritanism" have gone far astray as is proved conclusively by the length of time which elapsed between the emergence of English political liberty and the appearance of the crime of obscene libel. The crime of blasphemy still sufficed against the winds of doctrine. However much deism may have been popular in the upper reaches of English society, the masses were under the influence of religious orthodoxy, and blasphemy prosecutions of the eighteenth and nineteenth centuries still had public opinion behind them. It is a rule that when one of the safeguards against subversive doctrine is rendered less effective there is a compensating shift of emphasis toward another. The jurisdiction over blasphemy had been lodged in the ecclesiastical courts, but the pressure of political freedom transferred it to the temporal courts. The prominence of blasphemy prosecutions in England is no doubt partly to be explained by the English dread of Popery, a dread which had been ushered in with the uxorious Henry; but this was no less one of the signs of emancipation. The time had not yet arrived for the sex censorship in England, where the fear of blasphemy was so great that even in the middle of the nineteenth century successful prosecutions could be conducted against such rationalists as Carlyle, Cooper, Watts, Bradlaugh, Holyoake, and Foote.

If there is any doubt of the meaning of the application of the intermediate index, it is removed by the fact of the prolonged American insistence that it, no less than England, was a Christian country. It is true that political liberty under rigid constitutional guarantees became better established here at an earlier date than in the motherland. But the myth of the absolutely free and untrammeled American has become more and more discredited. The adoption of the Alien and Sedition Acts so soon after the great struggle over the Constitution is only one of the many qualifications which were made. The significant fact is, however, that in supposedly free America the necessity for maintaining the index of religion was recognized. The fact is that a direct union of Church and State obtained in the New England states and Maryland till the middle of the nineteenth century, and that England had effected complete Catholic and Jewish emancipation before at least one American state, New Hampshire. It is interesting that the greatest strides toward religious freedom were made in Virginia, the first of the Southern states which had a feudal aristocracy of slaveholders which was quite sure of itself. The First Amendment to the Federal Constitution was interpreted to limit only the powers of Congress in interfering with free worship. Christianity was declared to be the law of the land in the sense that it was entitled to preference and protection. Until the late years of the nineteenth century atheists were generally incompetent to testify in America, and still are in Arkansas, Maryland and North Carolina. Blasphemy was a crime in all American states no less than in England, and the American and English Puritan still refused to take alarm.

The sex censorship was the result of the secularization of life. From 1800, when the conventions of literary decency began to mature, to the time of Lord Chief Justice Campbell was the period of gradual transition. If the growth of the circulating libraries in England constituted a menace, a free public library was an even worse "evergreen tree of diabolical knowledge." The modern public libraries date from the middle of the nineteenth century in both England and America, but it took another quarter century before their resources became adequate. When the first public library in England was opened at Manchester, Thackeray improved upon Hogarth by picturing the Lancashire mechanic reading Carlyle, Dickens and Bulwer-Lytton. Popular education was introduced by Forster's Act in England in 1780, and alarmed satirists began to picture houses burning down while their cooks read hydrostatics in sixpenny tracts. The Civil War marked the same turning point in America. It is more than an extraordinary coincidence that Lord Campbell's Act, the final establishment of obscene libel as a crime at Common Law, the Comstock Acts in America, and the publication of *The Origin of Species* all occurred approximately in a decade. The cluster of the dates 1857, 1859, 1868, 1872 indicates that the late Puritanism which flowered in what we call mid-Victorianism was beginning to struggle with the monster it had created.

The organization of special vice societies seemed imperative in such an acute situation. The New York Society for the Suppression of Vice was becoming a terror which made its influence felt in all parts of the Anglo-Saxon world. Over three-quarters of a century of battle had apparently worn out the old English Society for the Suppression of Vice, and removed it far from its original inspiration. A successor arose in 1885 in the National Vigilance Association. It is almost a law of their evolution that vice societies arise to ideal with tangible evils and then soon turn to imaginary ones. The immediate cause for its organization was the existence of a con-

siderable white slave traffic which disgraced London at the
time. The cause was taken up at the instigation of several
ladies by the eccentric W. T. Stead, who, as the result of a
number of investigations, published that never-to-be-for-
gotten series of articles in his *Pall Mall Gazette* entitled *The
Maiden Tribute of Modern Babylon*. The revelations were
so graphic, startling, and specific that the starved Victorians
devoured the editions almost before they came off the press,
and "a wave of public indignation" swept London. To deal
with them the Vigilance Society was organized at a great
all-day meeting in St. James's Hall followed by a monster
demonstration in Hyde Park to which contingents from all
ends of London went singing hallelujahs. The first contribution was a five pound note from none other than His Eminence Cardinal Manning. It was significant that now the
Anglicans and the Catholics were lying down together like
the lion and the lamb. The Vice Secretary chosen was William Alexander Coote, whose exploits came to rival Comstock's. Within three years he was leading the attack against
the novels of Zola.

When Darwinism burst upon a frightened world, the fear
that was most expressed was that its materialism would
shake the ethical foundations of society. Without belief in
the Christian religion, men would relapse into savagery.
Without a system of rewards and punishments, there could
be no compelling reason for right conduct. With the religious
test of life undermined, the Victorian world set out upon a
quest for a secular system of ethics, and discovered its basis
naturally in sex. With the powers of the state also limited,
the family was of peculiar importance as a medium through
which to bind the conscience of the individual, and the deep
loyalties of the family became paramount. When a modern
employer, for instance, asks an applicant for work if he is
married, he is only using a test of dependability and regularity
which elevates the Home as the fountain-head of the State.
With the secularization of life, a special stress is placed upon

the institution of marriage, and the whole sexual life becomes a matter of grave concern. The secularization of life means, too, the triumph of individualism, and sex is the center of the individual's life forces. The evolution of the sex censorship occurred so long before the advent of Freudianism that it is a remarkable tribute to the practical genius for government which marks the Anglo-Saxon. The use of the law of criminal obscenity for the regimentation of life is an instinctive historical anticipation of the vast import of the libido. When we understand the multiple sublimations of which it is capable in all the avenues of life, we are no longer surprised that sex control has become the very crux of the political means. The sex censorship is Freudianism in action. It was accomplished by the gradual dissociation of the carnal and spiritual aspects of sex.

The old Puritan horror of lewdness and obscenities is also part of the modern sex censorship. To the extent that they are identical we are not mystified. It is often recognized as a characteristic of autocrats that they permit greater sexual laxity while they savagely curb political freedom: the brothel and vodka performed the same function in Tzarist Russia. But in a democracy, which simply means a state which is concerned with the welfare of the individual, it is natural that an attempt be made to guard against the deleterious effects of obscenity *per se*. The tendency is for an excessive pornography to be envisaged as a dangerous drug which interferes with the life of democratic citizenship. When obscenity is so regarded, its relation to the political means is very slight. To regard it even as the very mildest excitant to unconformity, one has to imagine a citizen in the lower ranks of society who has been so debauched by obscenities that he begins to give ear to the voices of disaffection.

At first blush, the transformation of the law of criminal obscenity into a normal method for the censorship of ideas is less obvious. Its duplicity has often been observed. There is a comparative frankness and straightforwardness about a charge of sedition or blasphemy. It is true that there may be differences of opinion as to the nature of an actionable sedition or blasphemy but the political dangers of such opinions are palpable. All the absurdities of the political censor or ecclesiastical inquisitor do not leave us in the dark as to his central object. Indeed his greatest alarm arises naturally from the fact that the tendency of treasonable and irreligious doctrine is more immediately convulsive. Sex, however, is a far more subtle index of virtue. A political censor objecting to such an expression in a geography as a "union of two rivers" as treasonable in its implications appears less egregious than the secretary of a vice society who objects to a union of lips for three minutes.

Nevertheless, it is true that the sex censorship is also a new metamorphosis in the control of opinion. The very name of the crime in English law, "obscene libel," shows that it is a substitution for "seditious libel" and "blasphemous libel." It has become one of the peace-time limitations upon free speech. It happens, for instance, that in war periods the barriers of the index of sex are always relaxed, since the state grows omnipotent and the censor turns his attention to patriotism. This was as true during the Great War as during the American revolutionary period, when *Charlotte Temple* was the most popular American novel. If censorship of jazz is unknown, the reason is that music has no articulate relation to ideas. If neo-Puritanism has receded from its early antipathy for the nude in painting, it is from a gradual realization that the same is true of art. But such old Puritans as Jeremy Collier and Anthony Comstock, who appreciated obscenity *per se,* knew better. The former remarked: "Music is almost as dangerous as gunpowder," and the latter hunted *September Morns*.

Very gradually the obscenity laws have been adapted to the safe-guarding of the most vital interest of modern civilization. We may speak freely upon any subject except the one in which our age is most absorbed. There is an implicit line of demarcation drawn between the type which questions those sexual morals themselves. Where the injury is offered to the sense of shame, it has to be gross before action will be taken. When it is existing sexual morality that is attacked, the degree of offensiveness need often be very slight. A Shubert review may approach the limits with impunity when a *God of Vengeance* or a *Mrs. Warren's Profession* are at once suppressed. An E. M. Hull and a Marie Corelli who do not attack the established order but indeed base themselves upon its standards in their exhibitionism of sex passion are exempt, but such writers as Zola, Dreiser, and W. L. George, whose work reflects upon current morality, have been subjected to prosecution. For instance, the Secretary of the New York Society for the Suppression of Vice publicly stated that the trouble with *The Genius* was that "there are very vivid descriptions of the activities of certain female delinquents who do not, apparently, suffer any ill consequence from their misconduct but, in the language of the day, 'get away with it.'" George Moore will probably never achieve a state of grace, for *Esther Waters* has actually led to the foundation of an Esther Waters Home for Girl Mothers. The works of Shelley have been haled into the Old Bailey but Byron has always lain upon drawing-room tables, even though the editor of *My Grandmother's Review* protested. A criticism of established sin tends to become criminal obscenity. That many more authors are not called to account is due to the limitations of human energy and the stupidity of authorities who do not always fully appreciate when morality is involved. A few sacrificial victims are simply chosen every now and then to remind the iconoclasts that virtue is not to be flouted with impunity. This periodic character of all censorship makes its rules merely the rules of a game, and leaves only the central reality significant.

The modern sex censorship concentrates more and more upon the creative artist. A theorist is often left unmolested where a novelist, especially if he is a realist, has to show cause. When sex is the index of virtue, it is natural for the novelist to attract the first attention. The love story is watched far more carefully than in ages when theological and political dispute was the main theme of authors. It is through the vehicle of persuasive fiction that corrupting ideas are popularized nowadays. Long ago Anthony Trollope declared: "I have always thought of myself as a preacher of sermons"; and Galsworthy has commented on one of his characters: "Like most novel readers of his generation, literature colored his view of life." Where once the great agitator moved the multitude, and the great preacher his congregation, it is the creative artist who has become the middle man through whom the revolutionary ideas of the thinkers are spread. It is he who represents philosophy in action. It is the creative artist who is the true performer and revolutionist, however unconscious he may be of such a mission. Mill's *The Subjection of Women* had gathered dust for many a year, but no sooner had H. G. Wells published *Ann Veronica*, which sounded the keynote of English feminism, than the hue and cry was raised. Hegel was called "an obscene bird of the night," but he elicited hardly more than this epithet, while Dreiser, who swallowed Hegelianism in his youth, has been the pet of the vice societies for a generation.

It is easy to fall into too great a Machiavellian acuteness if the qualification is not understood that sex censorship has a direct and indirect operation. The secretaries of vice societies are not philosophers and they are quite unconscious usually of the forces which support them. But that does not gainsay their reality. Many prosecutions are inspired simply by the hysterical attitude toward sex which the standards of censorship have themselves created. When they are a manifestation only of the tendency of the times, they are comparatively benign. But more often an ulterior motive, a personal animus, a political hostility is to be found.

The adoption of the index of sex was bound to make censorship far more sinister and dishonest than under the older tests. There are certain reticences which accompany sex in savage as well as in civilized societies, however much these may vary. An injury offered to the vital instincts of sex at once invokes the sacred name of morality, under which all sorts of crimes can be accomplished with convenience. The tests of obscenity are so comfortably vague. And many a man who will brave a charge of open atheism with impunity will fly when the specter of obscenity is raised. There can hardly have been a worse infidel than Ingersoll; yet when it was rumored that he was for the total repeal of the Comstock Laws, he resigned from the vice-presidency of the Liberal League. A combination charge of blasphemy and obscenity was too much for him to bear. The Anglo-Saxon who regards an assault upon free speech with horror views with equanimity its suppression as obscenity. Sir James Stephens has remarked upon the difficulty of distinguishing between simple obscenity and immorality in sexual ethics. Even more often heterodoxy in sex matters is confused with radicalism in general. The wise radical instinctively realizes that he must avoid the bugaboos of sex if he wishes to speak against social and economic evils. But he discovers soon that this is the most difficult thing in the world. The Achilles heel of the sex censorship is so large that a hidden motive is behind most prosecutions. It is usually radicals, reformers, eccentrics and trouble makers of one kind or another who are involved.

It is important to understand that sex radicalism in modern life is the best general index of radicalism in other spheres. The man who publicly upholds birth control, the single standard, free love, companionate marriage, easy divorce, and legitimization is a man prone to play with subversive ideas on private property, to be attracted by criminal syndicalism, to be dubious about the House of Lords, or about the fitness of the Republican Party to govern, and to question the general efficacy of prayer. When such an individual is attacked under the sex censorship, it is assumed that no very great tenderness for his rights need be shown.

From the very earliest days, the sex censorship has exhibited its affinities in this way. Charles Bradlaugh, Charles Watts, Annie Besant, who were all notorious infidels or rationalists, had to stand trial for publishing Malthusian pamphlets and were the first victims of Lord Chief Justice Cockburn's revolution in the law. The fact that they all had been indicted for blasphemy not many years before this indicates neatly, moreover, the transition to the sexual index of virtue. The Comstock Laws found their first victims in such vigorous apostles of discontent as Bennett, the Woodhull sisters, Harmon and Ezra Heywood, who were the subjects of prosecution again and again. When criminal obscenity laws are invoked for dealing with intemperate denunciation of the Catholic Church, it is really religious controversy that is thus controlled. The same use has been made in America of the Postal Laws to keep anti-Catholic literature from the mails. When such action is taken a Catholic bishop or the Knights of Columbus are often discovered in the background.

The desire to dispose of a vexing radical publisher is as manifest in the repeated indictments against certain publishers now as in the repeated indictments of Vizetelly in the eighties. The social and economic radicalism of the *New Masses* and the *American Mercury* supplies the impetus behind the crusade against them as it did against the *Adult Review* in 1898, when its editor, who also kept a bookstore, sold a copy of Havelock Ellis' *The Psychology of Sex,* unmolested till then. The hardest motive to trace is the gratification of private malice but it undoubtedly can be seen in the *Madeleine* case. The demand for censorship was raised by politicians who had been investigated by the grand jury of which an officer of Harper's was a member.

The most constant ulterior use which has been made of the obscenity laws is in the battle against birth control. This has almost the dignity of a settled policy. It has lapsed from its early virulence in England since the famous prosecutions against Bradlaugh, Annie Besant, and Edward Truelove because the law itself was amended, but it has not abated in America, where this ulterior motive still constitutes the greatest incubus of the Comstock Laws. The hazards of Dr. Marie Stopes in England were mild compared to the perils of Margaret Sanger in New York. It must be obvious that there is nothing inherently obscene in the rational exposition of an argument for the prevention of conception. But the fact that sex is involved has been seized as a pretext to charge birth control reformers with purveying obscene literature. In one-half of the American states there are no laws against giving contraceptive information but the same result is effected under the obscenity laws. Where there are such combination laws a great deal could be accomplished by a preliminary campaign to separate the provisions against obscene literature and birth control information which are mingled in the same statute. To the Anglo-Saxon mind they are, however, almost inseparable. The greatest obstacle is the example of the Federal Postal Laws. The best known case is that of Carlo Tresca, who, offending the Italian Government, found himself in the penitentiary ostensibly for publishing an "obscene" birth control advertisement of two lines! Speaking generally the United States federal sex censorship is more frequently invoked against radicalism than is the state or English censorship. Its remoteness and irresponsibility give it the greater elasticity necessary for this purpose.

The index, after all, matters little. A book which is obscene is very often also seditious or irreligious. It was G. B. Shaw who once pointed out that *King Lear* constituted an obscene, seditious, and blasphemous libel all in one. Life is too complex for these elements ever to be completely isolated. Walt Whitman's democracy, for instance, is a political nuisance, his sanctification of the Life Force is irreligious, and his frankness in sex matters is obscenity. It is interest-

ing that while the latter character has condemned him in
England and America, he has recently been proscribed as
an anarchist in reactionary Hungary. Conversely, not so long
ago a shipment of Lenin's and Trotsky's work, *The State
and the Revolution,* was seized as obscene in Boston. Birth
control is blasphemy as well as obscenity; it is an attempt to
undo God's command: "Increase and multiply." Hawthorne's
The Scarlet Letter is sacrilegious in the slur which it casts
upon the uprightness of the clergy, and obscene in the sexual
immorality which is the clergyman's sin. If the state assumed to protect the reputation of ministers, such a book
would also be treasonable. *Elmer Gantry,* its modern successor, has been condemned in Boston as obscene because of
the seductions of its religious hero. A hundred years ago, it
would have constituted a blasphemous and impious libel upon
religion. Two hundred years ago *The President's Daughter*
would have constituted a seditious libel upon the person of
His Majesty if written of an English king. As it is, an attempt was made to suppress the book as obscene and the
Vice Society states its regret that it could not prevent a libel
on a dead statesman. Shelley's *Queen Mab* was the subject
of a prosecution for blasphemy in 1842. By the end of the
century, the printed copies of *The Cenci* would have been
attacked.

Mutatis mutandis, the very same rules of the game of censorship have always prevailed. The sergeant-at-law who de-
fended *Queen Mab* employed the *reductio ad absurdum* of
the classics in the same manner as Vizetelly, except that he
chose the examples of blasphemy. He pointed to the slurs
upon infant Christianity which are contained in the polished
sarcasms of Gibbon's *Decline and Fall of the Roman Empire,*
and he asked if Milton had not let his imagination run away
with him to the point where he invested the Satanic Ad-
versary with too great nobility of soul and splendor. Now
the Song of Solomon is adduced from the Bible just as the
story of Job, who wished to curse God and die, was then.

404 SEX ATTITUDES IN MODERN SOCIETY

Always censorship has been aimed at the lower orders of society, and always directed particularly against "penny treason" and "penny blasphemy." Pitt refused to prosecute Godwin's *Political Justice* because it was published at three guineas a set, and he said, "a three guinea book could never do much harm among those who had not three shillings to spare." The gratification of private malice as a motive for censorship is one of the ulterior objects which has always been the same. Socrates was not attacked for corrupting morals of youth until after he had done so for decades, and the real animus of the prosecution was political, to punish him for his resistance to Athenian politicians.

Only the fashions change. The old game of censorship continues, even at the cost of all the psychic derangements of sex which sex control imposes.

THE END